Studies in Emotion and Social Interaction

Paul Ekman
University of California, San Francisco

Klaus R. Scherer
Université de Genève and
Justus-Liebig-Universität Giessen

General Editors

Judgment Studies

Studies in Emotion and Social Interaction

This series is jointly published by the Cambridge University Press and the Editions de la Maison des Sciences de l'Homme, as part of the joint publishing agreement established in 1977 between the Fondation de la Maison des Sciences de l'Homme and the Syndics of the Cambridge University Press.

Cette collection est publiée en co-édition par Cambridge University Press et les Editions de la Maison des Sciences de l'Homme. Elle s'intègre dans le programme de co-édition établi en 1977 par la Fondation de la Maison des Sciences de l'Homme et les Syndics de Cambridge University Press.

Judgment studies
Design, analysis, and meta-analysis

Robert Rosenthal
Harvard University

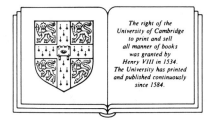

The right of the
University of Cambridge
to print and sell
all manner of books
was granted by
Henry VIII in 1534.
The University has printed
and published continuously
since 1584.

Cambridge University Press

Cambridge
London   New York   New Rochelle
Melbourne   Sydney

Editions de la Maison des Sciences de l'Homme

Paris

Published by the Press Syndicate of the University of Cambridge
The Pitt Building, Trumpington Street, Cambridge CB2 1RP
32 East 57th Street, New York, NY 10022, USA
10 Stamford Road, Oakleigh, Melbourne 3166, Australia

First published 1987

Printed in the United States of America

Library of Congress Cataloging-in-Publication Data
Rosenthal, Robert, 1933–
Judgment studies.
(Studies in emotion and social interaction)
Bibliography: p.
Includes index.
1. Judgment – Research – Methodology.   2. Nonverbal
communication (Psychology) – Evaluation.   3. Experimental
design.   4. Meta-analysis.   I. Title.   II. Series.
BF441.R67   1987   153.4′6   86-26337
ISBN 0 521 33191 9

British Library Cataloguing in Publication Data
(Applied for)

To my sisters:
Trude Parzen and Lottie Philipp
for their judgment and their friendship

Contents

Preface

My interest in conducting judgment studies began over twenty-five years ago. I had been doing experiments showing that psychological experimenters might unintentionally affect the results of their research by virtue of their personal characteristics and, especially, by virtue of their expectations for experimental outcomes. Judgment studies were needed to try to find out how subtle aspects of the experimenter-subject interaction were predictive of the results of the research. Later, in our so-called "Pygmalion" studies we discovered that teachers' expectations for pupils' performance could also come to serve as self-fulfilling prophecies. Judgment studies were again needed to try to find out how teachers treated differently those students for whom they held favorable versus unfavorable expectations. In more recent years, my collaborators and I have continued conducting judgment studies examining not only experimenter-subject and teacher-student interactions but such other interactions as counselor-client, employer-employee, physician-patient, psychotherapist-patient, and other dyads of everyday life.

The contents and the introductory chapter tell in detail the content and purpose of this book. Very briefly, its purpose is to describe the design, analysis, and meta-analysis of judgment studies in sufficient detail (a) so that they can be conducted by readers of this book and (b) so that they can be wisely evaluated when they have been conducted by others.

To give some focus to the content being investigated, this book addresses primarily the research domain of nonverbal behavior. Most of the examples are drawn from research on nonverbal behavior. However, this book is designed for any investigator employing judges, observers, raters, coders, or decoders whether the behavior being judged is nonverbal or not.

The book is intended for advanced undergraduate and graduate students and researchers in the behavioral and social sciences. The level of mathematical sophistication required is high school algebra. The level of statistical sophistication required is about half-way through a second course in data analysis (e.g., Rosenthal & Rosnow, 1984).

I am twice grateful to the National Science Foundation: first for having supported, since 1961, the substantive research on such processes of unintended social influence as interpersonal expectancy effects; and second, for having supported, in part, the development of some of the methodological procedures to be described in this book.

Most of the material of this book has been used for years as handouts in various courses in research methods and data analysis and many students and colleagues have provided valuable feedback. Special thanks for such feedback is due Pierce Barker, Rita Coleman, Bella DePaulo, Robin DiMatteo, Susan Fiske, Howie Friedman, George Gitter, David Goldstein, Judy Hall, Dan Isenberg, Chick Judd, Dave Kenny, Mark Pavelchak, Ralph Rosnow, Gordon Russell, Charles Thomas, Ed Tufte, and Miron Zuckerman.

Paul Ekman and Klaus Scherer, editors of this series, read and improved the book greatly. Susan Milmoe, Cambridge University Press editor and psychologist, helped to shape the book and facilitated its preparation.

Let me also thank William Cochran, Jacob Cohen, Paul Holland, Frederick Mosteller, and especially, Donald Rubin, who were very influential in developing my conception of data analytic procedures.

Most of the material in this book has appeared earlier in journal articles and book chapters but in widely scattered places. This book depends most heavily on four sources: (a) my chapter titled "Conducting Judgment Studies" in the *Handbook of Methods in Nonverbal Behavior Research,* edited by Klaus Scherer and Paul Ekman, and published by Cambridge University Press in 1982; (b) some of my sections of *Essentials of Behavioral Research,* by Robert Rosenthal and Ralph Rosnow, published by McGraw-Hill in 1984; (c) some of my sections of *Contrast Analysis,* by Robert Rosenthal and Ralph Rosnow, published by Cambridge University Press in 1985; and (d) some sections of my book *Meta-analytic Procedures for Social Research,* published by Sage in 1984.

The statistical tables in the appendix were reproduced with the generous permission of the American Statistical Association, Houghton Mifflin, Iowa State University Press, Joseph Lev, and McGraw-Hill.

Blair Boudreau typed the entire manuscript with her legendary accuracy; an accuracy that has ruined my skill at, and motivation for, proofreading.

MaryLu Rosenthal prepared the index over a period of about one week and she has prepared (and sustained) the author over a period of about thirty-five years.

PART I
The design of judgment studies

1. The nature of judgment studies

Some dimensions of judgment studies

Research in nonverbal communication very often requires the use of observers, coders, raters, decoders, or judges. Although distinctions among these classes of human (or at least animate) responders are possible, we shall not distinguish among them here but rather use these terms more or less interchangeably.

Judgment studies may focus on nonverbal behaviors considered as independent variables; for example, when the corners of the mouth rise, do judges rate subjects as being happier? Judgment studies may also focus on nonverbal behaviors considered as dependent variables; for example, when subjects are made happier, are the corners of the subjects' mouths judged as having risen more?

Judgment studies may employ a variety of metrics, from physical units of measurement to psychological units of measurement. For example, the movement of the corner of the mouth can be given in millimeters and judges' ratings of happiness may be given on a scale, perhaps of seven points, ranging from "not at all happy" to "very happy."

The judgments employed in a judgment study may vary dramatically in their reliability. Thus, judgments based on physical units of measurement are often more reliable than are judgments based on psychological units of measurement, although, for some purposes, the latter may be higher in validity despite their being lower in reliability (Rosenthal, 1966). This may be due to the lower degree of social meaning inherent in the more molecular physical units of measurement compared to the more molar psychological units of measurement. Table 1.1 shows some of the dimensions upon which it is possible to classify various judgment studies.

Table 1.1. *Dimensions tending to distinguish various types of judgment studies*

Dimension	Examples		
Type of variable	Dependent	vs.	Independent variables
Measurement units	Physical	vs.	Psychological units
Reliability	Lower	vs.	Higher levels
Social meaning	Lower	vs.	Higher levels

The judgment study model

The underlying model of a basic judgment study is shown in Figure 1.1. One or more encoders characterized by one or more attributes (e.g., traits, states, etc.) (A) are observed by one or more decoders who make one or more judgments (C) about the encoders on the basis of selectively presented nonverbal behavior (B). The AB arrow refers to the relationship between the encoder's actual attribute (e.g., state) and the encoder's nonverbal behavior. The AB arrow reflects the primary interest of the investigator who wishes to employ the nonverbal behavior as the dependent variable. The BC arrow reflects the primary interest of the investigator who wishes to employ the nonverbal behavior as the independent variable. The AC arrow reflects the primary interest of the investigator interested in the relationship between the encoder's attribute and the decoders' judgment, for example, the decoders' accuracy.

The nonverbal behavior (B) presented to the decoders tends to be highly selected as part of the research design. Investigators interested in facial expressions might present still photographs of the face (e.g., Ekman, 1973) while investigators interested in tone of voice might present speech that is content-standard (Davitz, 1964), randomized-spliced (Scherer, 1971), or content-filtered (Rogers, Scherer, & Rosenthal, 1971). Investigators interested

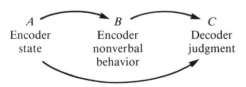

Figure 1.1. A simple model of judgment studies

in comparing the relative efficiency of cues carried in various channels of nonverbal communication might provide access to different channels of nonverbal cues (e.g., face, body, tone of voice; Rosenthal, Hall, DiMatteo, Rogers, & Archer, 1979; Scherer, Scherer, Hall, & Rosenthal, 1977).

To summarize the simple judgment model, then, we have encoder attributes, say, states (A), manifested behaviorally (B), and decoded by judges (C). The states then generate both the nonverbal behaviors and the decoders' judgments.

A more complex judgment study model based on Brunswik's (1956) lens model has been described by Scherer (1978).

The purposes of judgment studies

Judgment studies serve many purposes. In terms of our simple model of judgment studies (Figure 1.1) the focus of a judgment study may be on the encoder state or other attribute (A), the encoder's nonverbal behavior (B), the decoder's judgment itself (C), the AB, AC, and BC arrows, or the ABC chain.

Encoder state
Suppose we wanted to develop a system for the diagnosis of anxiety in college students from various nonverbal cues. Suppose further that we had available film clips of thirty students being interviewed. Before we could correlate various nonverbal behaviors with the degree of anxiety of the students we would have to ascertain their "actual" anxiety level. One way of defining the students' actual level of anxiety might be to show the thirty film clips to a sample of experienced clinical psychologists or other experts on anxiety and obtain ratings of the degree of anxiety shown by each college student.[1] The mean rating of anxiety of each stimulus person (encoder) becomes the operational definition of the true state of the encoder. Note that our emphasis here was on defining the encoder state, not on specifying the cues that might have led the expert judges to decide on what ratings they would give. In addition, note that this particular judgment study, done for the purpose of estimating parameters (mean anxiety) rather than establishing relationships, was a kind of preliminary study to be followed up by a study linking the state of anxiety to the nonverbal concomitants (an AB arrow), (Rosenthal & Rosnow, 1975a, 1984).

[1] An alternative way of defining actual level of anxiety in terms of test scores is described in the subsequent paragraph on *AC arrows*.

Encoder nonverbal behavior

Suppose we wanted to study the mediation of teacher expectancy effects (Rosenthal, 1966, 1969, 1974, 1976, 1985; Rosenthal & Jacobson, 1968; Rosenthal & Rubin 1978a, 1978b). One of our hypotheses might be that teachers who expect more from their students treat them more warmly. Furthermore, we may believe that this warmth will be expressed in part through tone of voice. Before we can examine the relationship between teachers' expectations and teachers' warmth in tone of voice, however, we must be able to define tonal "warmth." One way of defining warmth would be to ask judges to make ratings of the degree of warmth shown in the content-filtered voices of teachers talking to their students. The mean rating of warmth obtained for each stimulus teacher's content-filtered voice becomes the definition of the warmth of the nonverbal behavior. This particular judgment study, like the one just described, was done for the purpose of estimating parameters (mean warmth) rather than establishing relationships. As such it might serve as a kind of preliminary study that would be followed up by a study relating the nonverbal behavior to a teacher state or some other type of variable. Such studies have been conducted focusing on the tone of voice shown by, for example, teachers, psychotherapists, counselors, physicians, and by mothers (Harris & Rosenthal, 1985; Rosenthal, Blanck, & Vannicelli, 1984; Blanck & Rosenthal, 1984; Milmoe, Rosenthal, Blane, Chafetz, & Wolf, 1967; Milmoe, Novey, Kagan, & Rosenthal, 1968).

Decoder judgment

In the case of the two purposes of judgment studies described so far, judges' ratings were employed to provide the definitions of encoder states and encoder nonverbal behavior, usually in the context of a preliminary study, or a simple descriptive study (e.g., what proportion of experimenters smile at their research subjects?, Rosenthal, 1967). Sometimes, however, it is the judgments themselves we want to study. The interpretation of nonverbal cues may depend heavily on personal characteristics of the judges. Thus, we might not be surprised to find that aggressive, delinquent boys will tend to interpret nonverbal cues as more aggressive than would less aggressive boys (Nasby, Hayden, & DePaulo, 1980). Or, we might be interested to learn that blind children may be more sensitive to tone of voice cues (content-filtered and randomized-spliced) than are sighted children (Rosenthal et al., 1979). One of the earliest uses of decoders' judgments was to help establish that nonverbal behavior could, in fact, be decoded accurately (Allport, 1924; Ekman, 1965a, 1973).

AB arrows

If we record therapists' expectations for their patients and observe their non-verbal behaviors as they interact with their patients we have the ingredients of an AB arrow study. Therapists' nonverbal behaviors could be defined in terms of muscle movements in millimeters or voice changes in Hz or in terms of warmth, pride, esteem, and expectation, as rated on nine-point scales. In either case, we regard the nonverbal behaviors as the dependent variable, and the therapists' expectations as the independent variable (Blanck, Rosenthal, & Vannicelli, 1986).

BC arrows

A common type of BC arrow judgment study might experimentally manipulate various encoder nonverbal cues and observe the effects on decoders' ratings of various encoder characteristics (e.g., Friedman, 1976, 1978, 1979a). Questions addressed might include: are smiling faces rated as more friendly? Are voices with greater pitch range judged more pleasant? Are louder voices judged more extraverted? (Scherer, 1970, 1978, 1979a, 1979b, 1982; Scherer, Koivumaki, & Rosenthal, 1972; Scherer & Oshinsky, 1977).

AC arrows

AC arrow judgment studies are common in the general research domains of clinical diagnosis and person perception. The general paradigm is to ask decoders to assess the encoders' true attributes (e.g., diagnosis, anxiety level, adjustment level) and to correlate decoders' judgments with independently determined definitions of encoders' true traits or states. Thus, for example, clinicians' ratings of adjustment and anxiety might be correlated with encoders' scores on various subscales of such tests as the MMPI, or scores based on the Rorschach, TAT, or life history data.

When AC arrow judgment studies are employed in research on nonverbal communication it is often in the context of accuracy studies. Encoders might, for example, show a variety of posed or spontaneous affects, and judgments of these affects made by decoders are evaluated for accuracy. Sometimes these accuracy studies are conducted to learn the degree to which judges show better than chance accuracy (Allport, 1924; Ekman, 1965a, 1973). At other times these accuracy studies are conducted to establish individual differences among the judges in degree of accuracy shown. These individual differences in decoding accuracy may then be correlated with a variety of personal attributes of the judges (e.g., gender, age, ethnicity, psychopathology, cognitive attributes, personality attributes, etc., Rosenthal et al., 1979). It should be noted that such individual difference studies can be meaningfully conducted even when the mean level of accuracy shown by the entire sample of judges does not exceed the chance expectation level as in comparisons of people scoring above chance with those scoring below chance.

ABC chains

Sometimes we are simultaneously interested in the AB arrow and the BC arrow; such studies can be viewed as studies of the ABC chain. Suppose we want to study the mediation of teacher expectancy effects. We begin with a sample of teachers known to vary in their expectations for their pupils' intellectual performance, that is, known to vary in encoder states (A). These teachers are observed interacting with pupils for whom they hold higher or lower expectations and a sample of judges rates the teachers' behavior on degree of smiling, forward lean, and eye contact, that is, encoder nonverbal behaviors (B). Finally, a sample of judges rates the nonverbal behavior of the teachers for degree of overall warmth and favorableness of expectancy, that is, makes decoder judgments (C) of a fairly molar type. We would now be in a position to examine the effects of teacher expectation on teacher nonverbal behavior and the social impact of these effects on nonverbal behavior, all in the same study (Harris & Rosenthal, 1985).

Designing judgment studies

The particular purpose of any judgment study should determine the particular procedures of any judgment study. Given the diversity of purposes of judgment studies we have discussed above, it is not possible to prescribe the detailed procedures that should be employed for any particular judgment study. However, because judgment studies do have certain communalities, it is possible to discuss issues likely to be confronted in many judgment studies. In the following chapters we address some of these issues.

2. Sampling judges and encoders

Sampling judges

How many judges shall we employ in a judgment study in which our primary interest is in the encoders rather than the judges, and who should they be? The major factors determining the answers to these questions are (1) the average reliability coefficient (r) between pairs of judges chosen at random from a prescribed population and (2) the nature of the population of judges to which we want to generalize our results.

Effective reliability
Suppose our goal were to establish the definition of the encoder's state (A) or of some encoder nonverbal behavior (B). We might decide to employ judges' ratings for our definition. As we shall see shortly, if the reliability coefficient (any product moment correlation such as r, point biserial r, or phi) were very low we would require more judges than if the reliability coefficient were very high. Just how many judges to employ is a question for which some useful guidelines can be presented (Rosenthal, 1973; Uno, Koivumaki, & Rosenthal, 1972).

If we had a sample of teachers whose nonverbal warmth we wanted to establish we might begin by having two judges rate each teacher's warmth based on the videotaped behavior of each teacher. The correlation coefficient reflecting the reliability of the two judges' ratings would be computed to give us our best (and only) estimate of the correlation likely to be obtained between any two judges drawn from the same population of judges. This correlation coefficient, then, is clearly useful; it is not, however, a very good estimate of the reliability of our variable, which is not the rating of warmth made by a single judge but rather the mean of two judges' ratings. Suppose, for example, that the correlation between our two judges' ratings of warmth

9

were .50; the reliability of the mean of the two judges' ratings, the "effective" reliability, would then be .67 not .50. Intuition suggests that we should gain in reliability in adding the ratings of a second judge because the second judge's random errors should tend to cancel the first judge's random errors. Intuition suggests further that adding more judges, all of whom agree with one another to about the same degree, defined by a mean interjudge correlation coefficient of .50 (for this example), should further increase our effective reliability. Our intuition would be supported by an old and well-known result reported independently by Charles Spearman and William Brown in 1910 (Walker & Lev, 1953). With notation altered to suit our current purpose, the well-known Spearman–Brown result is:

$$R = \frac{nr}{1 + (n-1)r} \qquad\qquad (2.1)$$

where R = effective reliability
$\qquad n$ = number of judges
$\qquad r$ = mean reliability among all n judges (i.e., mean of $n(n-1)/2$ correlations).

Use of this formula depends on the assumption that a comparable group of judges would show comparable "mean" reliability among themselves and with the actual group of judges available to us. This assumption is virtually the same as the assumption that all pairs of judges show essentially the same degree of reliability. It should be noted that the effective reliability, R, can also be obtained computationally by means of the Kuder–Richardson 20 formula or by means of Cronbach's coefficient alpha (Guilford, 1954).

As an aid to investigators employing these and related methods, Table 2.1 has been prepared employing the Spearman–Brown formula.

The table gives the effective reliability, R, for each of several values of n, the number of judges making the observations, and r, the mean reliability among the judges; it is intended to facilitate rapidly obtaining approximate answers to each of the following questions:

(1) Given an obtained or estimated mean reliability, r, and a sample of n judges, what is the approximate effective reliability, R, of the mean of the judges' ratings? The value of R is read from the table at the intersection of the appropriate row (n) and column (r).

(2) Given the value of the obtained or desired effective reliability, R, and the number, n, of judges available, what will be the approximate value of the required mean reliability, r? The table is entered in the row corresponding to the n of judges available, and is read across until the value of R closest to the one desired is reached; the value of r is then read as the corresponding column heading.

Table 2.1. *Effective reliability of the mean of judges' ratings*

Number of judges (n)	Mean reliability (r)																				
	.01	.03	.05	.10	.15	.20	.25	.30	.35	.40	.45	.50	.55	.60	.65	.70	.75	.80	.85	.90	.95
1	01	03	05	10	15	20	25	30	35	40	45	50	55	60	65	70	75	80	85	90	95
2	02	06	10	18	26	33	40	46	52	57	62	67	71	75	79	82	86	89	92	95	97
3	03	08	14	25	35	43	50	56	62	67	71	75	79	82	85	88	90	92	94	96	98
4	04	11	17	31	41	50	57	63	68	73	77	80	83	86	88	90	92	94	96	97	*
5	05	13	21	36	47	56	62	68	73	77	80	83	86	88	90	92	94	95	97	98	*
6	06	16	24	40	51	60	67	72	76	80	83	86	88	90	92	93	95	96	97	98	*
7	07	18	27	44	55	64	70	75	79	82	85	88	90	91	93	94	95	97	98	98	*
8	07	20	30	47	59	67	73	77	81	84	87	89	91	92	94	95	96	97	98	*	*
9	08	22	32	50	61	69	75	79	83	86	88	90	92	93	94	95	96	97	98	*	*
10	09	24	34	53	64	71	77	81	84	87	89	91	92	94	95	96	97	98	98	*	**
12	11	27	39	57	68	75	80	84	87	89	91	92	94	95	96	97	98	98	*	*	**
14	12	30	42	61	71	78	82	86	88	90	92	93	94	95	96	97	98	98	*	*	**
16	14	33	46	64	74	80	84	87	90	91	93	94	95	96	97	97	98	98	*	*	**
18	15	36	49	67	76	82	86	89	91	92	94	95	96	96	97	98	98	*	*	*	**
20	17	38	51	69	78	83	87	90	92	93	94	95	96	97	97	98	98	*	*	*	**
24	20	43	56	73	81	86	89	91	93	94	95	96	97	97	98	98	*	*	*	**	**
28	22	46	60	76	83	88	90	92	94	95	96	97	97	98	98	98	*	*	*	**	**
32	24	50	63	78	85	89	91	93	95	96	96	97	98	98	98	*	*	*	*	**	**
36	27	53	65	80	86	90	92	94	95	96	97	97	98	98	*	*	*	*	**	**	**
40	29	55	68	82	88	91	93	94	96	96	97	98	98	98	*	*	*	**	**	**	**
50	34	61	72	85	90	93	94	96	96	97	97	98	98	*	*	*	**	**	**	**	**
60	38	65	76	87	91	94	95	96	97	98	98	98	*	*	*	*	**	**	**	**	**
80	45	71	81	90	93	95	96	97	98	98	98	*	*	*	*	**	**	**	**	**	**
100	50	76	84	92	95	96	97	98	98	*	*	*	*	*	**	**	**	**	**	**	**

Note: Decimal points omitted.
*Approximately .99.   **Approximately 1.00.

(3) Given an obtained or estimated mean reliability, r, and the obtained or desired effective reliability, R, what is the approximate number (n) of judges required? The table is entered in the column corresponding to the mean reliability, r, and is read down until the value of R closest to the one desired is reached; the value of n is then read as the corresponding row title.

Product moment correlations.   It should be noted that the mean reliability (r) of Table 2.1 is to be a product moment correlation coefficient such as Pearson's r, the point biserial r, or the phi coefficient. It is not appropriate to employ such indices of "reliability" as percentage agreement (number of agreements (A) divided by the sum of agreements (A) and disagreements (D), A/(A+D)) or net agreements, (A−D)/(A+D). These indices should not only be avoided in any use of Table 2.1 but they should be avoided in general because of the greatly misleading results that they can yield. For example, suppose two judges are to evaluate 100 film clips for the presence or absence of frowning behavior. If both the judges see frowns in ninety-eight of the film clips and disagree only twice they would show 98 percent agreement; yet the χ^2 testing the significance of the product moment correlation phi would be essentially zero! Thus two judges who shared the same perceptual bias (e.g., almost all behavior is seen as a frown) could consistently earn nearly perfect agreement scores while actually correlating essentially zero with one another (phi = .01). Table 2.2 shows two cases of 98 percent agreement between judges. In case 1, judges' variability (S^2) is very low and

Table 2.2. *Two cases of 98% agreement with very different product moment reliabilities*

		Case 1			Case 2		
		Judge A			Judge A		
		Frown	No frown	Σ	Frown	No frown	Σ
Judge B	Frown	98	1	99	49	1	50
	No frown	1	0	1	1	49	50
	Σ	99	1	100	50	50	100

$\chi^2(1) = .01$
phi = .01
Judge A $S^2 = .01$
Judge B $S^2 = .01$

$\chi^2(1) = 92.16$
phi = .96
Judge A $S^2 = .25$
Judge B $S^2 = .25$

accuracy is indistinguishable from rating bias. In case 2, judges' variability is maximal and accuracy is not confounded with rating bias. The two product moment correlations (phi) associated with cases 1 and 2 are dramatically different: .01 versus .96.

Reliability and analysis of variance

When there are only two judges whose reliability is to be evaluated it is hard to beat the convenience of a product moment correlation coefficient for an appropriate index of reliability. As the number of judges grows larger, however, working with correlation coefficients can become inconvenient. For example, suppose we employed forty judges and wanted to compute both their mean reliability (r) and their effective reliability (R). Table 2.1 could get us R from knowing r but to get r we would have to compute $(40 \times 39)/2 = 780$ correlation coefficients. That is not hard work for computers but averaging the 780 coefficients to get r is very hard work for investigators or their programmers. There is an easier way and it involves the analysis of variance.

Table 2.3 shows a simple example of three judges rating the nonverbal behavior of five encoders on a scale of 1 to 7, and Table 2.4 shows the analysis

Table 2.3. *Judges' ratings of nonverbal behavior*

| | | Judges | | |
Encoders	A	B	C	Σ
1	5	6	7	18
2	3	6	4	13
3	3	4	6	13
4	2	2	3	7
5	1	4	4	9
Σ	14	22	24	60

Table 2.4. *Analysis of variance of judges' ratings*

Source	SS	df	MS
Encoders	24.0	4	6.00
Judges	11.2	2	5.60
Residual	6.8	8	0.85

of variance of these data. Our computations require only the use of the last column, the column of mean squares (Guilford, 1954). Examination of the computational formulas given below shows that they tell us how well the judges can discriminate among the sampling units (e.g., people) minus the judges' disagreements controlling for judges' rating bias or main effects (e.g., *MS* encoders − *MS* residuals), divided by a standardizing quantity.

Our estimate of *R*, the effective reliability of the sum or the mean of all of the ratings of the judges is given by:

$$R \text{ (est.)} = \frac{MS \text{ encoders} - MS \text{ residual}}{MS \text{ encoders}} \tag{2.2}$$

Our estimate of *r*, the mean reliability or the reliability of a *single* average judge is given by:

$$r \text{ (est.)} = \frac{MS \text{ encoders} - MS \text{ residual}}{MS \text{ encoders} + (n-1)MS \text{ residual}} \tag{2.3}$$

where *n* is the number of judges as before (Formula 2.3 is known as the intraclass correlation). For our example of Tables 2.3 and 2.4 we have:

$$R \text{ (est.)} = \frac{6.00 - 0.85}{6.00} = .858$$

and

$$r \text{ (est.)} = \frac{6.00 - 0.85}{6.00 + (3-1)0.85} = .669$$

In the present example it will be easy to compare the results of the analysis of variance approach with the more cumbersome correlational approach. Thus the correlations (*r*) between pairs of judges (r_{AB}, r_{BC}, and r_{AC}) are .645, .582, and .800, respectively, and the mean intercorrelation is .676 which differs by only .007 from the estimate (.669) obtained by means of the analysis of variance approach.

If we were employing only the correlational approach we would apply the Spearman–Brown formula (2.1) to our mean reliability of .676 to find *R*, the effective reliability. That result is:

$$R = \frac{(3)(.676)}{1 + (3-1)(.676)} = .862$$

which differs by only .004 from the estimate (.858) obtained by means of the analysis of variance approach. In general, the differences obtained between the correlational approach and the analysis of variance approach are quite small (Guilford, 1954).

It should be noted that in our present simple example the correlational approach was not an onerous one to employ, with only three correlations to compute. As the number of judges increased, however, we would find ourselves more and more grateful for the analysis of variance approach, or for such related procedures as the Kuder–Richardson formulas, Cronbach's alpha, or similar methods available in commonly used data analytic packages.

Reliability and principal components

In situations where the ratings made by all judges have been intercorrelated, and a principal components analysis is readily available, another very efficient alternative to estimate the reliability of the total set of judges is available. Armor (1974) has developed an index, *theta,* that is based on the unrotated first principal component (where a principal component is a factor extracted from a correlation matrix employing unity (1.00) in the diagonal of the correlation matrix). The formula for theta is

$$\text{theta} = \frac{n}{n-1}\left(\frac{L-1}{L}\right) \tag{2.4}$$

where n is the number of judges and L is the latent root or eigenvalue of the first unrotated principal component. The latent root is the sum of the squared factor loadings for any given factor and can be thought of as the amount of variance in the judges' ratings accounted for by that factor. Factor analytic computer programs generally give latent roots or eigenvalues for each factor extracted so that theta is very easy to obtain in practice. (Armor (1974) has pointed out the close relationship between theta and Cronbach's coefficient alpha.)

For an illustration of the use of theta we refer to the standardization of a test of sensitivity to nonverbal cues, the Profile of Nonverbal Sensitivity (PONS) (Rosenthal et al., 1979). When the 220 items of that test were subjected to a principal components analysis, the eigenvalue or latent root (L) of the first (unrotated) component was 13.217. Therefore, from equation 2.4 we find

$$\text{theta} = \frac{n}{n-1}\left(\frac{L-1}{L}\right) = \frac{220}{219}\left(\frac{13.217-1}{13.217}\right) = .929$$

In this particular example the variables were test items; in other examples they might have been judges. In general, when reliabilities are being assessed, items of tests and judges of behaviors are equivalent.

Reporting reliabilities

Assuming we have done our reliability analyses well, how shall we report our results? Ideally, reports of reliability analyses should include both the mean reliability (the reliability of a single judge) and the effective reliability (reliability of the total set of judges or of the mean judgments). The reader needs to know the latter reliability (R) because that is, in fact, the reliability of the variable employed in most cases. However, if this reliability is reported without explanation, the reader may not be aware that the reliability of any one judge's ratings are likely to be lower, often substantially so. A reader may note a reported reliability of .80 based on twelve judges and decide that the variable is sufficiently reliable for his or her purposes. This reader may then employ a single judge only to find later that this single judge was operating at a reliability of .25, not .80. Reporting both reliabilities avoids such misunderstandings.

Split-sample reliabilities.   A related source of misunderstanding is the reporting of correlations between a mean judge of one type with a mean judge of another type. For example, suppose we had ten male and ten female judges, or ten black and ten white judges. One sometimes sees in the literature the reliability of the mean male and mean female judge or of the mean black and mean white judge. Such a correlation of the mean ratings made by all judges of one type with the mean ratings made by judges of another type can be very useful but they should not be reported as reliabilities without the explanation that these correlations might be substantially higher than the average correlation between any one male and any one female judge or between any one black and any one white judge. The reasons for this are those discussed in the earlier section on effective reliability.

As an illustration of the problem of split-sample reliabilities consider the following example. Two samples of judges were employed (one week apart) to rate the nonverbal behavior of a set of psychotherapists. There were ten judges in each of the two groups and the mean ratings assigned to each psychotherapist by the first set of ten judges were correlated with the mean ratings assigned to each psychotherapist by the second set of ten judges. The obtained r was .818. Reporting this r as "the reliability" could be misleading to other investigators since it represents neither the reliability of the total set of twenty judges nor the typical reliability computed from any pair of individual judges.

To obtain the reliability of the total set of twenty judges we employ the Spearman–Brown formula (2.1) with $r = .818$ and $n = 2$ since there were two *sets* of judges (each with ten judges whose ratings had been averaged). Our effective reliability, R, therefore, is found to be:

$$R = \frac{nr}{1+(n-1)r} = \frac{2(.818)}{1+(2-1).818} = .900$$

If we want to find the typical reliability of the twenty individual judges taken one at a time we rewrite the Spearman–Brown equation to solve not for R but for r, as follows:

$$r = \frac{R}{n + R - nR} \tag{2.5}$$

which, for the present example yields

$$r = \frac{.900}{20 + .900 - (20).900} = .310$$

To summarize, the group ($n = 10$) to group ($n = 10$) reliability was .818, the Spearman–Brown "upped" reliability was .900, and the Spearman–Brown "downed" reliability was .310. It should be noted that we could also have obtained this latter r from the original group ($n = 10$) to group ($n = 10$) reliability of .818 with .818 regarded as R and with $n = 10$.

Trimming judges. It sometimes happens that when we examine the intercorrelations among our judges we find one judge who is very much out of line with all the others. Perhaps this judge tends to obtain negative correlations with other judges or at least to show clearly lower reliabilities with other judges than is typical for the correlation matrix. If this "unreliable" judge were dropped from the data the resulting estimates of reliability would be biased, that is, made to appear too reliable. If a judge must be dropped, the resulting bias can be reduced by equitable trimming. Thus, if the lowest agreeing judge is dropped, the highest agreeing judge is also dropped. If the two lowest agreeing judges are dropped, the two highest agreeing judges are also dropped, and so on. Experience suggests that when large samples of judges are employed the effects of trimming judges are small as is the need for trimming. When the sample of judges is small, we may feel a stronger need to drop a judge, but doing so is more likely to leave a residual biased estimate of reliability. A safe procedure is to do all analyses with and without the trimming of judges and to report the differences in results from the data with and without the trimming. Although the method of trimming judges seems not yet to have been systematically applied, the theoretical foundations for the method can be seen in the work of Barnett and Lewis (1978), Huber (1981), Mosteller and Rourke (1973), and Mosteller and Tukey (1977), and, in particular, in the work of Tukey (1977).

Judge characteristics

Individual differences. So far in our discussion of the sampling of judges we have not considered systematic individual differences among our judges.

Typically, there is no special interest in individual differences among judges when we consider issues of reliability. We simply decide on the type of judges we want – for example, college students, clinical psychologists, linguists, dance therapists, mothers, and so forth – and then regard each judge within that sample as to some degree equivalent to or interchangeable with any other judge within that sample.

Sometimes, however, our interest focuses directly on individual differences among judges as when we want to know about the relationships of these individual differences with accuracy (or systematic inaccuracy) of encoding and decoding nonverbal behavior. Interest in such relationships has been increasing (e.g., Blanck, Buck, & Rosenthal, 1986; Buck, 1975, 1979; DePaulo & Rosenthal, 1979a, 1979b; DiMatteo, 1979; Friedman, 1979b; Hall, 1979; Nasby, Hayden, & DePaulo, 1980; Rosenthal, 1979c; Rosenthal & De-Paulo, 1979a, 1979b; Rosenthal et al., 1979; Uno, Koivumaki, & Rosenthal, 1972; Weitz, 1979; Zuckerman & Larrance, 1979).

The types of variables that have been studied for their degree of relationship to skill in decoding nonverbal cues include judges' age, sex, cultural background, cognitive attributes, psychosocial attributes, special skills and impairments, training, and experience (e.g., Rosenthal et al., 1979).

If we are planning a judgment study and want simply a prototypic sample of judges, we may be content to select a sample of college or high school students. If our aim is simply to define the encoder's state or the encoder's nonverbal behavior by means of the judges' ratings, we need not even be overly concerned about the common problem of volunteer bias, that is, the problem that volunteers for behavioral research may differ systematically from nonvolunteers. If our interest, however, is to estimate the average degree of accuracy for the population selected (e.g., students) we should be aware of the potentially large effects of volunteer bias. This problem is addressed in detail by Rosenthal and Rosnow (1975b) and somewhat more briefly later in this volume.

Recent research with high school students has suggested that the correlation between volunteering for behavioral research and accuracy of decoding nonverbal cues may be on the order of .40 (Rosenthal et al., 1979). Such a correlation reflects the situation obtained when 70 percent of the volunteers achieve the median level of accuracy compared to only 30 percent of the nonvolunteers given that about half the judges were volunteers and half were nonvolunteers (Rosenthal & Rubin, 1979b, 1982b).

Maximizing judge accuracy.   Sometimes our intent in a judgment study is not to find prototypic judges but the best judges for our purpose. Thus, if we wanted judgments of nonverbal cues to psychoses we might want clinical

Table 2.5. *Psychosocial variables likely to be useful in selecting judges of greater sensitivity to nonverbal cues* ($r \geq .20$)

Variables	Number of studies	Median r	Equivalent to increasing success rate[a]	
			From	To
Volunteering for research	2	.40	.30	.70
Achievement potential	5	.31	.34	.66
Social-religious values	1	.28	.36	.64
Interpersonal adequacy	5	.25	.38	.62
Democratic orientation	2	.24	.38	.62
Intellectual and interest modes	5	.23	.38	.62
Maturity	5	.22	.39	.61
Interpersonal sensitivity	22	.22	.39	.61
Task orientation	1	.21	.40	.60
Nondogmatic	2	.20	.40	.60
Spouses report of nonverbal sensitivity	2	.20	.40	.60

Note: For this Table, sensitivity to nonverbal cues was defined by performance on the PONS test (Rosenthal et al., 1979).
[a] Based on the Binomial Effect Size Display (Rosenthal & Rubin, 1979b, 1982b).

psychologists or psychiatrists for our judges. If we wanted judgments of nonverbal cues to discomfort in infants we might want pediatricians, developmental psychologists, or mothers. If we wanted judgments of nonverbal cues of persuasiveness we might want trial lawyers, fundamentalist clergymen, or salespersons.

If there is no very specialized type of judgment we are after but we would like to obtain the highest level of accuracy possible in a general way, we might want to select our judges on the basis of prior research suggesting characteristics of those more sensitive to nonverbal cues. A recent review of research suggests that to optimize overall sensitivity we might select judges who are female, of college age, cognitively more complex, and psychiatrically unimpaired (Rosenthal et al., 1979). Actors, students of nonverbal communication, and students of visual arts tend to perform better than do other occupational groups, and among teachers and clinicians, the more effective teachers and clinicians are likely to be the better decoders of nonverbal cues (Rosenthal et al., 1979). Finally, if we were to base our selection of more accurate judges of nonverbal behavior on psychosocial variables, we might want to consider results of the type shown in Table 2.5 based on research reported elsewhere in detail (Rosenthal et al., 1979). Users of Table 2.5 should note that the correlations given are medians of varying numbers of studies conducted so that greater confidence may be placed in those relationships based on a larger number of studies. Even in those cases, however, it is possible for any one study to show a much higher or a much lower correlation.

Sampling encoders

The basic issues that must be faced in our sampling of encoders are very similar to the issues that must be faced in our sampling of judges. One decision that must be made is how many encoders to employ. Should the researcher's finite resources be allocated to increasing the number of different encoders (with a concomitant decrease in the number of scenes encoded by each sender) or to increasing the number of scenes encoded by each sender (with a concomitant decrease in the number of encoders)? The purpose of a recent study was to address this question in a preliminary manner by comparing the internal consistency of tests comprised of many encoders, each sending the same scene, with the internal consistency of a standardized test comprised of a single encoder who sends many different scenes (Rosenthal, Hall, & Zuckerman, 1978).

When this question is rephrased as a substantive rather than as a methodological one, it may become more generally interesting. Am I, as a judge of other people's nonverbal communication, more consistent in the accuracy of my repeated judgments of a single other person than I am in the accuracy of my single judgments of a host of different people? To put this still another way, could one predict the accuracy of my future judgments of the single person better than one could predict the accuracy of my future judgments of new people?

Tests employing many encoders

We made two tests comprised of many encoders. The procedural details are given elsewhere (Zuckerman, Hall, DeFrank, & Rosenthal, 1976). Here it is enough to say that two groups of encoders ($N = 30,29$) were videotaped while they reacted spontaneously to four different videotaped scenarios (pleasant adult–child interaction, comedy scene, murder scene, and auto accident). Encoders were also videotaped while talking about the four scenarios and while *trying* to communicate via facial expression the nature of the stimuli they had been exposed to. Thus, each encoder sent twelve scenes: four scenarios in each of three modes (spontaneous, talking, and posed). For each group of encoders, a group of thirty judges "decoded" the encoders' scenes by viewing them on a videotape and making multiple-choice judgments of which one of the four scenarios was being expressed in each. These judgments were then scored for accuracy.

For each of our two samples of encoders (and separately for each of the twelve encodings), we were able to intercorrelate the accuracy scores earned by the encoders. In psychometric terms, encoders were analogous to test items and judges were analogous to test-taking subjects. The average of the intercorrelations among single test items, or among senders in this case, when corrected for the number of test items or encoders by the Spearman–Brown procedure described earlier, becomes an index of internal consistency known as K–R 20, coefficient alpha, or effective reliability (R) (Guilford, 1954; Rosenthal, 1973).

Test employing one encoder

Our goal was to compare the length-corrected internal consistency coefficients based on intercorrelations among encoders encoding the same scene in the same mode (many-encoder tests described above) with the intercorrelations among many different scenes sent by the same encoder. The latter intercorrelations were already available from psychometric research conducted with the Profile of Nonverbal Sensitivity, the PONS test (Rosenthal et al., 1979). In that test twenty different scenes are encoded by a single sender in eleven different channels of nonverbal communication (e.g., face, body, content-filtered speech, random-spliced speech, and various combinations of these) yielding 220 different items. The internal consistency coefficient for the 220-item PONS test was .86 for the norm group of nearly 500 high school students. When the analogous internal consistency coefficient was computed for the twenty scenes showing only the face (i.e., the modality employed in the many-sender tests), the reliability was nearly identical (.88) after correcting for the difference in length (from 20 to 220 items) by the Spearman–Brown procedure described earlier (Guilford, 1954; Rosenthal, 1973).

Internal consistency data

Table 2.6 shows the internal consistency coefficients for our many-encoder tests: two samples of encoders in three modes of sending each of the four scenes. All coefficients of internal consistency are corrected using the Spearman–Brown formula to the same number of items as the PONS (220). This is done merely to make results of one kind of test comparable to the results of the other; since coefficients of internal consistency go up as the number of test items goes up, it is essential to control for that fact when comparing two such coefficients. (It would have been equally informative, though less common in practice, to apply the Spearman–Brown formula downward from the 220-item length to the 30-item length for the single-encoder tests.) The grand mean of all twenty-four alphas of Table 2.6 was .83 and the grand median was .90. Because all of the items of the PONS test were posed, it was of specific interest also to note that the mean and median internal consistencies of

Table 2.6. *Length-corrected internal consistency coefficients for two many-encoder tests*

	Scene				
	Pleasant		Unpleasant		
Mode	Child	Comedy	Murder	Accident	Mean
Test A					
Spontaneous	.96	.91	.94	.98	.95
Talking	.67	.82	.85	.94	.82
Posed	.86	.77	.92	.96	.88
Mean	.83	.83	.90	.96	.88
Test B					
Spontaneous	.92	.89	.93	.93	.92
Talking	.71	.31	.89	.52	.61
Posed	.67	.91	.81	.90	.82
Mean	.77	.70	.88	.78	.78
Grand mean	.80	.77	.89	.87	.83

Table 2.6 for just the posed scenes were .85 and .88, respectively. The latter value was identical to the internal consistency coefficient for the face items of the PONS test corrected for length. In short, the reliability of the ability to decode different encoders sending the same scene was, on the average, the same as the reliability of the ability to decode different scenes sent by the same encoder.

Table 2.7 shows the analysis of variance of the data of Table 2.6. The three factors were: (1) test (two groups of encoders), (2) mode (spontaneous, talking, or posed), and (3) scene (child, comedy, murder, and accident). The last factor was decomposed into a contrast for pleasant versus unpleasant scenes with the two pleasant scenes and the two unpleasant scenes nested within those categories. The purpose of this analysis was not to test for significance in particular, but to examine the relative magnitude of effects. Results showed that encoder equivalence (internal consistency) was greatest for spontaneous encoding, lowest for talking about a stimulus, and intermediate for posed encoding. Although the magnitude of the effect was smaller, there was also a tendency for unpleasant scenes to show greater sender equivalence (.88) than did pleasant scenes (.78). In the PONS test, internal consistency was similarly greater for unpleasant than pleasant scenes (.87 versus .81).

Table 2.7. *Analysis of variance of length-corrected internal consistency coefficients for the two many-encoder tests of Table 2.6*

Source	SS	df	MS	F	p	eta
Test	.0590	1	.0590	[a]		
Mode	.1953	2	.0976	6.92[b]	.006	.65
(Scene)	(.0608	3	.0202)			
Pleasantness	.0570	1	.0570	4.04[c]	.06	.42
Residual	.0038	2	.0019	[d]		
Test × mode	.0391	2	.0196	[d]		
(Test × scene)	(.0202	3	.0067)			
Test × pleasantness	.0001	1	.0001	[d]		
Test × residual	.0201	2	.0101	[d]		
(Mode × scene)	(.0650	6	.0108)			
Mode × pleasantness	.0218	2	.0109	[d]		
Mode × residual	.0432	4	.0108	[d]		
(Test × mode × scene)	(.1396	6	.0233)			
Test × mode × pleasantness	.0028	2	.0014	[d]		
Test × mode × residual	.1368	4	.0342	[d]		
Pooled residual	.2677	19	.0141			

[a] Untestable.
[b] Mean alphas for spontaneous, talking, and posed modes were .93, .71, and .85, respectively.
[c] Mean alphas for pleasant and unpleasant scenes were .78 and .88, respectively.
[d] Pooled.

Implications

We found that the consistency of the ability to decode different encoders sending the same scenes was essentially identical to the consistency of the ability to decode one encoder sending different scenes. This in no way means, however, that being able to decode one encoder assures being able to decode a different encoder. Indeed, applying the Spearman–Brown formula in the downward direction from our standard length of 220 items shows that the average correlation between ability to decode any two encoders encoding only a single item is very low ($r = .03$) but just as high as the correlation between ability to decode any two scenes encoded by a single encoder ($r = .03$).

What our results do indicate is that no greater gain in generality results from adding encoders sending the same scene than from adding different scenes encoded by the same sender. Our results provide no basis for deciding whether a decoding task should employ more encoders (and fewer scenes) or more scenes (and fewer encoders). Only further empirical research with new stimulus materials can inform us of whether there are circumstances under which any particular combination of j senders and k scenes (where

$j \times k = N$ stimuli) would be optimal (e.g., in the sense of maximizing validity coefficients) for any specific research purpose. Thus, there is no sense in which our results should be interpreted as an argument for employing only a single sender any more than our results should be interpreted as an argument for employing only a single scene.

Further research might show that internal consistency would go up for judgments of a more homogeneous group of many encoders (e.g., all of one sex) or for judgments of a more homogeneous group of scenes or affects sent by a single gender. For the researcher, however, increases in validity due to increasing internal consistency in these ways might be offset for some purposes by a loss of generality in the stimulus materials. In short, we may have to pay for increases in internal consistency with a decrease in external validity.

Encoder sampling and decoder validity.   The foregoing discussion assumes that we do indeed want to generalize to encoders and to the variety of scenes or affects encoded by them. The stimulus sampling required to permit such generalization is often highly desirable and probably practiced too rarely (Brunswik, 1956; Clark, 1973; Ekman, Friesen, & Ellsworth, 1972; Hammond, 1954; Rosenthal, 1966). Before leaving this discussion, however, it should be pointed out that there are times when our goals are more modest and when there is no intrinsic interest in generalizing to encoders. Such would be the case when our intent is only to differentiate among decoders.

Suppose, for example, that we want to develop a test that would differentiate psychotherapists of greater and lesser sensitivity to the nonverbal cues of their patients. The validity of our test might be assessed by the correlation between test scores and ratings of the therapists made by their supervisors, their peers, and their patients. Suppose further that we select one male encoder and one female encoder, to portray fifty scenes or affects, the nonverbal aspects of which are to be decoded by our psychotherapist decoders. Our test might turn out to have fairly substantial validity coefficients (e.g., .30, Cohen, 1977; Rosenthal & Rubin, 1979b, 1982b) even though one male and one female encoder will not normally permit secure generalization to the parent populations of male and female encoders. In short, it is not necessary to be able to generalize to a population of *encoders* when our goal is only to generalize to a population of *decoders*. Sometimes we do want to be able to generalize to both the population of decoders and to the population of encoders and that situation raises interesting questions of data analysis that will be discussed shortly.

Encoder characteristics
So far in our discussion of the sampling of encoders we have not considered systematic individual differences (e.g., traits, states) among our encoders.

Typically, there is no special interest in individual differences among encoders when we consider issues of generalizability over encoders. We simply decide on the type of encoder we want, for example, college students, actors, children, and so forth, and then regard each encoder within that sample as to some degree equivalent to or interchangeable with any other encoder within that sample. Indeed, much of the pioneering work on nonverbal aspects of emotion expression has been within the biological framework that emphasizes the basic similarities of the encoding of emotions even cross-culturally (Darwin, 1872; Ekman, 1973; Izard, 1971).

There are times, however, when our interest does focus directly on individual differences among encoders as when we want to know about the relationships of these individual differences with accuracy of encoding nonverbal behavior (Rosenthal, 1979a). Compared to the wealth of studies examining the personal correlates of nonverbal decoding ability, there are relatively few studies examining the personal correlates of nonverbal encoding ability (Knapp, 1978). Among the better established findings are those suggesting that females are better encoders than males (Hall, 1979, 1980) and that better encoders are less responsive electrodermally than are poorer encoders (for an overview of this literature see Buck, 1979).

Simultaneous sampling

We have seen that there is a growing tradition of research on individual differences among judges in the ability to decode nonverbal cues and a more recent tradition of research on individual differences among encoders in the ability to encode nonverbal cues. Still more recent is the investigation of individual differences in skill at nonverbal decoding and encoding in the same study (e.g., DePaulo & Rosenthal, 1979a, 1979b; Zuckerman, Hall, DeFrank, & Rosenthal, 1976; Zuckerman, Lipets, Koivumaki, & Rosenthal, 1975). This is a very desirable development, one permitting the examination of personal correlates of both encoding and decoding skills as well as the examination of the relationship between the skills of decoding and of encoding nonverbal cues.

The purpose of the present section is to call attention to, and to suggest solutions for, a special problem created when both decoders and encoders are included in the same analysis. This problem is also found in other studies of person perception and, more broadly, in any study in which groups of judges make observations of groups of stimulus persons. Briefly, the problem is that regarding encoders as a between-subjects factor and decoders as a within-encoders (i.e., repeated measures) factor can yield tests of significance that are markedly different from those based on an equally defensible analysis regarding decoders as a between-subjects factor and encoders as a within-decoders (i.e., repeated measures) factor. In a recent study (see below), we found that when decoders were regarded as a between-subjects factor, sex of decoder made no significant difference, $F(1,34) = 1.77$, but when decoders were regarded as a within-encoders factor the *same data* showed an enormous effect of decoder gender with $F(1,34) = 35.60$! In what follows, this problem is explained in some detail and solutions are suggested (Rosenthal & DePaulo, 1980). To anticipate the discussion somewhat, the problem and its solutions are associated with the greater precision of repeated measures (within sampling units) compared to ordinary between-sampling units analyses because of the correlation with each other of the levels of a repeated-measures factor (Winer, 1971).

The encoder–decoder data matrix

In a hypothetical example, four encoders, two males and two females, have each encoded one positive affect and one negative affect. Four decoders, two males and two females, have rated each of the two encodings of each of the four encoders. For each pair of encodings by a single encoder, the decoder's rating, (on a scale of positiveness) of the negative affect is subtracted from the decoder's rating of the positive affect. These difference scores are shown

Table 2.8. *Illustration of results of study of encoding and decoding skill: hypothetical data*

		Encoders				
		Male		Female		
Decoders		1	2	3	4	Mean
Male	1	1	0	3	2	1.5
	2	0	−1	2	1	0.5
Female	3	3	2	3	2	2.5
	4	2	1	2	1	1.5
Mean		1.5	0.5	2.5	1.5	1.5

Subtable of means

Decoders	Encoders		
	Male	Female	Mean
Male	0.0	2.0	1.0
Female	2.0	2.0	2.0
Mean	1.0	2.0	1.5

in Table 2.8. A large difference score means both that a given decoder has done a "good job" of decoding that encoder's affects and that the encoder has done a "good job" of encoding the two affects. The row or decoder means define the individual differences among decoders while the column or encoder means define the individual differences among the encoders.

The key source of the problem is that the standard analysis of these data is a two-way analysis of variance with either encoders or decoders as the between-subjects factor (ordinarily regarded as a random factor) and the other as the within-subjects factor (ordinarily regarded as a fixed factor). One is equally justified in calling the encoders or the decoders the between factor depending on one's purpose. If encoders are regarded as a random between factor because we wish to generalize to other encoders, each decoder's score is a repeated measurement of the encoder's skill. If decoders are regarded as a random between factor because we wish to generalize to other decoders, each encoder's score is a repeated measurement of the decoder's skill.

A standard analysis of variance of the data of Table 2.8 is shown in Table 2.9. For the sake of this example, the encoder factor was arbitrarily chosen as the between factor, and the decoder factor was the within factor. The data of Table 2.8 were chosen so that the results of the analysis would be identical if the labels Encoders and Decoders were interchanged. The encoder gender effect, a between-subjects (fixed) effect of Table 2.9, was not significant with an F of only 2.00. However the decoder gender effect, a within-subjects (fixed) effect, was very significant with $F = \infty$. This great difference in the value of F was obtained despite the fact that the sex of encoder and sex of

Table 2.9. *Standard analysis of results of study of encoding and decoding skill of Table 2.8*

Source	df	MS	F	r
Between encoders				
Encoder gender (E)	1	2.00	2.00	.71
Encoders within gender (R)[a]	2	1.00	—	
Within encoders				
Decoder gender (D)	1	2.00	∞	1.00
DE	1	2.00	∞	1.00
DR[a]	2	0.00	—	

Note: Based on eight observations obtained from four encoders each observed twice; once for the average female decoder and once for the average male decoder.
[a]Error terms for the just-preceding sources.

decoder effects were of identical size as defined by the column and row means of Table 2.8. The data of Table 2.8 could also have been analyzed by regarding decoders as the between-subjects factor and encoders as the within-subjects factor. That analysis would have yielded results showing a nonsignificant effect of decoder gender ($F = 2.00$) but a very significant effect of encoder gender ($F = \infty$). These analyses suggest that when encoder or decoder effects are viewed as within-subjects effects they may be more significant statistically than when they are viewed as between-subjects effects even when they are of exactly the same size. To document that the results of this illustration are reasonably realistic, the results of a series of analyses of real data investigating sex differences in skill at encoding and decoding nonverbal cues, are now presented.

Actual analyses of encoder–decoder data

The details of the research are given elsewhere (DePaulo & Rosenthal, 1979b). Here it is sufficient to note that thirty-eight encoders, twenty males and eighteen females, were videotaped while describing (1) a person they liked (*Like*), (2) one they disliked (*Dislike*), (3) one they both liked and disliked (*Ambivalent*), (4) the person they really liked as though they disliked that person (*Like as though Dislike*), and (5) the person they really disliked as though they liked that person (*Dislike as though Like*). The first two descriptions, then, were of pure affects, the third description was of mixed affect, and the last two descriptions were of deceptive affects.

The same thirty-eight persons serving as encoders also served as decoders. Half the male and half the female encoders served as the decoders of the remaining half of the encoders. Thus, encoders 1–19 were decoded by encoders 20–38, and encoders 20–38 were decoded by encoders 1–19. For each of the five encodings made by encoders an accuracy of encoding score was computed for each decoder. For example, accuracy of encoding (or decoding) Like might be defined by the ratings of liking made to the Like encoding minus the ratings of liking made to the Dislike encoding.

Table 2.10 shows the F ratios obtained when the independent variables of encoder gender and decoder gender were studied by means of both a between-subjects analysis and a within-subjects analysis for the five different dependent variables, the accuracy scores. For both encoder and decoder gender the within-subjects analysis led to larger F ratios than did the between-subjects analysis. For the ten F ratios obtained when the independent variable was a between-subjects factor, the median F was 1.54 ($p = .222$); for the ten F ratios obtained when the same independent variable was a within-subjects factor, the median F was 8.77 ($p = .006$).

The F ratios of Table 2.10 were transformed to normalized ranks (Walker & Lev, 1953) and a $2 \times 2 \times 5$ analysis of variance-type of analysis (between/

Table 2.10. F-*tests obtained in actual studies of skill in nonverbal communication as a function of type of analysis*

| | Independent variable | | | |
| | Encoder gender | | Decoder gender | |
Dependent variable	Between analysis	Within analysis	Between analysis	Within analysis
Like	8.30**	19.60***	1.77	35.60***
Dislike	4.53*	10.81**	0.78	13.29***
Ambivalent	1.43	9.38**	1.66	8.16**
Like as though Dislike	0.17	0.71	1.24	1.55
Dislike as though Like	3.62	7.13**	0.00	0.10
Median	3.62	9.38**	1.24	8.16**

Note: dfs for all $Fs = 1,34$.
  $*p < .05$, $r = .34$.
  $**p < .01$, r's range from .42 to .49.
  $***p < .001$, r's range from .53 to .72.

within) × type of independent variable (encoder gender/decoder gender) × type of dependent variable (like accuracy/dislike accuracy. . . dislike as though like accuracy) – was computed, not primarily for purposes of significance testing but for examination of relative magnitudes of effects. Table 2.11 shows the results of this analysis. Type of analysis made a very big difference but neither the type of independent variable (encoder vs. decoder gender) nor the interaction of the independent variable with the type of analysis showed a detectable effect. The mean square for the dependent variable (regarded as a random effect) though not testable (unless the pooled error is viewed conservatively as an estimate of σ_e^2) was very substantial with an eta of .792 ($F(4,12) = 5.04$, $p = .013$, but this is a very conservative estimate). This simply means that some type of nonverbal encoding and decoding skills show larger effects of encoder and decoder gender than do other such skills. In the present studies the pure affects of liking and disliking showed greater sex differences in nonverbal skill than did the deceptive affects, $r = .777$ ($F(1,12) = 18.29$, $p = .001$).

The analyses presented show clearly that the choice of analysis (between vs. within subjects) can make a substantial difference in the inferences we draw via standard analyses from our studies about both encoder and decoder effects because of the greater power of within subject effects. There is less of an analytic problem, however, when we consider the interaction of encoder and decoder effects. That is because whether encoder or decoder

Table 2.11. *Analysis of variance of results of studies of skill in nonverbal communication obtained as a function of type of analysis*

			Basic analysis		Pooled error	
Source	df	MS	$F(1,4)$	p	$F(1,12)$	p
Dependent variable (R)	4	223.88	[a]		[a]	
Type of analysis (A)	1	405.00	14.40^b	.019	$9.12^{c,d}$	.011
AR	4	28.12	[a]		[a]	
Independent variable (B)	1	57.80	<1	—	1.30	.276
BR	4	87.92	[a]		[a]	
BA	1	28.80	1.68	.265	<1	—
BAR	4	17.18	[a]		[a]	
Pooled error (AR, BR, BAR)	12	44.41				

Note: This analysis was based on normalized ranks of original F ratios. The analysis based on the untransformed data yielded essentially the same results.
[a]Not testable.
[b]Effect size $r = .88$.
[c]Effect size $r = .66$.
[d]$F(1,12)$ based on original untransformed data $= 8.68$, $p = .012$.

is considered a between factor or a within factor, the interaction of these two factors is always a within factor. For the five dependent variables of our study we computed the interaction of encoder and decoder gender, once for encoder as the between factor and once for decoder as the between factor. None of the ten F's was significant. The five F's obtained when encoder was the between factor ranged from 0.00 to 2.06 with a median of .10, while the five F's obtained when decoder was the between factor ranged from .01 to 3.55 with a median of .08. For the five dependent variables, the correlation (r) between the F for interaction obtained when encoder versus decoder was the between factor was .998, $df = 3$, $p < .0001$. For the purpose of testing the interaction of encoder and decoder effects, therefore, it appears to make much less of a difference whether we consider the encoders or the decoders as the between factor.

Some alternative procedures

We have seen both for our hypothetical example and for our real data, that the statistical significance of studies of individual differences in nonverbal communication may depend heavily on whether the encoder or the decoder factor is regarded as the between-subjects factor rather than as the within-subjects factor because of the greater power of repeated-measures factors. Although the implications for analysis and statistical inference have apparently not been noted for very long (Rosenthal & DePaulo, 1980) it seems that investigators have generally made their decisions about analysis on the basis of relative size of sample of encoders versus decoders. Indeed, Hall (1980) has shown that investigators employing larger samples of encoders tend to employ smaller samples of decoders, $r = -.47$. Thus if fifty subjects are to decode the nonverbal cues of one male and one female encoder, it is the decoders that will be regarded as the (random) between-subjects factor and the two encoders will be regarded as the two levels of the (fixed) within-decoders factor. Or, if two judges, one black and one white, are to decode the behavior of thirty classroom teachers, it is the encoder factor that will be regarded as the (random) between-subjects factor while the two decoders will be regarded as two levels of the (fixed) within-encoder factor.

Such usage is neither unreasonable nor "wrong." It does appear, however, that the implications of such practice should be clear. Whatever the basis of the decision, the random between-factor type of analysis permits generalization of results to the population from which the encoders or decoders may be viewed as a random sample. However, since between-subjects error terms are typically larger than within-subject error terms, these analyses will lead to smaller F's. The (fixed) within-factor type of analysis does not permit generalization of the results, that is, estimates of effects to the population from which the encoders or decoders may be viewed as a random sample. That is, the within factor is typically analyzed as a fixed effect while the between factor is typically analyzed as a random effect. The loss in generality that occurs for the within-subject analysis is accompanied, however, by relatively larger F's because within-subject (repeated measures) error terms are typically smaller than between-subject error terms – sometimes *much* smaller because of the correlated nature of repeated measures.

One alternative procedure requires that we perform our analyses twice; once with encoders as the (random) between-subjects effect and the decoders as the (fixed) within-subjects effect, and again with decoders as the (random) between-subjects effect and the encoders as the (fixed) within-subjects effect. This solution is reasonable only if the smaller of the two sample sizes (i.e., of encoders and of decoders) is not *too* small.

A more comprehensive but often more complicated analysis requires that we simultaneously regard the between- and the within-subjects factors as random. Such analyses ordinarily require the computation of quasi-F's which typically work quite well but may turn out to be quite conservative in well-designed studies. Wickens and Keppel (1983) have shown that when stimulus materials (e.g., encoders) have been carefully selected as representative of their populations, when blocking has been employed to assign encoders to conditions so that encoder samples are fairly similar from condition to condition, the likelihood of serious errors of statistical inference is substantially decreased. Wickens and Keppel have also found that when the treatment × decoder variation is very large relative to the encoder variation, more decoders than encoders should be employed to maximize power. However, when the encoder variation is very large relative to the treatment × decoder variation more encoders than decoders should be employed to maximize power. Wickens and Keppel's work is too rich, detailed, and complex to be fully summarized here but readers seeking deeper insights into this problem will profit from close study of their work.

Judges and encoders as volunteers

We have now examined the topics of sampling judges, sampling encoders, and sampling both judges and encoders simultaneously. So far, however, we have only alluded briefly to the problem of volunteer bias, that is, the problem that those judges and/or encoders who find their way into our research may not be representative of the populations of judges and/or encoders to which we would like to generalize. A very detailed analysis of the problem of volunteer bias is available (Rosenthal & Rosnow, 1975b) and here it is only possible to draw from the summary of that work. The summary presented by Rosenthal and Rosnow was not, of course, designed to address specifically the problem of volunteer bias among judges and encoders in studies of nonverbal communication. However, the results that were obtained from our analyses appear to hold over a fairly wide array of research participants.

Reliability of volunteering
How reliable is the act of volunteering to be a research subject? If volunteering were an unreliable event, we could not expect to find any stable relationships between it and various personal characteristics of willing and unwilling subjects. However, there are many personal characteristics that do relate predictably to the act of volunteering. Moreover, coefficients of reliability tend to be satisfactorily high whether the measure of volunteering is simply stating one's willingness to participate or whether it is defined in terms of volunteering for sequentially different types of research tasks. From the available data, the median overall reliability for volunteering was computed as .52, which, by way of comparison, is identical to the median reliability of subtest intercorrelations as reported by Weschsler for the WAIS.

For studies requesting volunteers for the same task the median reliability was .80, and for studies asking for volunteers for different tasks it was .42. Although the number of studies on the reliability of volunteering is not large (ten studies), the findings do suggest that volunteering, like IQ, may have both general and specific predictors. Some people volunteer reliably more than others for a variety of tasks, and these reliable individual differences may be further stabilized when the particular task for which volunteering was requested is specifically considered.

Assessing the nonvolunteer

How do researchers determine the attributes of those who do not volunteer to participate? Several procedures have been found useful, and they can be grouped into one of two types, the exhaustive and the nonexhaustive.

In the exhaustive method, all potential subjects are identified by their status on all the variables on which volunteers and nonvolunteers are to be compared. They may be tested first and then recruited, as when the investigator begins with an archive of data on each person and then, sometimes years later, makes a request for volunteers. For example, incoming freshmen are routinely administered a battery of tests in many colleges, and these data can then be drawn upon in future comparisons. Another variation is to recruit subjects and then test them. In this case subjects for behavioral research are solicited, usually in a college classroom context, and the names of the volunteers and nonvolunteers are sorted out by using the class roster; shortly thereafter, a test or some other material is administered to the entire class by someone ostensibly unrelated to the person who recruited the volunteers.

In the nonexhaustive method, data are not available for all potential subjects, but they are available for those differing in likelihood of finding their way into a final sample. Thus, one variation of the method uses the easy-to-recruit subject, although, because true nonvolunteers are not available, it requires extrapolation on a gradient of volunteering. The procedure in this case is to tap a population of volunteer subjects repeatedly so as to compare second-stage volunteers with first-stage volunteers, and so on. If repeated volunteers, for example, were higher in the need for social approval than one-time volunteers, then by extrapolating these data roughly to the zero level of volunteering it could be tentatively concluded that nonvolunteers might be lower still in approval need. Another variation gets at the hard-to-recruit subject by repeatedly increasing the incentive to volunteer, a method frequently used in survey research to recruit more respondents into the sampling urn. Still another variation focuses on the slow-to-reply subject. In this case only a single request for volunteers is issued, and latency of volunteering is the criterion for dividing up the waves of respondents, as well as the basis for extrapolating to nonrespondents.

Volunteer characteristics

Examining studies that used these various procedures for assessing the non-volunteers, we drew the following conclusions about characteristics that may reliably differentiate willing and unwilling subjects:

Conclusions warranting maximum confidence

1. Volunteers tend to be better educated than nonvolunteers, especially when personal contact between investigator and respondent is not required.
2. Volunteers tend to have higher social-class status than nonvolunteers, especially when social class is defined by respondents' own status rather than by parental status.
3. Volunteers tend to be more intelligent than nonvolunteers when volunteering is for research in general but not when volunteering is for somewhat less typical types of research such as hypnosis, sensory isolation, sex research, small-group and personality research.
4. Volunteers tend to be higher in need for social approval than nonvolunteers.
5. Volunteers tend to be more sociable than nonvolunteers.

Conclusions warranting considerable confidence

6. Volunteers tend to be more arousal-seeking than nonvolunteers, especially when volunteering is for studies of stress, sensory isolation, and hypnosis.
7. Volunteers tend to be more unconventional than nonvolunteers, especially when volunteering is for studies of sex behavior.
8. Females are more likely than males to volunteer for research in general, but less likely than males to volunteer for physically and emotionally stressful research (e.g., electric shock, high temperature, sensory deprivation, interviews about sex behavior).
9. Volunteers tend to be less authoritarian than nonvolunteers.
10. Jews are more likely to volunteer than Protestants, and Protestants are more likely to volunteer than Catholics.
11. Volunteers tend to be less conforming than nonvolunteers when volunteering is for research in general but not when subjects are female and the task is relatively "clinical" (e.g., hypnosis, sleep, or counseling research).

Conclusions warranting some confidence

12. Volunteers tend to be from smaller towns than nonvolunteers, especially when volunteering is for questionnaire studies.
13. Volunteers tend to be more interested in religion than nonvolunteers, especially when volunteering is for questionnaire studies.
14. Volunteers tend to be more altruistic than nonvolunteers.
15. Volunteers tend to be more self-disclosing than nonvolunteers.
16. Volunteers tend to be more maladjusted than nonvolunteers, especially when volunteering is for potentially unusual situations (e.g., drugs, hypnosis, high temperature, or vaguely described experiments) or for medi-

cal research employing clinical rather than psychometric definitions of psychopathology.

17. Volunteers tend to be younger than nonvolunteers, especially when volunteering is for laboraory research and especially if they are female.

Conclusions warranting minimum confidence

18. Volunteers tend to be higher in need for achievement than nonvolunteers, especially among American samples.
19. Volunteers are more likely to be married than nonvolunteers, especially when volunteering is for studies requiring no personal contact between investigator and respondent.
20. Firstborns are more likely than laterborns to volunteer, especially when recruitment is personal and when the research requires group interaction and a low level of stress.
21. Volunteers tend to be more anxious than nonvolunteers, especially when volunteering is for standard, nonstressful tasks and especially if they are college students.
22. Volunteers tend to be more extraverted than nonvolunteers when interaction with others is required by the nature of the research.

Situational determinants

What are the variables that tend to increase or decrease the rates of volunteering obtained? The answer to this question has implications both for the theory and practice of the behavioral sciences. If we can learn more about the situational determinants of volunteering, we will also have learned more about the social psychology of social influence processes and, in terms of methodology, be in a better position to reduce the bias in our samples that derives from volunteers being systematically different from nonvolunteers on a variety of personal characteristics. As with the previous list of conclusions, our inventory of situational determinants was developed inductively, based on an examination of a fairly sizable number of research studies:

Conclusions warranting maximum confidence

1. Persons more interested in the topic under investigation are more likely to volunteer.
2. Persons with expectations of being more favorably evaluated by the investigator are more likely to volunteer.

Conclusions warranting considerable confidence

3. Persons perceiving the investigation as more important are more likely to volunteer.
4. Persons' feeling states at the time of the request for volunteers are likely to affect the probability of volunteering. Persons feeling guilty are more

likely to volunteer, especially when contact with the unintended victim can be avoided and when the source of guilt is known to others. Persons made to "feel good" or to feel competent are also more likely to volunteer.

5. Persons offered greater material incentives are more likely to volunteer, especially if the incentives are offered as gifts in advance and without being contingent on the subject's decision to volunteer. Stable personal characteristics of the potential volunteer may moderate the relationship between volunteering and material incentives.

Conclusions warranting some confidence

6. Personal characteristics of the recruiter are likely to affect the subject's probability of volunteering. Recruiters higher in status or prestige are likely to obtain higher rates of volunteering, as are female recruiters. This latter relationship is especially modifiable by the sex of the subject and the nature of the research.

7. Persons are less likely to volunteer for tasks that are more aversive in the sense of their being painful, stressful, or dangerous biologically or psychologically. Personal characteristics of the subject and level of incentive offered may moderate the relationship between volunteering and task aversiveness.

8. Persons are more likely to volunteer when volunteering is viewed as the normative, expected, appropriate thing to do.

Conclusions warranting minimum confidence

9. Persons are more likely to volunteer when they are personally acquainted with the recruiter. The addition of a "personal touch" may also increase volunteering.

10. Conditions of public commitment may increase rates of volunteering when volunteering is normatively expected, but they may decrease rates of volunteering when nonvolunteering is normatively expected.

Suggestions for reducing volunteer bias

Our assessment of the literature dealing with the situational determinants of volunteering led us to make a number of tentative suggestions for the reduction of volunteer bias:

1. Make the appeal for volunteers as interesting as possible, keeping in mind the nature of the target population.

2. Make the appeal for volunteers as nonthreatening as possible so that potential volunteers will not be "put off" by unwarranted fears of unfavorable evaluation.

3. Explicitly state the theoretical and practical importance of the research for which volunteering is requested.

4. Explicitly state in what way the target population is particularly relevant to the research being conducted and the responsibility of potential volunteers to participate in research that has potential for benefiting others.

5. When possible, potential volunteers should be offered not only pay for participation but small courtesy gifts simply for taking time to consider whether they will want to participate.

6. Have the request for volunteering made by a person of status as high as possible, and preferably by a woman.

7. When possible, avoid research tasks that may be psychologically or biologically stressful.

8. When possible, communicate the normative nature of the volunteering response.

9. After a target population has been defined, an effort should be made to have someone known to that population make the appeal for volunteers. The request for volunteers itself may be more successful if a personalized appeal is made.

10. In situations where volunteering is regarded by the target population as normative, conditions of public commitment to volunteer may be more successful; where nonvolunteering is regarded as normative, conditions of private commitment may be more successful.

3. Stimulus selection and presentation

Stimulus selection

Once the encoders have been selected for a judgment study, further selection must be made of precisely which aspects of the encoders' nonverbal behavior will serve as the stimulus materials for the judges. Suppose, for example, that we have selected as our encoders a group of classroom teachers who have been videotaped for thirty minutes on each of three different occasions. Suppose further that we have calculated that six minutes of videotape per teacher is all we will have time to show our judges, given the total number of teachers in our sample. How shall we select the six minutes from the ninety minutes?

Behavior sampling

We might decide that we should have a sample of teacher behavior from each of the three videotape recording occasions. Perhaps we will decide to choose the first forty seconds, the last forty seconds, and the midmost forty seconds of the behavior we are studying from each of the three occasions. In this sampling procedure, we will be sure to examine at least some of the behavior of the early, middle, and late periods of each of the occasions of observation. Although the particular selection of segments to be judged must depend on the particular purpose, it seems to be wise to sample systematically the various occasions of observation, the phases of each occasion of observation, and the types of specific behavior we want to present to our judges for evaluation. It should be noted, however, that one price we pay for this systematic, objective sampling procedure is the possibility that particular behavior sequences will be interrupted by the beginning or end of the time sample. This problem tends to diminish as the length of each time sample is increased.

To illustrate sampling the types of specific behavior of interest we consider further our example of videotaped teachers. Our theory of teaching might

Table 3.1. *Illustrative plan for sampling nonverbal behavior*

	Type of classroom behavior					
	Class-directed			Individual-directed		
Occasion	Beginning	Middle	End	Beginning	Middle	End
First						
Second						
Third						

Note: Each element of this sampling plan consists of a 20-second stimulus presentation.

hold that to understand teaching behavior we must know how teachers interact with (1) the class as a group and (2) individual students. We might decide, therefore, that half our stimuli will be selected from teacher interactions with the class as a whole, while the remaining half of our stimuli will
be selected from teacher interactions with individual students. Table 3.1 illustrates a sampling plan that "stratifies" or "blocks" on three different variables: (1) type of classroom behavior, (2) phase of each teaching occasion,
and (3) occasion of teaching. Judges' ratings are thus available for each combination of levels of the three independent variables of Table 3.1, and analyses of judges' ratings will tell us whether teacher nonverbal behavior differs
detectably as a function of type of classroom interaction (class- versus indi-
vidual-directed), phase of interaction (beginning, middle, end), and occasion (first, second, third), or interactions among these three variables.

Modality sampling
Suppose we have decided on a sampling plan for our judgment study, perhaps one like that shown in Table 3.1. What shall be the specific stimuli presented to our judges? Depending on how we have videotaped the interactions, we could present any subset of the following aspects of behavior and
the listing is only a sampling:
  I. Video only; no audio
      A. Face only
          1. all of face
          2. part of face
      B. Body only
          1. all of body
          2. part of body

    C. Face plus body
      1. all of face plus body
      2. parts of face plus body (e.g., upper half of face blacked out)
    D. Interpersonal distance cues
  II. Audio only; no video
    A. Full sound track
      1. natural speech
      2. standard content
      3. foreign language
    B. Content removed
      1. content filtered
      2. randomized spliced
      3. speech played backwards
 III. Verbal only (transcript)
 IV. Combinations of above

The specific nature of our research question must determine the type of nonverbal cues we will present to our judges. However, it can be seen from the nonexhaustive listing above, that the same basic material can serve many times over as stimulus materials in different "channels" of nonverbal communication. The resources of real life ordinarily will not permit our employing the many forms of stimulus material that might be interesting and important.

Clip length.   How we decide the question of the specific type of nonverbal stimuli to employ also has implications for the length of each stimulus clip. Although it has been established that considerable nonverbal information can be communicated in just two seconds in both the video and audio channels (Rosenthal et al., 1979), there may be interactions of channel and length of exposure such that changes in length of exposure will affect the information channels in different ways. For example, we know that considerable nonverbal information can be extracted from face or body cues exposed for only one or three 24ths of a second, but it seems unlikely that as much nonverbal information could be extracted from tone of voice cues exposed for such short periods.

Stimulus sampling.   Once again, depending on our purpose, we may want to insure an adequate representation of the various attributes that have been identified reliably in the various modalities. Thus, for example, a number of affects have been reliably differentiated in facial expressions (Ekman, 1973; Ekman, Friesen, & Ellsworth, 1972; Izard, 1971, 1977) and we may want to assess individual differences in judges' ability to decode these various affects. Or, in the work of various workers, a number of dimensions have been found onto which it seemed possible to map the various affects (for reviews of this work see, e.g., Ekman, Friesen, & Ellsworth, 1972; Rosenthal et al., 1979) and we may want to assess individual differences in judges' ability to decode behavior varying along one or more of these dimensions. Examples of the affects that have been reliably described are happiness, disgust, surprise, sadness, anger, and fear; examples of the dimensions that have been described are positive-negative, dominant-submissive, and intense-superficial.

Posed versus spontaneous encoding

An important decision to be made in the process of selecting stimuli is whether to employ posed or spontaneous encoding. On a priori grounds, but not on empirical grounds, we might prefer spontaneous over posed stimuli because it is ultimately the encoding and decoding of everyday nonverbal cues about which we want to make inferences. However, it would be an error of logic, though a common one, to assume that because our ultimate interest is in spontaneous nonverbal cues, a better index of accuracy could be constructed from the use of such stimuli. Surface similarities between models and things modeled are no guarantee of predictive utility (e.g., it would be unwise to assume that the experimental stresses imposed on a perfect six-inch model of a giant commercial airliner would provide sufficient information about the airliner's "real-life" resistance to stress). A model's utility lies in our knowing the relationship between the properties of the model and the thing modeled (Kaplan, 1964). At the present time we do not know whether real-life stimuli would be better or worse or not different from posed stimuli in permitting us to predict accuracy in decoding of everyday nonverbal cues. What is known, however, that is useful to our understanding of any measure of nonverbal accuracy, is that those people who are good at decoding posed stimuli are also good at decoding spontaneous stimuli ($r = .58$, $p < .001$ [Zuckerman, Hall, DeFrank, and Rosenthal, 1976]; and $r = .32$, $p < .02$ [Zuckerman, Larrance, Hall, DeFrank, and Rosenthal, 1979]); in addition, people who send more accurately in the posed mode are also better at sending in the spontaneous mode (in four studies $r = .35$ [Buck, 1975]; $r = .75$ [Cunningham, 1977]; $r = .46$ [Zuckerman et al., 1976]; $r = .40$ [Zuckerman et al., 1980]).

Size of sample of stimuli

Once we have decided whether to employ posed or spontaneous encoding, who our encoders shall be, how we should sample their behavior, and what modality of stimuli should be employed (e.g., video or audio), we must still decide how many stimuli to employ altogether. That question is one of the most difficult to answer since it depends on the total number of encoders to a great extent. Earlier, evidence was presented to show that there might well be an even trade-off between the number of encoders encoding a given affect and the number of affects or scenarios encoded by each encoder. Only further research can tell us for what purpose we should employ what balance of j encoders each encoding k clips.

Until such research is done any advice can be only very tentative. It seems likely, however, that if we are approximately equally interested in generalizing to encoders and to clips or scenarios, and if encoders and clips are similarly variable we may want to have j nearly equal to k. If we are more interested in generalizing to encoders than to clips, and/or if encoders are more variable than clips, we may want to have j greater than k. However, if we are more interested in generalizing to clips than to encoders, and/or if clips are more variable than encoders we may want to have k greater than j.

Stimulus presentation

Medium of presentation
In addition to decisions of stimulus sampling the investigator must select a medium of presentation for the stimuli. For example, the selected behavior could be recorded on film or videotape, on a still photograph, in an artist's representational or stylized drawing, on audiotape, or on a combination of such media. Because real-life behavior flows in time, film or videotape, each accompanied by sound, are the potentially most informative media in terms of total cues available. However, if the focus were on facial expressions or on tone of voice, still photos or audiotape alone might be quite sufficient to the purpose at hand. As we might expect, the amount of nonverbal information in still photographs appears to be greater than that found in drawings, and the amount of nonverbal information in film or videotape appears to be greater than that found in still photographs (Ekman, Friesen, & Ellsworth, 1972; see also the earlier discussion of modality sampling).

All of the above media of presentation have in common that the stimulus materials are preserved more or less permanently so that they can be analyzed and reanalyzed. There are times, however, when the stimulus presentation is in a "live" mode either because live interaction is what we want to study or because we cannot obtain a more permanent record of the interaction. For example, if we were interested in a teacher's nonverbal behavior, but were unable to make a permanent record via film or videotape we might employ classroom observers to record various aspects of teachers' nonverbal behaviors. Because we cannot replay live behavior to conduct a reliability analysis, it is especially important that we employ enough observers for each nonverbal variable being judged to get our effective reliability (R) level to an acceptable level.

Maximizing efficiency of design

In recent years, investigators of nonverbal communication processes have become more interested in the simultaneous investigation of two or more channels of nonverbal communication (DePaulo, Rosenthal, Eisenstat, Rogers, & Finkelstein, 1978; Ekman, 1965b; Ekman & Friesen, 1969, 1974; Ekman, Friesen, & Scherer, 1976; Littlepage & Pineault, 1978; Maier & Thurber, 1968; Rosenthal, 1964, 1966; Rosenthal, Fode, Friedman, & Vikan, 1960; Rosenthal et al., 1979; Scherer, Scherer, Hall, & Rosenthal, 1977; Zuckerman, DeFrank, Hall, Larrance, & Rosenthal, 1979; Zuckerman, Hall, DeFrank, & Rosenthal, 1976).

In these multichannel studies, judges are required to rate behaviors in two or more channels of nonverbal communication. In addition to an interest in channel differences, other variables such as length of exposure of the stimulus material may be of interest. As we have more questions to ask about differences among stimulus modalities, media, length, and so forth, we can achieve greater and greater statistical power (and thereby help to keep down the increased cost of collecting more information) by designing our stimulus material array so as to form a fully crossed factorial analysis of variance with judges as the sampling units and the factors of the experimental design as largely, but not exclusively, within-subjects factors.

The basic reason for the statistical economies to be achieved is the generally greater power we obtain from within-subjects (repeated measures) factors compared to between-subjects factors. We have already discussed this in the section on simultaneous sampling of encoders and decoders where it was also noted that the subjects factor itself is typically regarded as a random factor while the within-subjects factors are typically regarded as fixed factors. Most between-subjects factors, *except* for subjects nested within conditions, are also regarded typically as fixed factors.

An illustrative design.   Let us say that we wanted to compare the information conveyed in facial expressions and body movements as these occurred in various everyday life situations. Suppose, in addition, that we wanted to evaluate the relative amounts of nonverbal information conveyed in exposure lengths of 50, 150, 450, and 1350 msec. The experimental design is shown in Table 3.2. If we had N judges available to participate in our research we could assign one-eighth of them to each of our eight experimental conditions and analyze the experiment as a 2×4 factorial analysis of variance with both factors as between-subjects factors. In most cases, however, we could have a far more powerful design if we had each of our N judges make ratings in all eight of the experimental conditions. Our analysis would still be a 2×4 analysis of variance, but now both factors would be within-subjects factors. Depending on the degree of correlation of ratings made

Table 3.2. *Illustrative experimental design*

Channel	Length of exposure (in msec)[a]			
	50	150	450	1350
Face				
Body				

[a]The four exposure lengths were selected to be linear in their logs.

Table 3.3. *Analysis of variance: between- versus within-subjects models*

Between model		Within model	
Source	*df*	Source	*df*
Channel	1	Channel	1
Exposure length	3	Channel × subjects[a]	9
Chan. × expos.	3	Exposure length	3
Subjects in conditions[a]	72	Expos. × subjects[a]	27
		Chan. × expos.	3
		Chan. × expos. × subj.[a]	27
		Subjects[b]	9
Total	79	Total	79

[a]Error terms for the just-preceding sources.
[b]This is the only "between" effect and the only random effect.

under the eight different conditions, we might be able to conduct our within-subjects analysis with far fewer judges than would be required for the between-subjects analysis. Table 3.3 shows the analyses of variance (without planned contrasts). To keep the total number of *df* equal, the within-subjects model was assigned only ten judges, each operating in all eight conditions; the between-subjects model was assigned eighty judges, ten of whom operated in each of the eight conditions. In many situations, the within-subjects model will serve us more efficiently (i.e., with greater statistical power) than the between-subjects model since the error terms will tend to be smaller. Within-subjects analyses are often characterized by a risk of such time-related effects as fatigue and carryover effects. Procedures for dealing with these problems will be taken up in the section on counterbalancing and blocking.

Table 3.4. *A more complex experimental design*

		Video							
		No cues		Body cues		Face Cues		Body + face cues	
Audio		Neg.	Pos.	Neg.	Pos.	Neg.	Pos.	Neg.	Pos.
No cues	Dom.	a	a						
	Sub.	a	a						
RS cues	Dom.								
	Sub.								
CF cues	Dom.								
	Sub.								

Note: Five stimulus items occur in each cell of the $2 \times 2 \times 2 \times 2 \times 3$ design.
[a]Empty cells in design; in statistical analysis these cells are given chance accuracy level scores (Rosenthal et al., 1979).

A more complex design. More complex designs than that shown in Table 3.2 have also been usefully employed. Earlier, in the section on sampling encoders, we described the PONS test designed to measure sensitivity to nonverbal cues found in eleven different channels (Face, Body, Face + Body; Randomized spliced (RS), Content filtered (CF), Face + RS, Face + CF, Body + RS, Body + CF, Face + Body + RS, Face + Body + CF). Within each of these eleven channels, half the items were positive in affect and half were negative in affect. Within the positive and negative items found in each of the eleven channels half were dominant in interpersonal orientation and half were submissive.

Table 3.4 shows the experimental design. There are four levels of video information (no cues, body cues, face cues, face + body cues), three levels of audio information (no cues, RS cues, CF cues), two levels of affect (positive, negative), and two levels of interpersonal orientation (dominant, submissive). Accordingly, decoding accuracy scores for any person or group taking the PONS test can be analyzed as a $4 \times 3 \times 2 \times 2$ repeated-measures analysis of variance. However, the four levels of the video factor can be more efficiently rewritten as a 2×2 design (face present/face absent × body present/body absent), so that our four-factor design becomes a five-factor ($2 \times 2 \times 3 \times 2 \times 2$) design. For some purposes, a sixth factor of order of presentation, or learning, is added. Thus, within each combination of channel and type of scene, there are five items that can be arranged for analysis into the order in which they are shown in the PONS test. This order or learning factor with its five levels, is fully crossed with the five factors listed above. The one-degree-of-freedom (df) contrast for linear trend is an overall index of improvement over time in PONS test performance. Individuals and groups can, therefore, be compared for their degree of learning as well as their level of performance. In addition, the interaction of the one-df learning contrast with other one-df contrasts provides interesting information on such questions as which channels show greater learning, which content quadrants show greater learning, and various combinations of these questions.

It should be noted that our data-analytic model does not make frequent use of all eleven channels or of all combinations of channels and affect quadrants. While the model employs all this information, it employs it in a more efficient and reliable manner by subdividing parts of the eleven-channel profile into larger subsections than channels based only upon twenty scenes each. Thus, all scenes employing the face can be compared to all scenes not employing the face, all scenes employing the body can be compared to all scenes not employing the body, all scenes employing audio information can be compared to all scenes not employing audio information, and so forth. This series of comparisons, or contrasts, is appreciably more reliable and powerful than the simultaneous examination of all eleven channels. This improvement in reliability and power will be discussed in more detail in subsequent chapters dealing with focused F tests or contrasts.

Counterbalancing and blocking

Suppose we decide to conduct the experiment of Table 3.2 as a within-subjects design with eight stimuli to be presented in each of the eight experimental conditions. How shall we decide the sequence of presentation of the sixty-four stimuli that are to be presented to our judges? Our first thought might be to arrange the sixty-four stimuli randomly; however, experience and reflection suggest that this procedure leaves too much to chance. Bad luck in the selection of the random sequence can leave us with a serious problem of confounding. (This problem of confounding is likely to be serious only when we select a small number of random sequences. When we select a large number of random sequences there is much less chance of a serious problem of confounding.)

In our example, a certain channel (face or body) or exposure length (50, 150, 450, 1350 msec) may wind up heavily overrepresented in certain regions of the random sequence so that apparent effects of channel or exposure length are really effects of serial position of stimulus presentation. If the random sequencing of stimuli has put substantially more than half the body channel items into the last half of the test, and if scores (e.g., ratings, accuracy, etc.)

for the body channel were found to be lower than those for the face channel, we could not tell whether body channel scores were "really" lower or whether there were only a boredom or fatigue effect that lowered performance on all later-presented stimuli (which just happened to affect body items more than face items because of our particular randomization sequence).

Blocking plans. The problem of confounding can be avoided to a great extent by the procedure of blocking on serial position. Alternative blocking plans for our present example include:

1. Let the first thirty-two items of the sixty-four include four stimuli from each of the eight experimental conditions (two channels × four exposure lengths). The four stimuli from each condition to be presented in the first thirty-two items are selected at random, and the sequence of presentation of the first thirty-two items is also decided randomly. The sequence of the last thirty-two items may either be decided randomly or the sequence of the first thirty-two items can be "run in reverse" such as to equalize more precisely the average serial position of each of the eight experimental conditions.
2. Let the first sixteen items of the sixty-four include two stimuli from each of the eight experimental conditions. The two stimuli per condition are assigned at random to each of the four blocks of sixteen items each. The presentation sequence for the four blocks of stimuli may be random, or two may be random while the remaining two are simple reversals of the random sequences.
3. Let the first eight items of the sixty-four include one stimulus from each of the eight experimental conditions. The particular stimulus per condition is assigned at random to each of the eight blocks of eight items each. The presentation sequence for the eight blocks of stimuli:
   a. may be random for all eight.
   b. may be random for four with the remainder as simple reversals of these four.
   c. may be fully counterbalanced in a Latin square.

The advantage of the Latin square is that each of the eight experimental conditions will occur once and only once in each of the eight blocks of stimuli and once and only once in each order of presentation within blocks so that the mean serial position of each of the eight conditions will be identical. Table 3.5 illustrates a Latin square we could employ for the study under discussion.

Carryover effects. Whenever we employ the powerful within-subjects designs, we must consider whether there will be any reasonable risk of carryover effects. That is, will the performance on the second item be affected

Table 3.5. *Latin square for presentation of 64 stimuli*

Block	Order of presentation within blocks							
	1	2	3	4	5	6	7	8
First	A	B	C	D	E	F	G	H
Second	B	C	D	E	F	G	H	A
Third	C	D	E	F	G	H	A	B
Fourth	D	E	F	G	H	A	B	C
Fifth	E	F	G	H	A	B	C	D
Sixth	F	G	H	A	B	C	D	E
Seventh	G	H	A	B	C	D	E	F
Eighth	H	A	B	C	D	E	F	G

by the *particular* item that preceded it, or, more generally, will the performance on the kth item be affected by the particular sequence of $(k-1)$ items preceding the kth item.

When each subject is measured repeatedly on items representing the experimental conditions, and when counterbalancing and blocking have been properly employed, carryover effects are not likely to invalidate the inferences we would like to draw. However, if we want to be *certain* to eliminate the risk of carryover effects, we can design our studies to employ both a within- and between-subjects design so that we can (1) have the unaffected results of the between-subjects design if there *were* carryover effects and (2) have the more precise, powerful results of the within-subjects design as well, if there were *no* carryover effects. Table 3.6 presents the design and analysis of an experiment to test for the major substantive hypothesis as well as the hypothesis of carryover effects.

Suppose we have thirty judges who are to make ratings of stimuli derived from three channels: face (A), body (B), and tone of voice (C). Assume the common situation wherein it is difficult to obtain judges in the first place, but once having obtained them, it costs very little more to have them make a few more ratings. Thus it would be very efficient to have each judge rate all three channels. To avoid confounding we counterbalance as shown in Table 3.6. Our judges are randomly assigned to our three sequences of presentation of stimuli (ABC, BCA, CAB).

However, we are concerned about possible carryover effects. The analysis of the data shown in Table 3.6 yields a test that tells whether sequence of presentation (e.g., ABC) of stimuli makes a difference and whether the order of presentation (e.g., first presented) makes a difference. If they do not make a difference (say a small and nonsignificant F) we feel comforted and can employ the full ninety observations provided by our thirty judges. If

Table 3.6. *Design and analysis of an experiment testing for carryover effects*

A. Design

Groups	Order		
	1	2	3
Sequence I (10 judges)	A	B	C
Sequence II (10 judges)	B	C	A
Sequence III (10 judges)	C	A	B

B. Analysis (prior to contrasts)

Source	df
Between judges	29
Sequence	2
Judges within sequences[a]	27
Within judges	60
Order	2
Channel (order × sequence)	2
Residual[a]	56

[a]Error terms for the just-preceding sources.

they *do* make a difference and we want an estimate of channel differences unaffected by carryover effects, we analyze only the data obtained from the stimuli we presented to the judges *first;* that is, the face stimuli as rated by group I, the body stimuli as rated by group II, and the tone of voice stimuli as rated by group III. It should be noted, however, that this act of purification was not without its cost; we lost sixty observations in the process!

Judging sessions

So far in our discussion of stimulus presentation we have not dealt explicitly with the issue of the total length of time required to judge all of the encoder behavior we want to have evaluated. The more items of behavior we want to have judged, the longer the exposure time of each item, and the longer period of time required for judges to make their ratings, the longer will be the total length of service required of each judge.

Session length. Theory, hunch, and prior research will determine the items of behavior, molar or molecular, that we will want to have judged. A common pattern of selection is to employ rating scales or coding categories that have been found useful in other studies, that make sense on theoretical grounds, and that fall within the budget available to our research. It is also common to add one or more variables that we feel have an especially good chance of yielding interesting results given the specific nature of our study. These are the high risk–high yield variables.

The exposure time per clip is also determined on the basis of theory, hunch, and prior research. One of the surprising features of research on nonverbal communication is the amount of information contained in even very short clips of behavior. Thus while it may sometimes be useful to have clips running for several minutes, a great deal of research shows that clips lasting only one minute, twenty seconds, ten seconds, or even two seconds, or less, contain a good deal of useful information (Rosenthal, Blanck, & Vannicelli, 1984; Rosenthal et al., 1979).

The time required for judges to make each rating is best determined by means of a pilot study. In some of our own research we have found it useful to allow judges more time early in the rating process, decreasing this time systematically on subsequent clips to be rated (Rosenthal et al., 1979).

Multiple sessions.   If the duration of a session required to make all ratings is too long, we may invite our judges back for future sessions to finish their rating task. Inviting our judges back for a second session runs the risk of introducing an effect of judging session due to fatigue, boredom, or practice on the part of our judges or due to such extraneous factors as changes in the environmental situation from one judging session to the next. This procedure also runs the risk that some judges will not return and their data will then be lost. If we employed six judges in the first session and only four appear for the second session, we will have lost one-third of our data. An alternative to having judges come back for subsequent sessions is to employ more judges, each judging fewer encoding behaviors; thus k times as many judges each judge only $1/k$ times as many items.

Suppose we decide to divide the total stimulus material we want to have rated into two halves ($k = 2$), each to be rated by a different group of judges, Our procedures for conducting such a study should minimize the danger of confounding characteristics of the particular items presented in each half with the differences in rating behavior between the two groups of judges. Simple random assignment of items to halves could result in serious confounding problems and we should employ the principles of counterbalancing and blocking described earlier to minimize these problems. Each half of the stimuli set should be as nearly equal to the other in type of item and number of items per type as possible.

Even if we could be sure that all of the judges employed in one session would be available for a second rating session, it could be very helpful to create two equivalent halves of our stimulus materials. In that way we could

Table 3.7. *Equivalent halves of stimuli presented in two judging sessions*

	Judging session	
	First	Second
Judge group I	Half A	Half B
Judge group II	Half B	Half A

avoid confounding the particular half of the items (A or B) with the judging session (1 or 2). Table 3.7 presents the appropriate design; half the judges are randomly assigned to the sequence AB while half the judges are randomly assigned to the sequence BA.

Randomization of judges. When more than one group of judges is employed we must decide how judges are to be allocated to judge group. Sometimes, for example, it is of little consequence whether judges are assigned at random to judge group; at other times it is essential that judge assignment be random.

If all judges are to rate all stimuli in the same sequence (assuming stimuli have been well counterbalanced and blocked), randomization of judges is of little consequence. If we need twelve judges but only four can come to our Tuesday judging session, only four can come to our Wednesday session, and only four can come to our Thursday session, it will normally make little difference to our results. It is true that order effects (first, second, third session), day of week effects (Tuesday, Wednesday, Thursday) are confounded with each other and with differences among judges related to their self-selection into these three groups. However, it seems unlikely that we would be interested in any of these effects in the first place. Indeed, the fact that three groups of judges are employed who differ at least in their availability for service serves to increase the external validity of our results without realistically decreasing the internal validity of our results.

If judges are not going to rate all stimuli, and in the same sequence, as was the case in Table 3.7, randomization may become more necessary. In Table 3.7 if we are interested in the sequence effect (AB vs. BA), judges must be assigned at random to these two sequences. Otherwise, sequence effects would be confounded with judge-group effects. If each half of the stimulus set (A and B) were well counterbalanced and blocked, we might have less interest in examining sequence effects and judge randomization would be less important.

A common situation in which judge randomization is essential is one in which the same clips or scenarios are to be rated in different channels. For example, forty teachers may have been videotaped while teaching and we want ratings of each teacher based on (a) their face during teaching (b) their tone of voice during teaching (content-filtered speech), and (c) the content of what they taught (transcript). If it were necessary that three different groups of judges rate the three different channels (face, content-filtered speech, transcript) and if we were interested in the main effects of channels, it would be essential that judges be assigned at random to their channel to avoid confounding channel differences with judge-group differences.

Independence of judges.   It is customary when presenting encoder behaviors to our judges that we employ judges in groups. This is an efficient procedure in that we can collect a great deal of data in just a single session. It would be very costly indeed if we had to present all our encoder behaviors to judges working just one at a time. There is, however, a frequently unrecognized and potentially serious risk in this custom of having judges work in groups. That risk is the loss of independence of ratings made by judges. Judges working in the same session may make ratings that are correlated with each other for many different reasons: judges glance at one another's ratings, judges are similarly affected by (1) the mood and manner of the experimenter and of other judges in that judging session, (2) the examinations that may be coming the next day, (3) their missing their favorite television show, (4) the rainstorm outside, (5) the evening news, and so forth. (It should be noted that the issue here is not the effect on the mean ratings made by any group of judges but the effect on the degree of similarity of the judges' ratings within a given group.)

If it is an explicit goal of the research to generalize to judges, the statistical tests of significance of the phenomena in which we are interested (e.g., differences between channels) require that judges' ratings be completely independent. If judges' ratings are not independent, the df for the denominators of our F tests are no longer a function of the number of judges but rather of the number of *groups* of judges. Thus, if there is only a single group of judges *no tests of significance are possible.* An alternative to the inefficient procedure of having all judging sessions take place with only a single judge (to avoid losing judges' independence) is available, and it requires employing several groups of judges.

Testing for independence.   The basic strategy is to permit us to test for judge independence and to base our decisions regarding tests of significance on the information provided by the experiment. Suppose we want to compare ratings made on the basis of encoder behavior presented in three channels: face,

Table 3.8. *Design and analysis of an experiment testing for judge independence*

A. Design

Channel:	Female			Male		
	Face	Body	Tone	Face	Body	Tone
Judge group I						
Judge group II						
Judge group III						
Judge group IV						

(header: Sex of judges)

B. Analysis (prior to contrasts)

Source	df
Between judges	39
Sex of judges	1
Groups	3
Sex × groups	3
Judges within conditions	32
Within judges	80
Channels	2
Channels × sex	2
Channels × groups	6
Channels × sex × groups	6
Channels × judges	64

body, and tone of voice. We have forty judges available, twenty females and twenty males. If we present the stimuli to all forty judges at a single session we will not be able to assess the independence of the judges and hence may have no defensible significance test available. If we present the stimuli to one judge at a time it will require forty rating sessions, an inefficiency we may not be able to afford. We can afford, let's say, to have judges make their ratings in one of four sessions. Table 3.8 presents the design and analysis of our illustrative experiment.

Five female and five male judges were assigned at random to each of our four judging sessions, and each judge rated behavior in all three channels of face, body, and tone. Suppose our first question is whether the average ratings made by male and female judges were significantly different in the population from which our judges were sampled. Our temptation is to test the sex-of-judges effect against the judges-within-conditions effect, so that our error term would have 32 *df*. Unfortunately, we may not be able to do so.

Assuming groups to be a random factor, the appropriate test of our hypothesis is to test the sex effect against the sex × groups interaction, the latter error term having only 3 df! However, if the sex × groups interaction is neither significant nor large (say, less than 2.0, Green & Tukey, 1960) when tested against the judges-within-conditions effect, these two terms may be pooled and this new term will then serve as the error term for the sex-of-judge effect. Optionally, the groups effect may also be pooled into this new error term. Poolability, as defined by a sufficiently small F, is an alternative way of stating that judges' ratings made within conditions are essentially independent.

Our primary interest in the present study is in the within-judge effects of channel and channel × sex. Our temptation is to test both effects against the channel × judges interaction with 64 df. Again, we may not be justified in doing so. Assuming groups to be a random factor, the proper error term for the channels effect is the channels × groups interaction while the proper error term for the channels × sex interaction is the channels × sex × groups interaction. Each of the latter two error terms has only 6 df rather than the 64 df we would no doubt prefer. However, if the channels × groups interaction is poolable with the channels × judges interaction, we may use this new pooled error term to test for the channels effect. If the channels × sex × groups interaction is poolable with the channels × judges interaction, we may use this new pooled error term to test for the channels × sex interaction. Testing for poolability is very much like testing for independence of judges within sessions; when $F = 1.00$, the correlation among judges (the intraclass correlation) is zero. (We should note that this low intraclass correlation does not mean low interjudge reliability. That reliability depends on the *difference* between the channels effect and its error term, and on the *difference* between the channels × sex effect and *its* error term.)

When we achieve poolability in the design above we not only gain the power to which we are entitled, we have also set our minds at rest that our observations were independent. But suppose our tests for poolability suggest that pooling is not warranted (e.g., F significant and/or greater than 2.00)? That leaves us in the difficult situation of having to use as error terms the effects of groups of judges or the interactions of groups of judges with other variables (e.g., sex, channels, etc). These error terms ordinarily have few df and we must be satisfied with the lower power that usually is associated with fewer df in the error term. Nevertheless, it is better to have an accurate test of significance with *known* low power, than an inaccurate test with *apparent* great power. If we have developed the very desirable habit of always reporting an effect size estimate along with our tests of significance, the "penalty" we pay for proper inference will be very much minimized. More will be said on effect size estimation and reporting in subsequent chapters.

Independence of ratings. Related to the issue of the independence of judges from one another is the issue of the independence of different ratings made by the same judges. It seems a good bet psychometrically that, because of various rating biases (e.g., halo effects, clinging to the center of the rating scale, positive rating bias, etc.), different ratings made by the same judges will tend to be more highly correlated than would different ratings made by different judges. Since it is logistically easier and far less expensive to have each judge make ratings on a variety of scales or dimensions, it is valuable to ask what the consequences of these inflated correlations are likely to be.

A definitive answer to this question depends on research comparing the results of judgment studies in which the independent variable is the number of different ratings made by each of the study's judges. For example, if we wanted a series of 100 clips or scenarios rated on fifteen different rating scales, each by five different judges, we could examine the consequences of having (a) five judges each make all fifteen ratings of the 100 clips versus (b) having fifteen judges each make five of the fifteen ratings of the 100 clips, versus (c) having twenty-five judges each make three of the fifteen ratings of the 100 clips, versus (d) having seventy-five judges each make only one of the fifteen ratings of the 100 clips.

Such a study might show that as the number of scales rated by each judge decreases the average (absolute) intercorrelation among the scales would also decrease with a resulting drop in the eigenvalue of the first extracted principal component. However, while we might have a good guess as to the psychometric consequences of decreasing the number of scales rated by each judge, it is much harder to guess what the substantive consequences might be.

The costs of employing so many more judges would be so high that it seems unrealistic to think that investigators would stop having judges make multiple judgments unless research indicated substantial negative effects of this practice.

4. Judges' responses

We have talked often of judges' ratings, evaluations, observations, and judgments, but we have not yet been very explicit about the precise nature of the dependent variable, the judge's response. What shall be the format in which the judges make their response?

There are two great traditions of response format in the area of nonverbal communication, the *categorical* and the *dimensional,* and each has been used in a wide variety of research studies (e.g., Argyle, 1975; Buck, 1979; DePaulo & Rosenthal, 1979a; Ekman, 1973; Ekman, Friesen, & Ellsworth, 1972; Izard, 1971, 1977; Mehrabian, 1970; Rosenthal, 1966, 1979c; Scherer, 1979a, 1979b; Zuckerman et al., 1979; Zuckerman et al., 1976). The categorical response presents the judge with two or more response alternatives of which one (usually) is selected. The dimensional response format presents the judge with some form of more or less continuous rating scale (e.g., 1–5, 1–7, or 1–9) of which one numerical value is to be circled, crossed out, or otherwise selected.

There is no evidence to suggest that one of these response formats is uniformly superior, but each seems especially well suited to certain research questions and orientations. For example, if one holds a theory that there are m basic emotions, it is reasonable to employ a categorical response format including some or all of these m basic emotions (Ekman, 1973; Izard, 1971). If one holds a view that nonverbal cues can be mapped into a semantic space of three dimensions, it is reasonable to employ a dimensional response format tapping the three dimensions of semantic space (Osgood, 1966). In this section we shall consider some of the issues arising in our use of various formats of judges' responses.

Categorical formats

Suppose we want to assess judges' accuracy at decoding the affects in sixty content-filtered speech samples. The samples were chosen to represent six emotions studied by Ekman (1973): Anger, Distrust, Fear, Happiness, Sadness, and Surprise. Of the sixty items, ten were intended to represent each of the six affects. One response format might simply list all six emotions and ask the judge to circle the one that was most like the affect represented in the sample of content-filtered speech. Judges' total accuracy score would simply be the number of affects out of sixty that were correctly chosen. In this example, the frequency of correct alternatives was properly balanced so that all six emotions occurred equally often (ten times). The advantage of this balancing is that a judge who is biased to see all affects as anger will still only score at the chance level of 10 out of 60. If the frequency of correct response alternatives had not been balanced, those judges biased to rate all affects in a certain way would earn accuracy scores too high if that affect to which they were attracted were overrepresented in the set of stimulus items. (A little further on we shall discuss the effects of guessing in more detail.)

Making use of more of the data. For some research purposes, in studies of nonverbal accuracy, the total accuracy score may be all the data we want from each judge. However, much more often than we now do, we may want to look more closely at our data, not only for purposes of testing specific hypotheses, but also to see what the data might have to teach us in a spirit of exploratory data analysis (Tukey, 1977).

For example, in addition to the total accuracy score we can construct six separate accuracy scores, one for each of the emotions, as well. This generates a profile of accuracy scores and judges, or groups of judges, can be compared on their profiles as well as on their total scores. Comparing judges on their profiles means that we can compare them on each of the elements (affects in this case) taken one at a time, several at a time, or all at once. When we compare profiles we can do so in several ways. One way is to think of our six-score profile as a single point located in a six-dimensional space so we can compute distances (similarities) among points or judges. Another way is to correlate the six scores of each judge with the six scores of other judges. Similarity in this case is given not by distance but by similarity in the shape of the profile as summarized by a product-moment correlation of some kind (e.g., Pearson's or Spearman's).

Rich as the yield in accuracy scores may be from the simple illustrative study under discussion, considerably more can be learned by a still closer look at the judges' responses, one that permits analysis of judges' errors as well as accuracies (Tomkins & McCarter, 1964; see also our later discussion of the two-step model of response quantification). Table 4.1 shows an illustrative (hypothetical) full data matrix that summarizes all sixty of the

Table 4.1. *Full data matrix for one judge employing a categorical response format*

Chosen category	Correct category						
	Anger	Disgust	Fear	Happiness	Sadness	Surprise	Σ
Anger	8[a]	4	3	1	2	2	20
Disgust	1	4[a]	2	1	3	1	12
Fear	1	1	3[a]	2	1	2	10
Happiness	0	0	0	3[a]	0	1	4
Sadness	0	1	2	1	4[a]	2	10
Surprise	0	0	0	2	0	2[a]	4
Σ	10	10	10	10	10	10	60

[a] Items scored as accurate; total accuracy = 24.

judge's responses. For each of the correct categories of emotion, given in the columns, we can see the distribution of responses according to the category chosen by the judge, given in the rows. This illustrative judge correctly identified 8 of the 10 Anger stimuli but missed two; one was mistakenly called Disgust, the other was mistakenly called Fear.

The column totals of the full data matrix are fixed by the design of the study. In this case, each column totals 10 because we were careful to balance our set of stimuli for the frequency with which each emotion was the correct alternative. The row totals define the judge's bias. Fully unbiased judges, regardless of their total level of accuracy, would show no real differences among their row totals. The illustrative judge of Table 4.1 did show a significant bias $(\chi^2(5) = 17.6, p = .0035)$ that was characterized by choosing the category Anger too often, and the categories Happiness and Surprise not often enough.

The bias of seeing "too much" of one category (e.g., anger) tends to inflate accuracy for the biased category. Thus if there were perfect bias for one category (e.g., anger), all categories chosen would be *that* category, and all items for which that category (i.e., anger) is the correct answer would be scored correct. Thus, there tends to be a positive correlation between bias toward a category and accuracy in that category. For the data of Table 4.1 the correlation between bias (the column on the far right) and accuracy (the entry of each column with the superscript *a*) is .93, $p = .007$. Since the accuracy score is one component of the row total, or bias, we naturally expect a positive correlation between accuracy and bias. It often happens, however, that even when the row total is corrected for accuracy by subtracting the accurately categorized items from the row total, the correlation between accuracy and bias remains. For the data of Table 4.1, for example, the row totals of 20, 12, 10, 4, 10, 4, become 12, 8, 7, 1, 6, 2 when corrected by the accuracy scores of 8, 4, 3, 3, 4, 2, that is, when this last set is subtracted from the first. Still, the correlation between these accuracy scores and the accuracy-corrected bias scores remains substantial: $r(4) = .85$, $p = .033$. We could also compute our test for bias on the accuracy-corrected row totals, if we should want an estimate of bias omitting items categorized accurately. In this example, the test for bias remains significant when we employ the accuracy-corrected row totals, $\chi^2(5) = 13.67$, $p = .018$.

Further insight into the patterning of responses made in a full data matrix of the type shown in Table 4.1 can often be had by examining the differences between each cell entry and the value expected for that cell entry given its row and column total (row total × column total divided by grand total). These differences, or residuals, highlight the frequencies that are much too large or much too small and are, therefore, in need of close examination. An additional procedure for gaining such insight is a procedure called *standardizing the margins* developed by Mosteller (1968) and described in a more elementary context by Rosenthal and Rosnow (1975a, 1984). The procedure shows what the cell entries are like after the row totals have all been made equal to each other and the column totals have all been made equal to each other.

Standardizing the margins. We illustrate Mosteller's method by means of a simple set of hypothetical pilot study data. We have available fifty-three film clips of affect being expressed in the facial channel. Of the 53 clips 34 were intended to communicate happiness, 13 were intended to communicate surprise, and 6 were intended to communicate fear. Our pilot study judge made the selections shown at the top of Table 4.2.

We begin the procedure by dividing each cell count by the sum of the column in which we find the count yielding the center display of Table 4.2. This first step has equalized the column totals by setting them all equal to 1.00. We note, however, that the row totals are far from equal. To set them equal we divide each entry of this new table by its row total yielding the bottom display of Table 4.2.

For clarity, only two decimal places have been presented but it is usually best to employ at least three decimal places while calculating. We continue dividing the counts of each new table by the column totals which unequalizes the row totals; then dividing the counts of the following table by the row totals and so on until the row totals are all equal and the column totals are all equal. The individual row totals will not equal the individual column totals except in cases where the number of rows and columns are equal as they often will be in judgment studies of the type under discussion. Table 4.3

Table 4.2. *Results of a pilot study and the first two steps of standardizing the margin*

	Pilot study results			
	Intended affect			
Chosen affect	Happiness	Surprise	Fear	Σ
Fear	0	3	3	6
Surprise	10	3	2	15
Happiness	24	7	1	32
Σ	34	13	6	53
	Equating columns			
Chosen affect	Happiness	Surprise	Fear	Σ
Fear	.00	.23	.50	.73
Surprise	.29	.23	.33	.85
Happiness	.71	.54	.17	1.42
Σ	1.00	1.00	1.00	3.00
	Equating rows			
Chosen affect	Happiness	Surprise	Fear	Σ
Fear	.00	.32	.68	1.00
Surprise	.34	.27	.39	1.00
Happiness	.50	.38	.12	1.00
Σ	.84	.97	1.19	3.00

continues this process for the data of Table 4.2 where the displays on the right always follow the display immediately to their left.

The row and column totals have now all converged to unity and we have finished standardizing the margins. There is one more step, however, that will throw our results into still bolder relief and that is to subtract from each entry of the final table the grand mean of all cells. In this case that value is $3.00/9 = .33$, yielding the residuals shown in Table 4.4.

The interpretation of this display is quite straightforward. The greatest relative overrepresentation is in the upper right and lower left corners meaning that fear displays and happiness displays are particularly likely to be selected as fear displays and happiness displays, respectively. The greatest relative underrepresentation is in the upper left and lower right corners meaning that happiness displays and fear displays are particularly *unlikely* to be selected as fear displays and happiness displays, respectively.

Table 4.3. *Standardizing the margins of Table 4.2*

	Dividing by column totals				Dividing by row totals			
	Happi-ness	Sur-prise	Fear	Σ	Happi-ness	Sur-prise	Fear	Σ
Fear	.00	.33	.58	0.91	.00	.36	.64	1.00
Surprise	.41	.28	.32	1.01	.40	.28	.32	1.00
Happiness	.59	.39	.10	1.08	.55	.36	.09	1.00
Σ	1.00	1.00	1.00	3.00	.95	1.00	1.05	3.00
Fear	.00	.36	.61	0.97	.00	.37	.63	1.00
Surprise	.42	.28	.30	1.00	.42	.27	.31	1.00
Happiness	.58	.36	.09	1.03	.56	.35	.09	1.00
Σ	1.00	1.00	1.00	3.00	.98	.99	1.03	3.00
Fear	.00	.37	.62	0.99	.00	.38	.62	1.00
Surprise	.43	.27	.30	1.00	.43	.27	.30	1.00
Happiness	.57	.36	.08	1.01	.57	.35	.08	1.00
Σ	1.00	1.00	1.00	3.00	1.00	1.00	1.00	3.00

Table 4.4. *Table of residuals after standardizing the margins of Table 4.2*

	Intended affect		
Chosen affect	Happiness	Surprise	Fear
Fear	−.33	.05	.29
Surprise	.10	−.06	−.03
Happiness	.24	.02	−.25

These results suggest a linear relationship among the three affects on some underlying dimension of positiveness, for example, with happiness most positive and fear least positive. As the positiveness of the encoded affect increases so does the positiveness of the selected affect. This relationship can easily be quantified by the use of contrast weights discussed in subsequent chapters and elsewhere in more detail (Rosenthal & Rosnow, 1985). If we assign the weights $+1, 0, -1$ to the happiness, surprise, and fear affects as encoded and the same weights to the affects as decoded we multiply the row weight by the column weight relevant to each cell to yield the nine contrast weights shown in Table 4.5. When we correlate these nine contrast weights with their nine corresponding residuals of Table 4.4 we obtain an $r(7)$ of .97 showing how well the data fit the conclusion that the more positive the affect intended the more positive the affect selected.

Table 4.5. *Contrast weights for rows, columns, and their products*

	Intended affect		
Chosen affect	Happiness (+1)	Surprise (0)	Fear (−1)
Fear (−1)	−1	0	+1
Surprise (0)	0	0	0
Happiness (+1)	+1	0	−1

Table 4.6. *Table of residuals after standardizing the margins of Table 4.1*

Chosen category	Correct category					
	Anger	Disgust	Fear	Happiness	Sadness	Surprise
Anger	.42[a]	.04	−.04	−.17	−.09	−.16
Disgust	−.02	.26[a]	.00	−.16	.08	−.16
Fear	.07	.00	.24[a]	−.15	−.04	−.13
Happiness	−.17	−.17	−.17	.45[a]	−.17	.17
Sadness	−.17	.00	.10	−.16	.36[a]	−.13
Surprise	−.17	−.17	−.17	.20	−.17	.43[a]

[a] These cells represent the judges' accuracy level.

Standardizing more complex tables.   As an example of standardizing the margins of a more complex or larger table we return to the data of Table 4.1. After some ten cycles of standardizing and then subtracting the grand mean we obtain the approximate residuals of Table 4.6. Inspection shows that in every row and every column the largest entry is the residual representing the judge's accuracy level. If we code these six residuals as +1 and all other cells as 0 we find the correlation (r) representing this definition of accuracy to be .83.

Close comparison of Tables 4.1 and 4.6 reveals some useful insights from the latter. For example Table 4.1 suggests that the judge sees anger as often as he sees disgust when disgust is the correct category. That is indeed the case, but it is due to the judge's bias to see anger too often. Table 4.6 shows that when we correct for bias, as we do when standardizing the margins, we find that both fear and sadness are nearly as frequently seen as anger when disgust is communicated, a result not apparent from Table 4.1.

Table 4.1 also suggests that anger is as frequently diagnosed as fear when fear is communicated. Table 4.6 shows, however, that after correcting for the judge's bias, it is sadness that is most overrepresented among the incorrect alternatives. Similarly Table 4.1 suggests that when happiness is encoded both surprise and fear are the runner-up selections but Table 4.6 shows, after adjustment for bias, that only surprise is overrepresented while fear is actually *under*represented. Finally, when surprise is encoded, happiness appears to be underrepresented as a choice in Table 4.1 but overrepresented in Table 4.6.

Number of categories. In the illustration we have been discussing, it was reasonable to employ a categorical format of six alternatives. Often, however, the design of the research requires only two or three response alternatives, and when the needs of the research speak clearly on the number of alternatives or categories to employ, we should listen. Frequently, however, there is no clear theoretical reason to prefer any particular number of categories; that was the situation in our development of the PONS test (Rosenthal et al., 1979). That test presents judges with 220 items of nonverbal behavior and asks judges to select one of just two alternatives as the correct response. From a theoretical point of view, there was no reason to employ only two alternatives. We might just as well have employed three, four, or even five alternatives. Indeed, everything else equal, tests tend to be more reliable when the number of alternatives is increased (Nunnally, 1978, pp. 652–53).

Our choice of only two alternatives or categories was based more on intuition than on strong evidence. We felt that with a test so long (220 items, forty-five minutes administration time with two response alternatives) adding even a third alternative might prove to make the task too onerous and perhaps too time-consuming as well. There is a very real logistic advantage in having tests or judging tasks kept under fifty or forty-five minutes: they can be more easily administered to intact classes of secondary school and college students.

In a test or judging task, if more categories are employed without sacrificing other desirable features of the task, there is a practical benefit to be had. It becomes easier to assess the probability that a *particular* judge has shown accuracy greater than chance. Normally, when samples of judges are employed, this is not a great advantage, since the number of judges gives us the power to establish that judges, in the aggregate, can do better than chance in decoding nonverbal cues. In clinical contexts, however, or in selection contexts, where we are very much interested in evaluating the performance of a single patient or applicant, a larger number of alternatives per item is very useful, especially when we must keep the total number of items administered fairly low.

Table 4.7. *Minimum number of items required to establish individual judge's accuracy at various levels of significance*

Number of alternatives	Chance level	Significance levels (one-tailed)				
		.10	.05	.01	.005	.001
2	.50	4	5	7	9	10
3	.33	3	3	5	5	7
4	.25	2	3	4	4	5
5	.20	2	2	3	4	5
6	.17	2	2	3	3	4
7	.14	2	2	3	3	4
8	.12	2	2	3	3	4
9	.11	2	2	3	3	4
10	.10	1	2	2	3	3
11	.09	1	2	2	3	3
12	.08	1	2	2	3	3

Table 4.7 shows the number of items required to show a single judge to be significantly accurate for each of several numbers of response alternatives. If our criterion of "real" accuracy were accuracy at a one-tailed p of .005, we would require nine items having only two response categories, but only three items having six response categories. Thus, if we wanted to evaluate nonverbal accuracy in each of eleven channels as in the PONS test, we would require ninety-nine items with only two alternatives, but only thirty-three items with six alternatives. Table 4.7 is useful not only for research applications in which only a single judge has been employed but also in clinical applications where we may wish to establish the accuracy of individual clinicians.

Effects of guessing.   The second column of Table 4.7 shows the probability of obtaining a correct response by random selection of a response alternative (guessing) as a function of the number of response categories or alternatives. With only two categories we have a probability of .50 of guessing the correct category; with ten categories we have a probability of only .10. Therefore, if we had a test of 100 items we would regard a score of 50 correct quite differently if the number of alternatives (A) were two versus ten. If A were two, the performance would be no better than chance; if A were ten, the performance would be very substantially better than chance ($\chi^2(1) = 178$, $Z > 13$, p close to zero). Our evaluation of the effects of guessing on the level of a judge's accuracy, then, depends heavily on the number of response alternatives.

Under many conditions, we may not be concerned with estimation of a judge's actual level of accuracy. In a great deal of research on individual differences, for example, we may be concerned only with judges' relative position on a distribution of accuracy scores. In such cases the number of response categories per item need not concern us. At other times, however, we do want some estimate of how well a judge or group of judges has done, taking into account the effect of successful guessing as a function of the number of response alternatives. The standard estimate is given by Nunnally (1978). The number of items that are correct after adjustment for guessing (R adjusted) is a function of the number of items that are correct, or right (R), the number of items that are incorrect, or wrong (W), and the number of categories of response for each item (A). The adjusted number correct is given by

$$R \text{ adjusted} = R - \frac{W}{A-1}$$

Thus, if we answer 50 of 100 items correctly, we will earn an adjusted score of zero if there are only two alternatives per item, since we did not do any better than randomly choosing (guessing) one alternative. However, had there been ten alternatives, our adjusted score would have been 44.4. Table 4.8 gives the adjusted accuracy scores for a 100-item test for varying numbers of response alternatives. The first column gives the number of correctly answered items (R) in steps of five. The second column gives the number of incorrectly answered items (W) which is simply $100 - R$ for this table. In each column of the body of the table, a perfectly chance level of performance is given by an adjusted accuracy score of zero. Because Table 4.8 employs steps of five items correct, a nearly exact score of zero is not found in each column; however, interpolation can be used to find the level of approximate zero or any other value located between adjacent entries. A more precise location for zero values of adjusted accuracy scores for Table 4.8 is given by:

$$R = \frac{100}{A}$$

or, more generally, by

$$R = \frac{K}{A}$$

where K is the total number of items or $R + W$.

We have defined the total number of items (K) as the sum of the right (R) and wrong (W) answers. That relationship holds only if we score as wrong

Table 4.8. *Estimated accuracy adjusted for guessing (100-item test)*

		Number of alternatives								
Number right	Number wrong	2	3	4	5	6	7	8	9	10
100	0	100	100	100	100	100	100	100	100	100
95	5	90	92.5	93.3	93.8	94	94.2	94.3	94.4	94.4
90	10	80	85.0	86.7	87.5	88	88.3	88.6	88.8	88.9
85	15	70	77.5	80.0	81.2	82	82.5	82.9	83.1	83.3
80	20	60	70.0	73.3	75.0	76	76.7	77.1	77.5	77.8
75	25	50	62.5	66.7	68.8	70	70.8	71.4	71.9	72.2
70	30	40	55.0	60.0	62.5	64	65.0	65.7	66.2	66.7
65	35	30	47.5	53.3	56.2	58	59.2	60.0	60.6	61.1
60	40	20	40.0	46.7	50.0	52	53.3	54.3	55.0	55.6
55	45	10	32.5	40.0	43.8	46	47.5	48.6	49.4	50.0
50	50	00	25.0	33.3	37.5	40	41.7	42.9	43.8	44.4
45	55	− 10	17.5	26.7	31.2	34	35.8	37.1	38.1	38.9
40	60	− 20	10.0	20.0	25.0	28	30.0	31.4	32.5	33.3
35	65	− 30	2.5	13.3	18.8	22	24.2	25.7	26.9	27.8
30	70	− 40	− 5.0	6.7	12.5	16	18.3	20.0	21.2	22.2
25	75	− 50	− 12.5	0.0	6.2	10	12.5	14.3	15.6	16.7
20	80	− 60	− 20.0	− 6.7	0.0	4	6.7	8.6	10.0	11.1
15	85	− 70	− 27.5	− 13.3	− 6.2	− 2	0.8	2.9	4.4	5.6
10	90	− 80	− 35.0	− 20.0	− 12.5	− 8	− 5.0	− 2.9	− 1.2	0.0
5	95	− 90	− 42.5	− 26.7	− 18.8	− 14	− 10.8	− 8.6	− 6.9	− 5.6
0	100	− 100	− 50.0	− 33.3	− 25.0	− 20	− 16.7	− 14.3	− 12.5	− 11.1

any items that are omitted. However, scoring omitted items as zero gives them too little credit in computing R. It seems preferable to credit omitted items with the score that would be obtained by purely random guessing, that is, the reciprocal of the number of alternatives $(1/A)$. Thus, if there are two categories of response we credit omitted items with .5 points, if there are three response alternatives, we credit omitted items with .33 points, and so forth (Nunnally, 1978, p. 650; Rosenthal et al., 1979). Because judges often know more than they think they do, and because factors other than actual skill at nonverbal decoding affect the frequency of omitted items, it seems best to do all one can to avoid omitted items. Judges can usually be successfully urged to "leave no blanks." If blanks *are* left and we do not credit them with $1/A$ points, we run the risk of having people who don't like to guess scoring significantly *below* chance.

Level of accuracy. So far we have talked only of the effect on item difficulty, or lack of "guessability," of an extrinsic factor of format: the number of response alternatives. There are also intrinsic factors contributing to item difficulty, for example, length of stimulus exposure time, quality of stimulus materials, and so forth. From the point of view of developing psychometrically sound stimulus materials or tests, what should be the level of difficulty of the items? If there were two response alternatives, an average accuracy rate of 50 percent would clearly be undesirable since that would suggest that judges were unable to decode the nonverbal materials better than chance. Similarly, if there were two response alternatives, an average accuracy rate of 100 percent would be undesirable since no individual differences in accuracy could be assessed, and since we would have no idea of how much more difficult the task might have been made without the average accuracy level dropping noticeably.

There is no uniformly correct answer to the question of a desirable level of average accuracy for stimulus materials of varying numbers of response categories. As a very rough rule-of-thumb, however, we might expect reasonably good performance (e.g., discrimination power) from items with accuracy adjusted for guessing (R adjusted) of approximately .7. Table 4.8 can be employed to obtain the raw score accuracies (R) equivalent to the adjusted accuracies for each column (number of categories). For most practical applications, the raw score accuracies (R) equivalent to the adjusted accuracy of .7 will range between .7 and .85, the latter value for the situation of only two response alternatives, the former value for the situation of a larger number of response alternatives (Guilford, 1954, p. 391; Nunnally, 1978, p. 273).

The two-step model of response quantification.   Suppose we ask our judges to select one of six emotions as the correct one. We must first quantify the response in some way before our computer, animate or inanimate, can take the next step. Quantification in this case is very conveniently carried out by "dichotomous coding," that is, assigning the value one to the chosen category and the value zero to *all* categories that were not chosen. If the response alternatives were:

A. Anger
B. Disgust
C. Fear
D. Happiness
E. Sadness
F. Surprise

and we selected C, Fear, we would record the score of one for C, Fear, and the score of zero for alternatives A, B, D, E, and F. It should be noted that what we have quantified is the judge's response, *not* whether that response is correct or incorrect. After we have quantified the judge's response we will ordinarily want to score that response as accurate or inaccurate. In the simplest case where one of the response alternatives has been defined by the investigators as the correct one, an item is counted correct if the judge has assigned the value one to the alternative defined as the correct one. (It should be noted that for the example under discussion there is a strong empirical basis for scoring certain errors as more serious than others [Ekman et al., 1972; Izard, 1971; Tomkins & McCarter, 1964]. On these grounds, Ekman [personal communication, 1979] has long suggested that we should take account of the evidence on difficulty level, or likelihood of confusion of affects, in our scoring of accuracy.)

The procedure advocated here is thus a two-step procedure:

1. Recording the response quantitatively (assigning 1 or 0 to each response alternative).
2. Scoring the response as accurate, for example, 1, if the response alternative scored 1 was the one designated as correct by the investigators and as inaccurate, for example, 0, if the response alternative scored 1 was not the one designated as correct by the investigators.

Why do we need step 1? Why don't we simply score each item as correct or incorrect in the first place, that is, score the item 1 if the judge's selection was the correct one and 0 if the judge's selection was the incorrect one? Sometimes, for some purposes, that is indeed a reasonable procedure but there are two reasons to think basically in terms of the two-step procedure. The first reason is that computers, the inanimate kind, generally require the two-step procedure. In the first step we tell the computer what the judge's response was; in the second, the computer tell us whether it was correct or incorrect depending on what we have told the computer to say. The second reason is that if we skip the first step we have thrown away a great deal of information for that item, if the item is answered incorrectly (see Table 4.1).

For any item of A alternatives, there are $A - 1$ incorrect alternatives and if a judge misses an item we cannot identify the wrong alternative that attracted his or her vote. A full data matrix of the type shown in Table 4.1 is possible only if we use the two-step procedure. If we skip step 1, the rich yield of Table 4.1 is reduced in the best case to knowing only the diagonal values of Table 4.1; in the worst case, to knowing only the total number correct. We may feel sure at the time of the research that we are not interested in judges' biases or sources of confusion, and we may decide, therefore, to skip step 1 of our two-step approach. Experience suggests, however, that often it turns out that we do indeed want to look at these variables at some future time. It is, therefore, more efficient to design the quantification procedure with that possibility in mind.

Finally, there are situations in which the focus of research is entirely on step 1 – there is no step 2. That, for example, is the case for research on characteristic or "average" nonverbal demeanor (DePaulo & Rosenthal, 1979a, 1979b, 1982). Personal correlates of these characteristic nonverbal demeanors are being investigated. More generally, of course, it is the case that *all* research in which judges' responses provide the definition of encoder state is research involving only step 1. That is the case whether judges are asked to employ categorical formats or other formats to be discussd later in this chapter.

Multiple response quantification.   So far in the discussion we have assumed that in research on nonverbal decoding accuracy, only one of the categories offered as an alternative was the correct one. We need not restrict ourselves to that situation, however. Suppose, for example, that we wanted to replicate research suggesting that female superiority at decoding nonverbal cues was greater for more negative affects (Hall, 1979; Rosenthal et al., 1979). If we were employing the six response alternatives we have been discussing, we might decide that four of these comprised clearly negative affects (anger, disgust, fear, sadness) while the remaining two (happiness, surprise) did not. We might decide to form two categories of response: the four negative categories and the two nonnegative categories. For our first step, then, we would score as 1 *all* of the negative affects if any one of them were chosen and we would score as 0 *both* of the nonnegative affects if either one of them were chosen. For our second step, we would score the item as correct if the new larger category (negative, nonnegative) selected by the judge were the correct new category.

The example that we have chosen to examine here is made more complex by having the probability of a correct guess vary with the new category of the correct alternative. Thus when the correct answer is a negative affect, the probability of guessing it correctly is .67; when the correct answer is a nonnegative affect, the probability of guessing it correctly is only .33. A judge whose response bias was to see all affects as negative would earn a score of 67 percent correct if our test represented the basic six emotions equally often. A judge whose response bias was to see all affects as nonnegative would earn a score of only 33 percent correct. If we wanted to make our test equally fair to persons of both types of bias, we would simply insure that the total number of times negative and nonnegative alternatives were the correct answer had been made equal.

Scoring by unweighted proportions.   It sometimes happens that although we would like to make our test equally fair to persons of various types of bias, the nature of the research requires that we employ unequal numbers of stimuli (e.g., negative and nonnegative). In that case, scoring by the method of unweighted proportions (or unweighted means) can be used to maintain equity for various types of bias.

Table 4.9 illustrates the method for a simple case of a test made up of forty negative affect items and twenty positive affect items. The left half of Table 4.9 shows the results for a judge with maximum negative bias; the right half shows the results for a judge with maximum positive bias. Because the test has twice as many negative affect items (40) as positive affect items (20) the judge with maximum negative bias earns twice the score as the judge with maximum positive bias in raw score units (40 vs. 20) or in weighted proportion correct (.67 vs. .33). However, if we score the negative and positive items separately in terms of proportion correct and then simply average these proportions correct, without weighting them, both our judges will have earned the same score of .50. Neither judge, of course, has performed any better than "chance," a fact easy to verify by computing the $\chi^2(1)$ for each judge's 2×2 table of counts. Both $\chi^2(1)$'s are zero and the correlations (phi) between category encoded and category decoded are similarly zero for both judges.

Category ranking.   We began our discussion of response quantification by describing the simple case of coding one response alternative as one and all others as zero. We then discussed the somewhat more complex case of coding each of several response alternatives as one and the remaining response

Table 4.9. *Scoring by unweighted proportions to control judges' bias*

Chosen category	Negatively biased judge			Positively biased judge		
	Correct category			Correct category		
	Negative	Positive	Σ	Negative	Positive	Σ
Negative	40[a]	20	60	0[a]	0	0
Positive	0	0[a]	0	40	20[a]	60
Σ	40	20	60	40	20	60
Proportion correct	1.00	.00	.67[b]	.00	1.00	.33[b]
Mean proportion correct	.50[c]			.50[c]		

[a]Correct choices.
[b]Weighted mean proportion correct.
[c]Unweighted mean proportion correct.

alternatives as zero. More complex forms of response quantification are also available. For example, judges may be asked to rank all of the response categories from most to least appropriate as a label for the nonverbal behavior serving as the stimulus item. This is a potentially more precise and discriminating procedure, usable whenever the investigators are able to rank the response alternatives from "most correct answer" to "least correct answer." (This "criterion ranking" is not always easy to achieve but it does not differ in principle from the selection of just one correct answer in the more traditional procedures; e.g., Ekman et al., 1972; Rosenthal et al., 1979.) Table 4.10 shows some hypothetical results for this ranking procedure. The first column lists the six response categories for a single item, while the second lists the ranking that has been defined as correct by the investigators. Four judges (A, B, C, D) have responded to this item by ranking the categories from most to least correct.

Two of the judges (A and B) would have been scored as correct if the item had been scored dichotomously because they ranked as most correct (rank of 1) the same item that the investigators defined as most correct. Two of the judges (C and D) would have been scored as incorrect if the item had been scored dichotomously because they did not rank as most correct the same item that the investigators defined as most correct.

The third from the last row of Table 4.10 gives the correlation between the ranks assigned by the judge of that column and the ranks assigned by the

Table 4.10. *Illustrative results of four rankings of six response categories for one item*

| | | Judges' rankings | | | |
| | | "Correct response" | | "Incorrect response" | |
Response categories	Criterion ranking	A	B	C	D
Happiness	1	1	1	2	6
Surprise	2	2	6	1	5
Anger	3	3	5	3	4
Fear	4	4	4	4	3
Disgust	5	5	3	5	2
Sadness	6	6	2	6	1
Rank correlation with criterion ranking		1.00	−.14	.94	−1.00
Dichotomous scoring		1	1	0	0
Sum of squared differences in ranks (ΣD^2)		0	40	2	70

investigators. The two judges who were correct when this item was scored dichotomously differed substantially from each other in their degree of correlation with the criterion ranking; one judge agreed perfectly (rho = +1.00), the other actually showed a slightly negative correlation (rho = −.14) with the criterion ranking.

The two judges who were both incorrect when this item was scored dichotomously differed even more from each other. One of these judges disagreed perfectly with the criterion ranking (rho = −1.00) while the other agreed very strongly (rho = .94). It is especially noteworthy that one of the judges who was incorrect by the dichotomous scoring criterion (judge C) was very much more accurate by the more sensitive category-ranking criterion than one of the judges who was correct by the dichotomous scoring criterion (judge B).

One of the advantages of this procedure of category ranking is that we can empoy fewer items per judge to establish that judges are more accurate than random guessers. For example, for a given item listing six response categories, a correct choice defined dichotomously has a probability of .17 of occurring by chance (random guessing). However, a perfectly accurate ranking performance has a probability of only .0014. If very small errors are made, as for judge C, the probability is only .01, and even if *none* of the ranks agree with the criterion ranks but are never off by more than one, the probability is still only .03, enough to establish statistically significant accuracy of nonverbal decoding with only a single item.

When the method of category ranking is employed, the correlation coefficient obtained for each item will be the more precise and efficient the greater is the number of response alternatives. Thus, if there are only two response alternatives, ranking them tells us no more than does selecting just one of them; the probability of getting it right by dichotomous scoring or of getting it perfectly right by ranking is still only .5. Even with as few as three response alternatives, however, the method of category ranking adds precision, and for only four response alternatives, a perfect ranking is significantly superior to random guessing at $p = .04$ while a correct response by dichotomous scoring could occur by guessing with probability $= .25$.

If we decide to employ category ranking, we could compute for each judge the mean (or median) correlation between his or her ranking of the categories and the criterion ranking of each of the items. This average correlation would be that judge's overall accuracy score. The formula for the correlation (rho) reflecting accuracy for each item is:

$$\text{rho} = 1 - \left(\frac{6}{A^3 - A}\right)\Sigma D^2$$

where A is the number of categories or response alternatives, and D is the difference between a judge's assigned rank and the criterion rank. Each of these D's is squared and these squared D's are added to get ΣD^2. For many practical purposes, it turns out that we do not need to compute rho at all. For any data analytic purpose other than estimating rho itself, we can do just as well using ΣD^2 instead of rho because these quantities are perfectly (negatively) correlated within a given study employing the same number of response alternatives (A) throughout.

Suppose we were comparing the nonverbal sensitivity of three groups of judges. We could work with the quantity ΣD^2 for each item, compute a mean ΣD^2 for each judge and for each group, and compute our test statistics (e.g., F) on these ΣD^2's. We could even report ΣD^2's as the means of our three groups and stop there since the metric ΣD^2 has meaning in and of itself when the number of alternatives is constant. If, however, we wanted to compute the mean rho for accuracy for each of our three groups we could do so simply by employing our mean ΣD^2's in the formula for rho given above. We can employ Table 4.10 as an illustration. If we wanted the mean accuracy score of all four judges we could add the ΣD^2's given in the bottom row, take the mean (which equals twenty-eight) and substitute into the formula for rho. Or, we could simply average the four rhos of Table 4.10 and get precisely the same answer: mean rho = .20 or rho of mean $\Sigma D^2 = .20$.

Dimensional formats

The dimensional response format usually presents judges with some form of more or less continuous rating scale. For example, judges may be asked to rate the degree of hostility in the tone of voice of a physician talking about alcoholic patients (e.g., Milmoe et al., 1967). Judges may be given anywhere between 2 and over 20 scale points to choose from to indicate the level of hostility they perceive in the doctor's tone of voice.

Relating the formats.   There is an interesting relationship between the dimensional and categorical response formats that is not generally recognized. A categorical response format with A alternatives to choose from is analogous to a set of A rating scales each offering only two scale points. Thus the categorical response format offering the alternatives:

A. Angry _____
B. Happy _____
C. Sad   _____

with the instruction to select one or more is analogous to the dimensional response format:

A. Angry 0____1
B. Happy 0____1
C. Sad   0____1

with the instruction to rate the nonverbal behavior on each of the three rating scales offered. The end points (0 and 1) of the rating scale might be labeled absent = 0, present = 1; low = 0, high = 1; does not apply = 0, does apply = 1, and so forth. However we may choose to label the end points, both the categorical and the dimensional response formats will give us one of two possible scores for each category or each dimension, where 0 for the dimensional is the same as unselected for the categorical, and where 1 for the dimensional is the same as selected for the categorical.

Scale points and labels.   The advantage of the dimensional response format begins to appear as the number of scale points increases. The greatest benefits to reliability accrue as we go from two to seven scale points but it may still be beneficial to reliability to employ up to eleven scale points (Nunnally, 1978). Indeed, there are some circumstances where as many as twenty scale points will prove useful (Guilford, 1954; Rosenthal, 1966, 1976). From a very practical point of view, there are some advantages to employing nine or ten scale points; that is enough points to reap most of the benefits of added reliability but it keeps each judge's response at a single digit which can effect some economies of data processing (i.e., 1–9 or 0–9; the former if a neutral midpoint is desired, the latter if not).

There is no clear agreement on the optimal number of labels to employ for our judges' rating scales. As a minimum, of course, we want to label the end points of our scale (e.g., warm–not warm, warm–cold, not cold–cold). Some additional benefits may accrue to us if we label some or all of the intermediate scale points. A useful practical solution is to label all the scale points when there are few of them (say five or less) and label only the areas of the rating scale when there are many scale points. For example, in a nine- or ten-point rating scale of warmth, we might label the end points "not at all warm" and "very warm," and distribute the three interior labels – "somewhat warm," "moderately warm," and "quite warm" – such that all five labels will be approximately equidistant. This would be an example of a unipolar scale, one that runs from the absence of a characteristic to a great deal of the characteristic. An example of a bipolar scale, one that runs from a great amount of a characteristic to a great amount of its opposite, might be a nine- or ten-point scale of warmth labeled as "very cold" and "very warm" at the end points, and with "somewhat cold," "neither cold nor warm," and "somewhat warm" as the interior labels to be spaced along the rating scale. (Some special problems of bipolar scales will be discussed shortly.)

It is easier to find nonredundant labels for bipolar scales, and some researchers might want to employ more than five labels for the cold–warm scale we have been considering. An example of the use of nine labels might be: very cold, quite cold, moderately cold, somewhat cold, neither cold nor warm, somewhat warm, moderately warm, quite warm, very warm. Experience suggests that judges used to making ratings (e.g., college students, college graduates, most high school students) can do about as well with just a few labels on a rating scale as with many such labels. Different judges will tend to use different sections of the rating scales more frequently, but these biases do *not* affect the judges' reliability.

When designing rating scales for our judgment studies, it is less confusing to judges and data processors always to place higher numbers on the right since most judges and data processors will have learned in elementary school that numbers increase to the right. In addition, given the choice of placing the "good end" (e.g., warm, friendly, empathic) on the left or right, experience suggests it is wiser to place it on the right. Although there *may* be a tendency for the grand mean ratings to increase somewhat thereby, it is likely that on the average, errors of judging, of coding, and of interpretation will be reduced by this practice (Guilford, 1954, p. 268). Numbers on our rating scales should of course be placed equidistantly apart and the physical format of the sheet of rating scales should be designed to make it unlikely that scales could be overlooked or "skipped."

The two-step model.   A major advantage of the dimensional response format over the categorical response format is that, for any given dimension, we have relatively much greater precision of judgment than we do for any one of the categories of the categorical response format, assuming we employ at least three scale points. Another advantage is that our judges' ratings in the dimensional format come "ready to use." That is, step 1 of the two-step model of response quantification described earlier is very easily accomplished; the rating *is* step 1. Often step 1 is all we need as when we are employing judges to define the encoder's true state. However, if we want to assess the judge's accuracy, step 2 is required and step 2 may be more complicated for the dimensional than for the categorical format.

In the case of the categorical format, step 2 required only that we compare the judge's response to the criterion. If the judge's response agreed with the criterion, (e.g., both listed happy as 1 and all other responses as 0) it was defined as correct. In the case of the dimensional format, however, there is no direct way to decide whether the judge's response "agrees" with the criterion. For example, suppose we have a group of encoders describe *honestly* someone they like and someone they dislike, and describe *dishonestly* someone they really like as though they disliked that person and someone they really dislike as though they liked that person. Judges are then asked to rate these four encodings of each of the encoders on a nine-point scale of deceptiveness (DePaulo & Rosenthal, 1979a, 1979b, 1982). How shall we score judges' accuracy in decoding deception on the part of the encoders?

Suppose we simply averaged the ratings of deceptiveness made to the dishonest encodings. Could we say that judges who rated dishonest encodings as more deceptive (than did other judges) were more accurate? There are two reasons why we might not want to do that. First, we might feel that not all the dishonest encodings were maximally dishonest, so we might not want to define as most accurate those judges who labeled all dishonest encodings as maximally dishonest. Second, there might be some judges who rated *all* behavior as deceptive whether the encodings were deceptive or not.

Comparison ratings.   We would do better to introduce a comparison rating against which to evaluate judges' ratings of the deceptiveness of the dishonest encodings. In the present example, we might compute the average rating of deceptiveness made when the encoder was instructed to be honest and subtract that average rating from the average rating of deceptiveness made when the encoder was instructed to be dishonest. The greater this difference score the more was that judge able to differentiate between the encoders' honest and dishonest states. Thus, a judge who saw deception everywhere and assigned a rating of 9 to all encodings would earn a difference score or accuracy score of zero. If we had not subtracted off this judge's ratings of deceptiveness on the comparison stimuli, we would have scored this judge as maximally accurate instead of as completely inaccurate.

The general principle for forming accuracy scores of this type is to subtract the average rating on dimension X of stimuli that should show little X from the average rating on dimension X of stimuli that should show much X. The major advantages of this type of accuracy score are that it (1) adjusts for a response bias on the part of the judge and (2) permits finer gradations of accuracy than the all-or-none levels of accuracy ordinarily employed with categorical response formats. This type of accuracy score does require, however, that each judge make at least two ratings for each accuracy score required. The judge's accuracy for that pair of ratings is defined by the difference between the rating that should be higher if the judge is accurate and the rating that should be lower.

Bipolar versus unipolar scales. The difference between bipolar and unipolar scales was briefly noted earlier in this section. Bipolar scales run from a great amount of a characteristic to a great amount of its opposite (e.g., warm–cold) while unipolar scales run from a great amount of a characteristic to the absence of that characteristic (e.g., warm–not warm; cold–not cold).

For many practical purposes it seems not to matter much whether we employ bipolar or unipolar scales; the correlation between judges' ratings of warmth on a scale of warm–cold and a scale of warm–not warm are likely to be quite substantial, perhaps as high as the retest reliability of either rating. Experience also suggests, however, that the expected negative correlation between ratings of warm–not warm and cold–not cold is not necessarily as high as we might expect. This potentially low correlation between unipolar rating scales that appear to be opposites has been superbly documented in recent work on masculinity-femininity (e.g., Bem, 1974; Spence & Helmreich, 1978). This research has shown that the obtained ratings on the unipolar scales of masculine and feminine are correlated sufficiently poorly that it is possible to identify a good proportion of people who score high on both or low on both, as well as those people who we would have expected to predominate, those who score high on one and low on the other.

More specific to research in nonverbal communication, DePaulo and Rosenthal (1979a, 1979b, 1982) have employed scales of liking and disliking as unipolar scales. Despite substantial negative correlations between ratings on these unipolar scales, we have found it possible to identify encodings in which a person being described was both liked and disliked considerably. We employ this as an operational definition of an ambivalent interpersonal affect. We have also found it possible to identify encodings in which a person being described was neither liked nor disliked. We employ this as an operational definition of an indifferent interpersonal affect.

The lesson to us of these recent developments has been that, although it may require employing more scales (e.g., like *and* dislike scales rather than one like–dislike scale), it may be worth it to employ more unipolar scales in hopes of turning up some other surprises.

Categories as dimensions.   We can combine the characteristics of dimensional formats with those of categorical formats. Suppose we want to evaluate encoders' nonverbal behavior as to the presence of six emotions or affects studied by Ekman (1973), for example. We could ask judges to rate the degree of presence of each of these emotions on a nine-point scale. Table 4.11 shows an illustrative profile of the rated presence of the six emotions listed in the first column.

Employing categories as dimensions (i.e., rating categories) is similar in spirit to the method of category ranking described earlier. However, there are several advantages to the former. First, in the method of category ranking, the number of categories to be ranked defines the number of scale points to be employed. In the method of category rating, we are free to decide the number of scale points and how they are to be labeled. Second, in the method of category ranking, the distance between any two adjacent ranks is forced to be the same while in the method of category rating, the rated difference between adjacent ranks can more accurately reflect the judge's assessment of the difference. Table 4.11 illustrates this. If we had employed category ranking, the distance between Happy and Sad (two units) would be treated as equivalent to the distance between Fearful and Disgusted (two units). However, the judge's actual rating of these emotions showed the distance between Happy and Sad to be much greater (four units) than the distance between Fearful and Disgusted (two units).

A third advantage of the method of rating categories over the method of ranking categories, applicable to studies evaluating judges' accuracy, is that it gives greater statistical power to reject the hypothesis that the judge is performing in a purely random (i.e., nonaccurate) manner. This gain in statistical power is not dramatic, but it is most noticeable where the number of

Table 4.11. *Illustrative profile of ratings of six categories of emotion*

Categories of emotion	Scale points								
	Not at all	Some-what		Moderately			Quite		Very
	1	2	3	4	5	6	7	8	9
Angry	1	②—	3	4	5	6	7	8	9
Disgusted	° 1	2	3	4	5	⑥	7	8	9
Fearful	1	2	3	4	5	6	7	⑧	9
Happy	①	2	3	4	5	6	7	8	9
Sad	1	2	3	4	⑤	6	7	8	9
Surprised	1	2	3	4	5	6	⑦	8	9

alternatives is small. Thus, when there are only three or four categories, it is not possible to reject the null hypothesis of no accuracy at $p = .01$ by the method of category ranking even when rankings are in perfect agreement with the criterion rankings. However, even when there are only three or four categories, it is possible to reject the null hypothesis of no accuracy at $p = .01$ by the method of category rating.

Table 4.12 shows the degree of correlation required for both methods to demonstrate significant levels of accuracy. For any number of alternatives (A), it requires a lower correlation to reject the null hypothesis of no accuracy when category rating is employed compared to when category ranking is employed. However, it can be seen that as the number of alternatives grows larger, the advantage of category rating becomes smaller.

By far the most dramatic information of Table 4.12, however, is the listing of the probabilities of accurate guessing for various numbers of alternatives when only the selection of a single category is employed. Even with twelve alternatives, it is not possible to reject the null hypothesis of no accuracy by the category selection method. Thus, although category rating may be more powerful than category ranking, both are very dramatically superior to simple category selection.

It is not only for purposes of testing accuracy for statistical significance that both category ranking and category rating are superior to category selection. The former two methods both provide greater potential for scoring partial credit for partial accuracy and for analyzing the nature of the errors

Table 4.12. *Degree of agreement between judges' responses and criterion required for establishing significant accuracy for a single item*

Number of alternatives (A)	Category selection p of accurate guess	Category ranking[a]		Category rating[b]	
		.05	.01	.05	.01
3	.33	–	–	.99	1.00
4	.25	1.00	–	.90	.98
5	.20	.90	1.00	.80	.93
6	.17	.83	.94	.73	.88
7	.14	.71	.89	.67	.83
8	.12	.64	.83	.62	.79
9	.11	.60	.78	.58	.75
10	.10	.56	.75	.55	.72
11	.09	.53	.73	.52	.68
12	.08	.51	.71	.50	.66

[a]From Siegel, 1956.
[b]From Walker and Lev, 1953.

made, both for the purpose of learning the source of errors for judges in general and for investigating individual differences among judges in factors associated with their mistakes in judgment.

The matter of partial credit may be especially important when we are working with a fairly homogeneous group of judges and/or are asking each to judge very few items. In the limiting case of a single item per judge, we might be unable to distinguish between two judges both of whom "missed" the item as defined by category selection but one of whom was very accurate ($r = .94$) while the other was truly very inaccurate ($r = -1.00$) in the sense of agreement with the profile of criterion ratings (see Table 4.10).

The methods of category ranking and category rating thus permit the correlation, for each item, of each judge's ranking or rating with (1) the criterion ranking, or (2) the grand mean rating by all judges. In addition, however, these methods also permit the correlation, for each item, of individual judges with one another. Investigators interested in individual differences in judges' ratings would be able to group, cluster, or factor judges into judge types whose personal characteristics could then be investigated.

Open-ended formats
Teachers' folklore has it that good objective test items (e.g., multiple-choice items) are difficult to construct but easy to score while good subjective (essay) test items are relatively more easy to construct but more difficult to score.

Open-ended response formats are like essay examinations. Judges may be asked simply to report, in their own words, the type of affect they have just seen or heard, the type of person who would behave in such a way, the type of situation in which one might find such behavior, and so forth.

Judges' responses to an open-ended format are likely to yield a quite diverse set of reactions that would be very useful for generating research (or clinical) hypotheses, but that usually require considerable effort to quantify if they were to be employed for hypothesis testing.

Diversity. In the categorical and dimensional formats, the investigator decides which categories or dimensions are required by, or at least useful to, the purposes of the research. In the open-ended, or free-response, formats, it is the judges who decide which categories or dimensions are to be employed. To some degree, the nature of the stimulus materials determines the categories or dimensions that will be employed. Some judges, for example, are likely to employ some category or dimension of power much more often than others, while other judges are likely to employ some category or dimension of affection much more often. Depending on the stimulus characteristics, there will be varying degrees of diversity among judges in how they evaluate encoders' nonverbal behavior.

The value to the investigator of introducing greater diversity into judges' response formats is that judges may see or hear things that the investigator neither planned to look for or listen to, nor was able to see or hear when the investigator assessed the stimulus materials. Thus, open-ended response formats are especially valuable in pilot work designed to generate the categories and/or dimensions to be employed in the more formal research to follow.

In addition to their use in *pilot studies,* open-ended formats can be employed as a *parallel enrichment procedure.* In this usage, a sample of judges is employed, part of which is to make categorical and/or dimensional responses, and part of which is to make open-ended responses. The quantitative data produced by the former subset of judges is then augmented by the more lively, real-lifelike sounding, descriptions of the latter subset of judges. Hypothesis testing is based on the quantitative data, while hypothesis generating (and perhaps the feeling of "understanding") is based on the qualitative data produced by the judges employing open-ended formats. This very promising procedure, because it requires more judges, does of course increase our research costs to some degree.

Quantification. Just about any kind of judge's response can be quantified, but usually the quantification of open-ended responses costs more in terms of time, effort, and often, money, than does the quantification of categorical or dimensional responses. The two most common approaches are (1) *the content analytic,* and (2) *the higher order judges'* approach.

The content-analytic approach may employ either predetermined or inductively derived content categories, and each judge's open-ended response is coded as falling into one or more of a set of exhaustive content categories. (Content categories can be made exhaustive by the addition of a category of "other.") Each item of encoder nonverbal behavior is then scored as 1 or 0 for each of the content categories that have been generated either a priori or on the basis of the categories found in the set of open-ended responses. In short, the content-analytic approach is quantified just like the categorical response format's step 1. The practical differences are that the content-analytic procedure (1) usually yields a much larger number of categories than does the categorical procedure, and (2) provides no guarantee that categories of interest to the investigator will even be considered by judges.

The higher order judge's approach employs an additional sample of judges who judge the open-ended responses on a series of dimensions (or categories) that have been selected by the investigator. The higher order judge might be asked, for example, to rate an open-ended response on a nine-point scale reflecting to what degree the responder felt the encoder's behavior was warm.

Although both practical experience and psychometric considerations have a great deal to offer us in deciding what type of response format we might want to employ to achieve any particular type of goal, we could benefit greatly from research designed specifically to test the relative merits of the various response formats, their variant forms, and the various combinations in which they might be employed.

Accuracy, error, and response bias

Much of the research on nonverbal communication has shown an interest in judges' accuracy. In our discussion of categorical and dimensional response format, we described methods for quantifying the accuracy of judges' responses including methods designed (1) to minimize the effects of various forms of response bias, or at least (2) to permit us to estimate the type and degree of such biases. Much more could be said of the problem of quantifying accuracy in nonverbal communication. An excellent introduction to some of the technical issues, general to various fields of interpersonal judgment, has been provided by Cline (1964), and the response bias built into some types of answer formats has been discussed by Rosenthal et al. (1979, pp. 35–7; 116–17).

The problem of the quantification of accuracy is somewhat less central to the open-ended format if only because that format is not used so frequently in the assessment of judges' accuracy. In principle, of course, it could be.

In general, response biases can be viewed in three ways: (1) as a source of artifact impairing our effective quantification of accuracy scores, (2) as a source of information about interesting individual differences among judges, and (3) as a source of information about the workings in general of the senses and the mind of "the" human observer, or of subtypes of the human observer. An interesting recent example of viewing response biases in all three ways is given by Nasby, Hayden, and DePaulo (1980).

PART II
The analysis of judgment studies

5. Forming composites and other redescriptions of variables

Forming composites

Suppose that our judges have rated the nonverbal behavior of a set of psychotherapists on three dimensions: warmth, empathy, and positiveness of regard. Suppose further that the retest reliabilities and the internal consistency reliabilities of all three variables are .75 and that each of our three variables is also correlated with the others .75. Under these conditions, when our variables are so highly correlated with each other, as highly correlated as they are with themselves, we may find no advantage to analyzing all our data separately for the three variables.

For most purposes we might well prefer to form a composite variable of all three. We might, therefore, standard score (z-score) each of the three variables we plan to combine and replace each therapist's three ratings by the mean of the three z scores the therapist earned from the judges. A mean z score of zero means the therapist scores as average on our new composite variable; a large positive mean z score means the therapist scores as very high on our new composite variable; and a large negative mean z score means the therapist scores as very low on our new composite variable of warmth, empathy, and positiveness of regard. It should be noted that the means of z scores are not themselves distributed as z scores and that if our composite variables are to be employed in the construction of further composites they should be z-scored again.

Benefits of forming composites

For the example given above, and for many more complex cases as well, there are conceptual and practical reasons for forming composite variables. Conceptually, if variables cannot be discriminated from one another (because they are as highly correlated with each other as they are with themselves) it is hard to defend treating them as separate variables. Practically, we are able to obtain more accurate (and usually larger) estimates of the

relationship of composites with other variables of interest than we are working with the individual variables before they were combined into a composite. In addition, reducing a larger number of variables to a smaller number
of composites makes it easier to interpret the obtained significance levels
accurately.

For example, if we are interested in the effects of therapists' training on
patients' nonverbal behavior, we might have employed five, or ten, or twenty
variables on which patients were to be rated by judges. If we find the relationship between therapists' training and patient behavior to be significant
at .05 for only one of ten behaviors it is very difficult to interpret what the
"true" level of significance of that result might be, given that ten tests of significance were performed. If our ten patient behaviors had been combined
into a single meaningful composite, we would be able to interpret the obtained significance level far more accurately. We return to this problem of
interpreting the results of numerous tests of significance later when we discuss the Bonferroni methods of adjustment for multiple tests of significance.

Forming composites and increasing effect sizes.   When each of the separate
variables shows approximately the same magnitude of correlation with some
other variable, and when the correlations among the various separate variables are also fairly homogeneous, we can estimate the effects of forming
composites on the magnitude of the effect size (correlation) of interest.

For example, suppose we examine the effects of therapists' training on ten
dependent variables. Suppose further that the correlation (r_i) between therapist training and each of the ten dependent variables is about .30 and that
the average correlation (r) among the ten dependent variables is .50. What
would be the new correlation (r_c) of a composite variable with the independent variable of therapist training? We estimate the answer to be a new r
(r_c) of .40 based on the rearrangement of terms of an equation (14.37) given
by Guilford (1954).

The general equation is:

$$r_{composite} = r_{individual} \times F \tag{5.1}$$

which states simply that the effect size based on the composite variable (r_c)
is the product of the typical effect size based on the individual variable (r_i)
multiplied by a factor F.

This factor F is defined as follows:

$$F = \left[\frac{n}{1 + \bar{r}(n-1)} \right]^{1/2} \tag{5.2}$$

where n is the number of variables entering into the composite and $\bar{r}$ is the
mean intercorrelation among the variables entering into the composite.

Table 5.1. *Factors* (F) *by which effect sizes* (r) *increase as a function of number of variables in a composite and mean intercorrelations among variables*

Mean inter-correlation $\bar{r}$	Number of individual variables (n)			
	2	5	10	20
1.00	1.00	1.00	1.00	1.00
.90	1.03	1.04	1.05	1.05
.75	1.07	1.12	1.14	1.15
.50	1.15	1.29	1.35	1.38
.25	1.26	1.58	1.75	1.87
.10	1.35	1.89	2.29	2.63
.00	1.41	2.24	3.16	4.47

Table 5.1 shows the values of F for varying levels of n and of $\bar{r}$. Only when the individual variables are perfectly correlated with each other is there no benefit from forming composites. In general, the more separate variables that are combined into a composite, the greater will be the increase in the effect size r obtained. In addition, the *lower* the mean intercorrelation among the individual variables, the greater the increase in the effect size r obtained. It should be noted, however, that as the mean intercorrelation becomes lower and lower it will be rarer and rarer that the effect sizes for the individual variables will be homogeneous. If they are, it means that each individual variable is equivalently related to the external or criterion variable but is "predicting" an independent portion of that criterion.

The values of F shown in Table 5.1 need only be multiplied by r_i, the typical effect size for individual variables, to yield r_c, the effect size based on the composite variable. There are also situations, however, when r_c is known and we would like to find r_i, the probable value of the typical effect size for individual variables. This is readily accomplished from the following relationship:

$$r_{\text{individual}} = \frac{r_{\text{composite}}}{F} \qquad (5.3)$$

Equation 5.3 would be useful in the following type of situation. Investigator A has reported a correlation between therapists' gender and perceived nonverbal warmth of .70. Investigator B feels that r must be too high and tries to replicate, obtaining an r of .40. Since both investigators employed large samples, the two r's of .70 and .40 differ very significantly. Investigator B wonders where A went wrong until she recalls that she used as her definition of warmth a single-rating scale whereas A used a composite variable made up of ten variables with average intercorrelation of .25. Using Table 5.1 and equation 5.3 she finds $F = 1.75$ and

$$r_i = \frac{r_c}{F} = \frac{.70}{1.75} = .40$$

a result suggesting that the data of investigators A and B were not discrepant after all. In both cases the "per single-variable effect size" was .40.

Principal components analysis: a fundamental redescriptor

There is a class of procedures intended to redescribe a set of variables in such a way as to meet one or more of the following goals:

1. *Reduce the number of variables* required to describe, predict, or explain the phenomena of interest.
2. *Assess the psychometric properties* of standardized measures or measures under construction.
3. *Improve the psychometric properties* of measures under construction by suggesting (a) how test and subtest reliability might be improved by adding relatively homogeneous items of variables, (b) how subtests are related to each other, and (c) what new subtests might usefully be constructed.
4. *Test hypotheses* derived from theories implying certain types or patterns of descriptors emerging from the analyses.
5. *Generate hypotheses* in the spirit of exploratory data analysis on the basis of unexpected descriptors emerging from the analyses.

Forming composites is one way of redescribing variables but our discussion of it so far has focused on the simple case in which the variables are homogeneously related to each other. In many, perhaps most, situations, however, the pattern of intercorrelations among our variables is more complex than that and a variety of procedures is available to help us redescribe our variables in these more complex situations. One of the most general and most useful procedures available is *principal-components analysis*.

Suppose that a number of variables, say eleven, have been administered to a large group of people and we want to know whether we could do an adequate job of describing the total variation in the data on all eleven variables with a much smaller number of "supervariables" or components. *Principal-components analysis* rewrites the original set of eleven variables into a new set of eleven components (usually) that have the following properties. The first principal component rewrites the original variables into the linear combination that does the best job of discriminating among the subjects of our sample. It is the single supervariable that accounts for the maximum possible variance in all of the original variables.

The second principal component is essentially the same *type* of supervariable except that it operates on the variation in the data remaining after removal of the variation attributable to the first principal component. Thus they are orthogonal, since there is no overlap between the first and second principal components. That is, the second operates only on the leftovers of the first. After the second principal component has been extracted, the third is computed, and so on until as many components have been computed as there are variables. (If one or more of the original variables is completely predictable from the other original variables, the total number of components computed is reduced accordingly.)

How does it help us in our search for supervariables to rewrite eleven variables as eleven components? The logic of the method is such that the first few components computed tend to account for much more of the total variation among subjects on the full set of variables than would be the case for an equal number of the original variables, chosen at random. Thus, the first principal component alone might account for 30, 40, or 50 percent of the total variation among the subjects on ten or twenty variables. In contrast, only 10 percent or 5 percent would be expected if the early components were no more supervariables than any variable chosen randomly from the original set.

We can illustrate with the small example of Table 5.2 how just a few components can reexpress most of the information in several variables. As in principal components (and related) procedures we begin with the matrix of intercorrelations. In this example, we show only five variables intercorrelated.

Since the lower left and upper right large triangles of this correlation matrix are mirror images, we can concentrate on just one of these, say the lower left. To call attention to the major features we decompose the large triangle into three smaller geometric shapes: a triangle, a rectangle, and a square, as shown in the lower half of Table 5.2.

The triangle of three correlations represents all the intercorrelations of variables A, B, and C which a more formal analysis would show to be important contributors to the first principal component. The median intercorrelation is .80. The square represents the intercorrelation (.80) of variables D and E which a more formal analysis would show to be important contributors to the second principal component. The rectangle shows the intercorrelations between the variables A, B, and C and the variables D and E. The median intercorrelation is .10. The median intercorrelations at the bottom of Table 5.2 permit a comparison of the typical intercorrelation *within* a group of variables comprising a supervariable and the average intercorrelation *between* the variables comprising a supervariable.

Table 5.2. *An illustration of variable reduction*

| | The correlation matrix | | | | |
| | Variables | | | | |
Variables	A	B	C	D	E
A	1.00	.80	.70	.10	.00
B	.80	1.00	.90	.20	.10
C	.70	.90	1.00	.10	.00
D	.10	.20	.10	1.00	.80
E	.00	.10	.00	.80	1.00

Decomposition of the lower left triangle

	A	B		A	B	C		D
B	.80		D	.10	.20	.10		
C	.70	.90	E	.00	.10	.00	E	.80

Median intercorrelations	.80		.10		.80

The difference between the median of all within and the median of all between correlations, .80 versus .10 in this case, provides information on the strength and "purity" of the supervariable. In this example the two supervariables are nearly independent of each other and highly consistent internally.

This example is not technically an example of principal components analysis, but it serves to convey the spirit of the enterprise. Actually the example is an illustration of one of the related procedures called *cluster analysis*.

The process of principal-components analysis also begins with the intercorrelation of all the variables. Then the components are computed, and the *loading* (or component loading or factor loading) of each variable on each component is computed. These loadings are the correlations between each variable (usually the rows) and the newly computed components (usually the columns). Each component is understood or interpreted in terms of the pattern of loadings. We illustrate this presently.

Typically, however, the components as first extracted from the correlations among the variables are not very interpretable (except perhaps the first component). They are typically made more interpretable by a process called *rotation*. We illustrate this process by showing in Figure 5.1 a plot of the data of a matrix of correlations of variables with components; just the first two components are shown (see the top of Table 5.3).

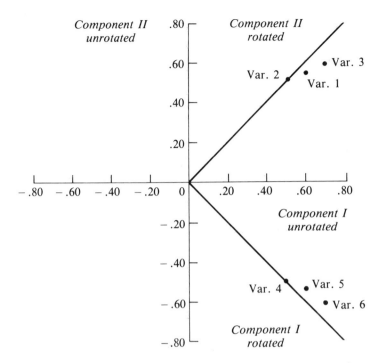

Figure 5.1. Plot of the loadings of six variables on two principal components before and after rotation (see Table 5.3)

With respect to the original unrotated Components I and II all the variables loaded highly on Component I while half the variables showed a strong positive and half showed a strong negative loading on Component II. However, when we rotate the axes, in this particular case 45 degrees clockwise, we find three of the variables load highly only on one rotated component while the other three load highly only on the other rotated component. The new *rotated component loadings* are shown in the lower half of Table 5.3.

If we were now told that variables 1, 2, 3 were alternative measures of sociability and variables 4, 5, and 6 were alternative measures of intellectual ability, the rotated components would be far more useful than the unrotated. The latter would be very difficult to interpret; the former would suggest that our six variables could be reduced to two supervariables (sociability and intellectual ability) which were independent of each other or *orthogonal*, because when we rotated the axes of Components I and II we kept them orthogonal, that is, at right angles to one another. Sometimes it is useful to allow the rotations to be nonorthogonal as when the hypothesized underlying supervariables are thought to be somewhat correlated in the real world. Such nonorthogonal rotations are called *oblique rotations*.

Table 5.3. *Loadings of six variables on two principal components before and after rotation*

	Loadings before rotation	
Variables	Component I	Component II
1	.60	.55
2	.50	.50
3	.70	.60
4	.50	−.50
5	.60	−.55
6	.70	−.60
Sum of squared loadings	2.20	1.82

	Loadings after rotation	
Variables	Component I	Component II
1	.04	.82
2	.00	.70
3	.06	.92
4	.70	.00
5	.82	.04
6	.92	.06
Sum of squared loadings	2.01	2.01

The most commonly used method of orthogonal rotation is called *varimax;* it tries to maximize the variation of the squared loadings for each component by making the loadings go to zero or to 1.00 to the extent possible. This method of rotation helps make components easier to interpret.

Principal components and construct validity

As part of the construct validation of a new measure of sensitivity to nonverbal cues, the PONS test, it was important to assess the independence of this measure from measures of intellectual functioning (Rosenthal et al., 1979). For a sample of 110 high school students we had available their PONS subtest scores to items reflecting sensitivity to nonverbal cues that were positive and submissive in content, positive and dominant, negative and submissive, and negative and dominant.

In addition, we had available scores on the verbal SAT, the math SAT, and the Otis IQ test. If the PONS test were really independent of intellectual ability as hoped and hypothesized, we should obtain two principal components which, after varimax rotation, should yield an intelligence component and an orthogonal nonverbal sensitivity component. Table 5.4 shows what was found.

Table 5.4. *Loadings of seven variables on two principal components after rotation*

	Loadings after rotation	
Variables	Component I	Component II
Otis IQ	.19	.64
Verbal SAT	−.02	.89
Math SAT	−.07	.84
PONS: Pos.-Sub.	.66	.02
PONS: Pos.-Dom.	.82	−.00
PONS: Neg.-Sub.	.77	.06
PONS: Neg.-Dom.	.78	.06
Sum of squared loadings	2.35	1.91

Table 5.5. *PONS test channels arranged in a 4×3 matrix*

	Visual channels			
Auditory channels	Face + Body	Face	Body	None
Random-spliced	1	4	7	10
Content-filtered	2	5	8	11
None	3	6	9	×

These results, then, were in good agreement with the predictions and the hopes. The first rotated component was essentially a PONS test component, the second was essentially an intellectual component. Just as had been the case for our simpler hypothetical example above, before rotation the first principal component had shown positive loadings by all the variables; the second principal component had shown positive loadings by some of the variables (the three intellectual variables) and negative loadings by some of the variables (the four sensitivity to nonverbal cues variables).

Principal components and subtest construction

The preceding application of principal-components analysis was to construct validation. The next application is to *subtest formation*. The PONS test of sensitivity to nonverbal cues was made up of 220 items, twenty in each of eleven channels. The channels were either in the visual or auditory domain as shown in Table 5.5.

Face channel items showed only facial cues, body channel items showed only body cues, while face + body channel items showed both. Content-fil-

Table 5.6. *Loadings of eleven variables on four principal components after rotation*

Variables	Loadings on components			
	1	2	3	4
Face	.62	.12	.10	.15
Face + Body	.68	.07	.11	.24
Face + Rand.-splice	.70	.02	.06	.22
Face + Cont.-filt.	.65	−.03	.09	.20
Face + Body + RS	.67	.30	.09	.05
Face + Body + CF	.70	.06	.10	.32
Random-spliced	.14	.95	.03	.12
Content-filtered	.20	.04	.96	.14
Body	.47	−.04	.02	.59
Body + Rand.-splice	.33	.07	.12	.57
Body + Cont.-filt.	.11	.13	.08	.82
Sum of squared loadings	3.11	1.04	1.01	1.66
Percentage of variance	28%	9%	9%	15%
Number of variables defining components	6	1	1	3
Number of items defining components (20 per variable)	120	20	20	60

tered items preserved tone but not content, by removing high frequencies. Random-spliced items preserved different aspects of tone but not content by random scrambling of speech.

After intercorrelating the eleven channels and channel combinations shown earlier, extracting four principal components and rotating orthogonally (varimax), we obtained the loadings shown in Table 5.6.

The first component was characterized by face presence, reflecting ability to decode nonverbal cues from any combination of channels as long as the face was included as a source of information. The second and third principal components each reflected a specific skill: decoding random-spliced and content-filtered cues respectively, in the absence of any visual cues. The fourth principal component reflected ability to decode body cues in the absence of facial cues.

The first row at the bottom of the matrix of loadings shows the sum of the squared loadings, the amount of variance accounted for by that factor. (Alternative terms for the sum of the squared loadings before rotation are *eigenvalue, latent root, characteristic root,* or just *root;* Armor, 1974.) The second row at the bottom of Table 5.6 shows the percentage of variance accounted for by each component. It is computed by dividing the sum of the squared loadings for that component by the total number of variables, eleven in this illustration. For the present analysis these first two rows show that the first and fourth components are more important in the sense of accounting for more variance than are the second and third components. Note that this can occur only after rotation. Before rotation no succeeding component can be larger than a preceding component because each succeeding component is extracted only from the residuals of the preceding component.

The third row at the bottom of Table 5.6 lists the number of variables serving to define each component and the last row lists the number of raw test items contributing to the variables defining each component.

Various procedures are available for forming scales from principal components analyses. Many of these generate scores for each subject for each component. In our own work, however, we have used a simple procedure that often leads to psychologically more interpretable scales, subtests, supervariables, or composites: We simply combine all the variables serving to define each component. How we combine variables depends on their form. If they are all measured on similar scales and have similar standard deviations, we simply add or average the variables. That was the situation for the preceding analysis. Since scores on each variable could range from 0 to 20 and standard deviations were similar, we simply added subjects' scores on the variables to define each component.

Thus, each subject could earn a score of 0 to 120 on the supervariable based on the first rotated component, scores of 0 to 20 on the second and third rotated component, and scores of 0 to 60 on the fourth rotated component.

When the variables are not all on the same scale or metric we would standard score all variables before adding or averaging. When there are no missing data it may not matter whether we add or average the scores on the variables defining each component. However, when there may be missing data as in many real-life applications, it is safer to use the mean of the variables rather than their sum as the new composite or supervariable. The use of sums can introduce very large errors since subjects with many missing data can earn bizarrely low composite scores.

When we are constructing composite variables by adding or averaging the individual variables (in raw or z score form) it is essential that all variables have loadings of the same sign on the component used to define the composite and that they are positively correlated with each other. A variable negatively correlated with the others can be added or averaged in only after changing its scale into the proper direction; for example, by multiplying each observation by -1.

If it is desired that the mean of the scores on the individual variables be interpretable in the original units, it is helpful to recode the raw score units. For example, if a nine-point rating scale was employed to rate warmth, empathy, and hostility, warmth and empathy will tend to be strongly positively correlated with each other but negatively with hostility. We can recode hostility into a variable of "nonhostility" by subtracting each rating of hostility (X_i) from the sum of the highest (X_{max}) and lowest (X_{min}) possible rating. Thus, recoding is accomplished as in equation 5.4:

$$X \text{ recoded} = (X_{max} + X_{min}) - X_i \qquad (5.4)$$

Therefore, if the rating scale runs from 0 to 9, X_i's of 0, 1, 2, 3, 4, 5, 6, 7, 8, 9 are recoded to 9, 8, 7, 6, 5, 4, 3, 2, 1, respectively. If a rating scale runs from 1 to 5, X_i's of 1, 2, 3, 4, 5 are recoded to 5, 4, 3, 2, 1, with $X_{max} = 5$ and $X_{min} = 1$.

A final note has to do with the number of principal components it will be useful to examine. One rarely is very interested in seeing all the principal components' loadings either unrotated or rotated. A number of quantitative criteria are available to help decide how many to examine. For subtest or supervariable construction we recommend a step-up approach in which we examine in turn the rotated first two components, then the first three, then the first four, and so on. Experience suggests that looking only at the rotated end result (i.e., the loadings of all variables on all the components extracted based on any of several quantitative rules for stopping the extraction process) typically yields more components than are needed to construct useful, meaningful subtests or supervariables and fewer components that are interpretable. It should be noted that at each step up, the definition of each component will change. Thus the first component after rotating two components will not be the same component as the first component after rotating three or four or more components.

Principal components and reliability analysis

Since the first unrotated principal component is the best single summarizer of the linear relationships among all the variables it can be employed as the basis for an estimate of the internal consistency reliability of a test. We would probably employ such an estimate only where it made substantive sense to think of an overall construct tapped by all the variables, more or less. Such might be the case for many measures of ability, adjustment, achievement, and the like.

It would make sense, for example, to think of an ability to decode nonverbal cues. We might, therefore, estimate the internal consistency of the

PONS test from the first principal component *before rotation.* After rotation it would no longer be the best single summarizer though it would probably give a far better structure to the data working in concert with other rotated components.

Armor's (1974) formula for the computation of his index of reliability, theta, is

$$\text{theta} = \frac{n}{n-1}\left(\frac{L-1}{L}\right) \tag{5.5}$$

where n is the number of variables and L is the latent root (eigenvalue or sum of squared loadings). We encountered this equation earlier as equation 2.4 in our discussion of judges' reliability. In that application it was judges' ratings that were intercorrelated and n referred to the number of judges.

For the 220 items of the PONS test with each item regarded as a variable we found

$$\text{theta} = \frac{220}{219}\left(\frac{13.217-1}{13.217}\right) = .929$$

The analogous reliability based on the 11 channels rather than the 220 items was

$$\text{theta} = \frac{11}{10}\left(\frac{4.266-1}{4.266}\right) = .842$$

It should be noted that the sum of the squared-factor loadings (latent root) of 4.266 for the eleven-variable analysis is substantially (37 percent) larger than the sum of the squared-factor loadings of 3.113 obtained for the first principal component after rotation.

The thetas reported for the PONS test are quite substantial. However, we saw earlier that the PONS test was made up of four orthogonal components (see Table 5.6). How is it possible that a test made up of four orthogonal components can have such substantial internal consistency reliability? The answer is that the internal consistency of a total test depends on (a) the typical intercorrelations among the items or subtests and (b) the number of items or subtests. Therefore, even when the typical intercorrelations among the items or subtests are lowered by the presence of orthogonal components, the internal consistency reliability of the total test can be maintained or even raised by the addition of items or subtests that correlate positively with at least some of the other items. Longer tests, therefore, can show high internal consistency reliability even when they are made up of orthogonal components or factors.

Other redescriptors

Factor analysis. The most commonly used alternative to the principal-components method for the redescription of variables is actually an entire family of alternatives called *factor analysis.* Sometimes principal-components analysis is viewed as a special type of factor analysis, but there are subtle differences between principal components and other forms of factor analysis. For example, some forms of factor analysis make more assumptions than are required for principal-components analysis and introduce a greater series of options for viewing the data. As a result, different investigators exercising different options will obtain different factor structures from the same data. Beginners do well to employ principal components with varimax rotation as their standard procedure. Stanley Mulaik (1972) and R. J. Rummel (1970) provide detailed comparisons of various types of factor analysis, and Jae-On Kim (1975) provides a briefer overview.

Cluster analysis. A flexible family of methods for grouping variables known as cluster analysis ranges from some very simple to some very complicated procedures. A very simple form of cluster analysis was illustrated when we first introduced principal-components analysis; there we used as a criterion of cluster tightness the difference between the average within-cluster intercorrelations and the average between-cluster correlations. We can illustrate this simple method by applying it to the eleven subtests of the PONS test which were also subjected to a principal-components analysis (Table 5.6).

Suppose that on theoretical grounds we had decided to form four composite subtests of the eleven subtests of the PONS test such that the largest composite would be made up of all six channels in which the face was shown (channels 1–6 of Table 5.5), the second largest composite would be made up of the three channels showing the body without the face (channels 7–9 of Table 5.5), and the third and fourth "composites" would be made up of the single channels of random-spliced and content-filtered speech, respectively (channels 10 and 11 of Table 5.5).

Table 5.7 shows the results of the process of simple clustering. The final column shows the median intercorrelation of the composite members with one another. Thus the fifteen $[n(n-1)/2$ or $6(5)/2]$ intercorrelations among the six variables of the face-present cluster showed a median intercorrelation of .40. The median correlation of the six variables of that cluster (a) with the three variables of the body-only cluster was .32, (b) with the random-spliced variable was .20, and (c) with the content-filtered variable was .25. The rest of Table 5.7 shows the median intercorrelations among the elements com-

Table 5.7. *Median intercorrelations among clusters of variables of the PONS test*

Clusters	Clusters				
	Face-present	Body-only	Random-spliced[a]	Content-filtered[a]	Median r intracluster
Face-present	—	.32	.20	.25	.40
Body-only	.32	—	.17	.24	.36
Random-spliced[a]	.20	.17	—	.12	1.00[a]
Content-filtered[a]	.25	.24	.12	—	1.00[a]
Median	.25	.24	.17	.24	.70

Note: All median intracluster r's are higher than any median intercluster r.
[a]Single variable.

prising the different clusters. It can be seen that the range of median *inter*cluster r's is from .12 to .32 (median $r = .22$) all of which are smaller than any of the *intra*cluster r's which range from .36 to 1.00 (median $r = .70$).

Table 5.8 gives an additional example of simple clustering. This clustering was of those nonverbal behaviors of psychological experimenters, as judged from their instruction-reading behavior, that significantly predicted the degree of the experimenters' subsequent expectancy effects. The more detailed data are given elsewhere (Rosenthal, 1966). Here it is enough to note that the twenty-one variables were "successfully" clustered into five clusters that predicted magnitude of experimenter expectancy effects. These clusters included behaving in a relaxed, dominant, and businesslike manner in the visual channel, behaving in an unpleasant manner in the auditory (tone of voice) channel, and behaving in a calm manner as judged from the visual plus auditory channel.

The "success" of the clustering can be indexed by comparing the (absolute) median *inter*cluster r of .11 with the median *intra*cluster r of .59. The difference between these median r's (.48) is equivalent to that found for the previous example of Table 5.7. There is no firm rule about the difference between *inter* and *intra* cluster median r's required for "successful" clustering. However, unless there is a lower median (or mean) *inter* than *intra* cluster r, no clustering can be said to have occurred in the psychometric sense. Never-

Table 5.8. *Mean intercorrelations among clusters of variables of psychological experimenters' nonverbal behavior*

	Clusters						
Cluster	Relaxed (visual)	Dominant[a] (visual)	Businesslike (visual)	Unpleasant (auditory)	Calmness (visual plus auditory)	Mean r intracluster	Number of variables per cluster
Relaxed (visual)	—	.13	.19	.00	−.29	.65	5
Dominant[a] (visual)	.13	—	.03	.12	.04	1.00[a]	1
Businesslike (visual)	.19	.03	—	−.10	−.46	.51	2
Unpleasant (auditory)	.00	.12	−.10	—	.07	.59	6
Calmness (visual plus auditory)	−.29	.04	−.46	.07	—	.51	7
Median of absolute values	.16	.08	.14	.08	.18	.59	

Note: All mean intracluster r's are higher than any (absolute value) mean intercluster r.
[a] Single variable.

Table 5.9. *Data matrices redescribing variables versus persons*

Data matrices	
IA Redescribing variables[a]	IIA Redescribing persons[b]

	Variables 1 2 3 4 5		Persons 1 2 3 4 5 6
Person 1		Variable 1	
Person 2		Variable 2	
Person 3		Variable 3	
Person 4		Variable 4	
Person 5		Variable 5	
Person 6			

[a]To redescribe the variables as clusters, factors, or types.

[b]To redescribe the persons as clusters, factors, or types.

Correlation matrices	
IB	IIB

	Variables 1 2 3 4 5		Persons 1 2 3 4 5 6
Variable 1		Person 1	
Variable 2		Person 2	
Variable 3		Person 3	
Variable 4		Person 4	
Variable 5		Person 5	
		Person 6	

Note: The matrix above has each correlation based on six observations, i.e., the six persons.

Note: The matrix above has each correlation based on five observations, i.e., the five variables.

theless, some grouping of variables might still be useful as in trying to replicate the correlates of earlier clusters which could not be reproduced in the subsequent study.

Clustering subjects.   In clustering, it is not necessary that it be variables that are clustered. We could instead cluster the subjects or other sampling units for whom measurements had been obtained. Then instead of grouping variables together that correlated highly over a list of persons we could group persons together that correlated highly over a list of variables. A typology of persons or other sampling units could thereby be constructed. It should be noted, however, that factor analysis and principal-components analysis can also be employed to the same end. We illustrate what is involved with a small example shown in Table 5.9; these procedures involve what amounts to an exchange of rows with columns assuming that we always intercorrelate columns with an eye to their redescription.

We call subtable IA and IIA of Table 5.9 *data matrices;* the one on the left (IA) has each person's scores on all variables in one row and the one on the right (IIA) has each variable's scores for each person in one row. From these data matrices we compute the correlation matrices IB and IIB shown below IA and IIA by correlating each column's scores with every other column's scores.

Clustering or factoring these correlation matrices would lead to a redescription of the five variables in terms of some (usually smaller) number of groupings of variables in the case of the matrix on the lower left (IB) and to a redescription of the six persons in terms of some (usually smaller) number of groupings of persons in the case of the matrix on the lower right (IIB).

A detailed summary of various cluster-analytic methods is given by Bailey (1974), and Kim and Roush (1980) give a brief but quite mathematical discussion.

Other methods.   Many other procedures have been developed to serve as redescriptors. They have in common that they examine the relationships among objects or stimuli in terms of some measure of similarity or dissimilarity and then try to infer some number of dimensions that would meaningfully account for the obtained pattern of similarities or dissimilarities among the objects or stimuli. The methods have been called *dimensional analysis,* a term referring to distance analysis, multidimensional scaling, multidimensional unfolding, proximity analysis, similarity analysis, smallest space analysis and other procedures summarized by Coombs, Dawes, and Tversky (1970) and Rummel (1967), and addressed in more detail by Guttman (1966), Lazarsfeld and Henry (1968), Torgerson (1958), and especially, by Shepard, Romney, and Nerlove (1972).

6. Significance testing and effect size estimation

Once we have defined the variables to be investigated in our research, perhaps first redefining them into composites as described in the last chapter, we can begin to analyze "the results" of our research. Too often in the behavioral sciences, however, the results are equated with a series of tests of significance that may be only tangentially related to the questions that motivated the research in the first place. Two reasons why tests of significance are not informative enough for them to serve as the definition of the results of our research are:

a. They give no indication of the magnitude of the effect under investigation, and

b. They are often based on more than a single df in the numerator of an F test or on more than a single df for a χ^2 test. In both cases a significant result alone does not tell us how a specific variable X is related to a specific variable Y.

It is more useful to think of the results as the answer to the question: What is the relationship between any variable X and any variable Y? (Rosenthal, 1984). The variables X and Y are chosen with only the constraint that their relationship be of interest to us. The answer to this question, however, must come in two parts: (a) the estimate of the magnitude of the relationship (the effect size) and (b) an indication of the accuracy or reliability of the estimated effect size (as in a confidence interval placed around the estimate). An alternative to the second part of the answer, one not intrinsically more useful but one more consistent with the existing practices of behavioral researchers, is the test of significance of the difference between the obtained effect size and the effect size expected under the null hypothesis of no relationship between variables X and Y.

A fundamental equation of data analysis

Since the argument has been made that the results of a study with respect to any given relationship can be expressed as an estimate of an effect size plus

105

Table 6.1. *Examples of the relationship between tests of significance and effect size:* $\chi^2(1)$, Z, *and* t

Equation	Test of significance	=	Size of effect	×	Size of study
6.1	$\chi^2(1)$	=	ϕ^2	×	N
6.2	Z	=	ϕ	×	$N^{1/2}$
6.3	t	=	$\dfrac{r}{[1-r^2]^{1/2}}$	×	$[df]^{1/2}$
6.4	t	=	$\left(\dfrac{M_1-M_2}{S}\right)^a$	×	$\left[\dfrac{1}{n_1}+\dfrac{1}{n_2}\right]^{-1/2}$
6.5	t	=	$\left(\dfrac{M_1-M_2}{S}\right)^a$	×	$\left[\dfrac{n_1 n_2}{n_1+n_2}\right]^{1/2}$
6.6	t	=	$\left(\dfrac{M_1-M_2}{\sigma}\right)^b$	×	$\left(\dfrac{[n_1 n_2]^{1/2}}{n_1+n_2}\times[df]^{1/2}\right)$
6.7	t	=	d	×	$\dfrac{[df]^{1/2}}{2}$

[a]Also called g (Hedges, 1981, 1982a).
[b]Also called d (Cohen, 1969, 1977).

a test of significance, we should make explicit the relationship between these two quantities. The general relationship constitutes a fundamental equation of data analysis:

Test of significance = Size of effect × Size of study

Tables 6.1 and 6.2 give useful specific examples of this general equation. Equation 6.1 shows that χ^2 on $df=1$ is the product of the size of the effect expressed by ϕ^2 (the squared product moment correlation) multiplied by N (the number of subjects or other sampling units). It should be noted that ϕ is merely Pearson's r applied to dichotomous data, that is, data coded as taking on only two values such as 0 and 1, 1 and 2, or +1 and −1.

Equation 6.2 is simply the square root of equation 6.1. It shows that the standard normal deviate Z (i.e., the square root of χ^2 on 1 df) is the product of ϕ (the product moment correlation) and $N^{1/2}$. Equation 6.3 shows that t is the product of the effect size $r/[1-r^2]^{1/2}$ and $[df]^{1/2}$, an index of the size of the study. The denominator of this effect size ($[1-r^2]^{1/2}$) is also known as the coefficient of alienation or k, an index of the degree of noncorrela-

Table 6.2. *Examples of the relationship between tests of significance and effect size:* F *and* t *for correlated observations*

Equation	Test of significance	=	Size of effect	×	Size of study
6.8	F^a	=	$\dfrac{r^2}{1-r^2}$	×	df error
6.9	F^b	=	$\dfrac{\text{eta}^2}{1-\text{eta}^2}$	×	$\dfrac{df \text{ error}}{df \text{ means}}$
6.10	F^b	=	$\dfrac{S^2 \text{ means}}{S^2}$	×	n
6.11	t^c	=	$\dfrac{r}{[1-r^2]^{1/2}}$	×	$[df]^{1/2}$
6.12	t^c	=	$\dfrac{\bar{D}}{S_D}$	×	$n^{1/2}$
6.13	t^c	=	d	×	$[df]^{1/2}$

[a] Numerator $df = 1$.
[b] Numerator df may take on any value.
[c] Correlated observations.

tion (Guilford and Fruchter, 1978). This effect size, therefore, can be rewritten as r/k, the ratio of correlation to noncorrelation. Equations 6.4 and 6.5 share the same effect size, the difference between the means of the two groups being compared divided by, or standardized by, the unbiased estimate of the population standard deviation.

This latter effect size $(M_1 - M_2)/S$ is the one typically employed by Glass and his colleagues (Glass, McGaw, & Smith, 1981) with the S computed as $[\Sigma(X - \bar{X})^2/(n_c - 1)]^{1/2}$ employing only the subjects or other sampling units from the *control group*. The pooled S, that is, the one computed from both groups, tends to provide a better estimate in the long run of the population standard deviation. However, when the S's based on the two different conditions differ greatly from each other, choosing the control group S as the standardizing quantity is a very reasonable alternative. That is because it is always possible that the experimental treatment itself has made the S of the experimental group too large or too small relative to the S of the control group.

Another alternative when the S's of the two groups differ greatly is to transform the data to make the S's more similar. Such transformations (e.g., logs, square roots, etc.) of course require our having access to the original data, but that is also often required to compute S separately for the control group. When only a mean square error from an analysis of variance is available we must be content to use its square root (S) as our standardizing denominator in any case. Or, if only the results of a t test are given, we are similarly forced to compute the effect size using a pooled estimate of S. (We could use equations 6.4 or 6.5 to solve for $(M_1 - M_2)/S$.)

Before leaving the topic of whether to compute S only from the control group or from both groups we should remind ourselves of the following. When S's differ greatly for the two groups so that we are inclined to compute S only from the control group, ordinary t tests may give misleading results. Such problems can be approached by approximate procedures (Snedecor & Cochran, 1980, pp. 96–8) but are perhaps best dealt with by appropriate transformation of the data (Tukey, 1977).

Equation 6.6 shows an effect size only slightly different from that of equations 6.4 and 6.5. The only difference is that the standardizing quantity for the difference between the means is σ (pooled sums of squares divided by N) rather than S (pooled sums of squares divided by $N-k$ for k groups). This is one of the effect sizes employed by Cohen (1969, 1977) and by Friedman (1968). Basically this index, Cohen's d, is the difference between the means of the groups being compared given in standard score units or z scores. Equation 6.7 shows $(M_1 - M_2)/\sigma$ expressed as d and the size of study term simplified considerably for those situations in which it is known or in which it can be reasonably assumed that the sample sizes (n_1 and n_2) are equal.

Equation 6.8 of Table 6.2 shows that F with one df in the numerator is the product of the squared ingredients of the right-hand side of equation 6.3 of Table 6.1. That is just as it should be, of course, given that $t^2 = F$ when $df = 1$ in the numerator of F.

Equation 6.9 is the generalization of equation 6.8 to the situation of $df > 1$ in the numerator. Thus eta^2 refers to the proportion of variance accounted for just as r^2 does, but eta^2 carries no implication that the relationship between the two variables in question is linear. Equation 6.10 shows the effect size for F as the ratio of the variance of the condition means to the pooled within-group variance, while the size of the study is indexed by n, the number of observations in each of the groups.

Comparing r *to* d

Equation 6.11 has for its test of significance a t for correlated observations or repeated measures. It is important to note that this equation for the correlated t is identical to equation 6.3 (Table 6.1) for the independent samples t. Thus, when we employ r as our effect size estimate, we need not make any

Table 6.3. *Underestimation of* d *by "equal* n*" formula*

Study	n_1	n_2	Accurate d^a	Estimated d^b	Raw difference	Percent under- estimate
1	50	50	.61	.61	.00	.00
2	60	40	.62	.61	− .01	.02
3	70	30	.66	.61	− .05	.08
4	75	25	.70	.61	− .09	.13
5	80	20	.76	.61	− .15	.20
6	85	15	.85	.61	− .24	.28
7	90	10	1.01	.61	− .40	.40
8	95	5	1.39	.61	− .78	.56
9	98	2	2.16	.61	−1.55	.72
10	99	1	3.05	.61	−2.44	.80

$^a d = t(n_1 + n_2)/([df]^{1/2}[n_1 n_2]^{1/2}) =$ general formula from rearranging equation 6.6.
$^b d = 2t/[df]^{1/2} =$ "equal n" formula from rearranging equation 6.7.

special adjustment in moving from t tests for independent to those for correlated observations. That is *not* the situation for equations 6.12 and 6.13, however. When the effect size estimates are the mean differences divided either by S or by σ, the definition of the size of the study changes by a factor of 2 in going from t for independent observations to t for correlated observations. This inconsistency in definitions of size of study is one of the reasons the present writer has recently grown to prefer r as an effect size estimate rather than d, after many years of using both r and d.

Another reason for preferring r over d as an effect size estimate arising in meta-analytic work especially, is that we are often unable to compute d accurately from the information provided by the author of the original article. Investigators sometimes report only their t's and df's but not their sample sizes. Therefore, we cannot use equations 6.4, 6.5, or 6.6 to compute the effect sizes. We could do so only if we assumed $n_1 = n_2$. If we did so, for example, from rearranging equation 6.7, we could get d as follows:

$$d = \frac{2t}{[df]^{1/2}} \tag{6.14}$$

If the investigator's sample sizes were equal, d would be accurate, but as n_1 and n_2 become more and more unequal, d will be more and more underestimated. Table 6.3 shows for ten studies, all with $t = 3.00$ and $df = n_1 + n_2 - 2 = 98$, the increasing underestimation of d when we assume equal n's and employ equation 6.14. It should be noted, however, that when the split is no more extreme than 70:30 the underestimation is less than 8 percent.

A third reason for preferring r to d as an effect size estimate has to do with simplicity of interpretation in practical terms. Later in this chapter we describe the BESD (Binomial Effect Size Display), a method for displaying the practical importance of the size of an obtained effect. Using this method we can immediately convert r to an improvement in success rate associated, for example, with employing a new treatment procedure or a new selection device, or a new predictor variable. Because of the probability of seriously misinterpreting its practical importance we shall not use r^2 as an effect size estimate (Rosenthal & Rubin, 1982b).

Although the present writer has grown to prefer r over d for the three reasons just given, the most important point to be made is that *some* estimate of the size of the effect should always be given whenever results are reported. Whether we employ r, g, d, Glass's Δ (difference between the means divided by the S computed from the control group only) or any of the other effect size estimates that could be employed (e.g., see Cohen, 1977) is less important than that *some* effect size estimate be employed along with the more traditional test of significance.

Computing effect sizes

Our own emphasis is on r as the primary effect size estimate. Fortunately, it is easy to obtain r from tests of significance. The following formulas can be found by rearranging equations 6.1, 6.3, and 6.8 (Cohen, 1965; Friedman, 1968):

$$\phi = \left[\frac{\chi^2(1)}{N} \right]^{1/2} \tag{6.15}$$

$$r = \left[\frac{t^2}{t^2 + df} \right]^{1/2} \tag{6.16}$$

where $df = n_1 + n_2 - 2$, and

$$r = \left[\frac{F(1, -)}{F(1, -) + df \text{ error}} \right]^{1/2} \tag{6.17}$$

where $F(1, -)$ indicates any F with $df = 1$ in the numerator.

If we are working with other people's data, as in a meta-analysis, and none of these tests of significance have been employed or reported, we can usefully estimate an effect size r from a p level alone as long as we know the size of the study (N). We convert the obtained p to its standard normal deviate equivalent using a table of Z values. We then find r from:

$$r = \left[\frac{Z^2}{N} \right]^{1/2} = \frac{Z}{[N]^{1/2}} \tag{6.18}$$

It should be noted that equations 6.15 to 6.18 all yield product moment correlation coefficients. It makes no difference whether the data are in dichotomous or continuous form, or whether they are ranked. Thus, correlations known as Pearson's *r*, Spearman's rho, phi, or point biserial *r*, are all defined in exactly the same way (though there are computational simplifications available so that some appear to be different from others) and are interpreted in exactly the same way.

If we should want to have *r* as our effect size estimate when only Cohen's *d* is available we can readily go to *r* from *d* (Cohen, 1977):

$$r = \frac{d}{[d^2 + 1/pq]^{1/2}} \tag{6.19}$$

where *p* is the proportion of the total population that is in the first of the two groups being compared and *q* is the proportion in the second of the two groups, or $1 - p$. When *p* and *q* are equal, or when they can be viewed as equal in principle, equation 6.19 is simplified to equation 6.20:

$$r = \frac{d}{[d^2 + 4]^{1/2}} \tag{6.20}$$

In most experimental applications we use equation 6.20 because we think of equal population sizes in principle. We might prefer equation 6.19 in situations where we have intrinsic inequality of population sizes as when we compare the personal adjustment scores of a random sample of normals and a random sample of hospitalized psychiatric patients.

In those cases where we want to work with Cohen's *d* but have only *r* available we can go from *r* to *d*:

$$d = \frac{2r}{[1 - r^2]^{1/2}} \tag{6.21}$$

Inferential errors

If the reported results of a study always include both an estimate of effect size and a test of significance (or a related procedure such as a confidence interval) we can better protect ourselves against the inferential invalidity of Type I and Type II errors. There is little doubt that in the social and behavioral sciences Type II errors (i.e., concluding that *X* and *Y* are unrelated when they really are related) are far more likely than Type I errors (Cohen, 1962, 1977). The frequency of Type II errors can be reduced drastically by our attention to the magnitude of the estimated effect size. If that estimate is large and we find a nonsignificant result, we would do well to avoid deciding that variables *X* and *Y* are not related. Only if the pooled results of a good many replications point to a very small effect size on the average, and to a

Table 6.4. *Population effect sizes and results of significance testing as determinants of inferential errors*

Population effect size	Results of significance testing	
	Not significant	Significant
Zero	No error	Type I error
Small	Type II error[a]	No error[b]
Large	Type II error[c]	No error

[a]Low power may lead to failure to detect the true effect, but if the true effect is quite small the costs of this error may not be too great.
[b]Although not an inferential error, if the effect size is *very* small and *N* is very large we may mistake a result that is merely very significant for one that is of practical importance.
[c]Low power may lead to failure to detect the true effect and with a substantial true effect the costs of this error may be very great.

combined test of significance that does not reach our favorite alpha level, are we justified in concluding that no nontrivial relationship exists between *X* and *Y*. Table 6.4 summarizes inferential errors and some possible consequences as a joint function of the results of significance testing and the population effect size.

A summary of some effect size indicators

In this section, we want to bring together the various effect size indicators that have been referred to so far as well as a few others that may prove useful. Table 6.5 serves as a summary. The first four indicators include the very general Pearson product moment correlation (r) and three related indices. The indicator r/k is not typically employed as an effect size estimate though it certainly could be. It is included here because of its role in equations 6.3 and 6.11; that is, it is an effect size estimate that needs only to be multiplied by $[df]^{1/2}$ to yield the associated test of significance, t. The index r/k turns out also to be related to Cohen's d in an interesting way – it equals $d/2$ for situations in which we can think of the two populations being compared as equally numerous (Cohen, 1977; Friedman, 1968). The indicator z_r is also not typically employed as an effect size estimate though it, too, could be. However, it is frequently used as a transformation of r in a variety of data analytic procedures (e.g., averaging r's). Cohen's q indexes the difference between two correlation coefficients in units of z_r.

Table 6.5. *Three types of effect size indicators*

	Effect size indicator	Definition
Product moment correlation (*r*) and functions of *r*	Pearson *r*	$\Sigma(z_x z_y)/N$
	r/k	$r/[1-r^2]^{1/2}$
	z_r	$\frac{1}{2}\log_e[(1+r)/(1-r)]$
	Cohen's *q*	$z_{r_1} - z_{r_2}$ [a]
Standardized differences between means	Cohen's *d*	$(M_1 - M_2)/\sigma$ pooled
	Glass's Δ	$(M_1 - M_2)/S$ control group
	Hedges's *g*	$(M_1 - M_2)/S$ pooled
Differences between proportions	Cohen's *g*	$P - .50$
	d'	$P_1 - P_2$
	Cohen's *h*	$P_1^b - P_2^b$

[a] This is an effect size indexing the magnitude of the difference between two effect sizes.
[b] *P*'s are first transformed to angles measured in radians: $2 \arcsin P^{1/2}$.

The next three indicators of Table 6.5 are all standardized mean differences. They differ from each other only in the standardizing denominator. Cohen's *d* employs the σ computed from both groups employing *N* rather than $N-1$ as the within-group divisor for the sums of squares. Glass's Δ and Hedges's *g* both employ $N-1$ divisors for sums of squares. Glass, however, computes *S* only for the control group, while Hedges computes *S* from both experimental and control groups.

The last three indicators of Table 6.5 include two from Cohen (1977). Cohen's *g* is the difference between an obtained proportion and a proportion of .50. The index *d'* is the difference between two obtained proportions. Cohen's *h* is also the difference between two obtained proportions but only after the proportions have been transformed to angles (measured in units called radians, equal to about 57.3 degrees).

Many other effect size indicators could have been listed. For example, Kraemer and Andrews (1982) and Krauth (1983) have described effect size estimates when medians rather than means are to be compared. These are not described here since the product moment correlations (based on continuous scores, ranks, or dichotomized data) can be employed in those situations. We have specifically not included any indices of proportion of variance accounted for such as r^2, eta^2, omega^2, epsilon^2, and so forth. As we shall see in the following section, all these indices tend to be misleading at the lower levels. In addition, those that are based on *F* tests with $df > 1$ in the numerator are generally of little value in the data analytic enterprise (Rosenthal, 1984; Rosenthal & Rosnow, 1984, 1985).

The practical importance of the estimated effect size

Mayo (1978) criticized Cohen (1977) for calling an effect size large ($d = .80$) when it accounted for "only" 14 percent of the variance. Similarly, Rimland (1979) felt that the Smith and Glass (1977) meta-analysis of psychotherapy outcome studies sounded the "death knell" for psychotherapy because the effect size was equivalent to an r of .32 accounting for only 10 percent of the variance.

The binomial effect size display (BESD)

Despite the growing awareness of the importance of estimating effect sizes, there is a problem in evaluating various effect size estimators from the point of view of practical usefulness (Cooper, 1981). Rosenthal and Rubin (1979b, 1982b) found that neither experienced behavioral researchers nor experienced statisticians had a good intuitive feel for the practical meaning of such common effect size estimators as r^2, eta^2, omega^2, epsilon^2, and similar estimates.

Accordingly, Rosenthal and Rubin introduced an intuitively appealing general purpose effect size display whose interpretation is perfectly transparent: *the binomial effect size display (BESD).* There is no sense in which they claim to have resolved the differences and controversies surrounding the use of various effect size estimators but their display is useful because it is (a) easily understood by researchers, students, and lay persons, (b) applicable in a wide variety of contexts, and (c) conveniently computed.

The question addressed by BESD is: what is the effect on the success rate (e.g., survival rate, cure rate, improvement rate, selection rate, etc.) of the institution of a new treatment procedure, a new selection device, or a new predictor variable? It, therefore, displays the change in success rate (e.g., survival rate, cure rate, improvement rate, accuracy rate, selection rate, etc.) attributable to the new treatment procedure, new selection device, or new predictor variable. An example shows the appeal of the display. Suppose the estimated mean effect size were found to be an r of .32, approximately the size of the effects reported by Smith and Glass (1977) and by Rosenthal and Rubin (1978a, 1978b) for the effects of psychotherapy and of interpersonal expectancy effects, respectively.

Table 6.6 is the BESD corresponding to an r of .32 and an r^2 of .10. The table shows clearly that it is absurd to label as "modest" an effect size equivalent to increasing the success rate from 34 percent to 66 percent (e.g., reducing a death rate from 66 percent to 34 percent). Even so small an r as .20,

Table 6.6. *The binomial effect size display*
(BESD) for an r of .32 that accounts for
"only" 10 percent of the variance

	Treatment result		
Condition	Alive	Dead	Σ
Treatment	66	34	100
Control	34	66	100
Σ	100	100	200

accounting for "only" 4 percent of the variance is associated with an increase in success rate from 40 percent to 60 percent, for example, a decrease in death rate from 60 percent to 40 percent, hardly a trivial effect. It might be thought that the BESD can be employed only for dichotomous outcomes (e.g., alive vs. dead) and not for continuous outcomes (e.g., scores on a Likert-type scale of improvement due to psychotherapy, or gains in performance due to favorable interpersonal expectations). Fortunately, however, the BESD works well for both types of outcomes under a wide variety of conditions (Rosenthal & Rubin, 1982b).

A great convenience of the BESD is how easily we can convert it to r (or r^2) and how easily we can go from r (or r^2) to the display.

Table 6.7 shows systematically the increase in success rates associated with various values of r^2 and r. For example, an r of .30, accounting for only 9 percent of the variance, is associated with a reduction in death rate from 65 percent to 35 percent, or, more generally, with an increase in success rate from 35 percent to 65 percent. The last column of Table 6.7 shows that the difference in success rates is identical to r. Consequently, the experimental group success rate in the BESD is computed as $.50 + r/2$ whereas the control group success rate is computed as $.50 - r/2$.

The propranolol study and the BESD

On October 29, 1981, the National Heart, Lung, and Blood Institute officially discontinued its placebo-controlled study of propranolol because the results were so favorable to the treatment that it would be unethical to keep the placebo-control patients from receiving the treatment (Kolata, 1981). The two-year data for this study were based on 2,108 patients and $\chi^2(1)$ was approximately 4.2. What, then, was the size of the effect that led the Institute to break off its study? Was the use of propranolol accounting for 90 percent of the variance in death rates? Was it 50 percent or 10 percent, the overly

Table 6.7. *Changes in success rates (BESD) corresponding to various values of* r^2 *and* r

Effect sizes		Equivalent to a success rate increase		Difference in success rates[a]
r^2	r	From	To	
.00	.02	.49	.51	.02
.00	.04	.48	.52	.04
.00	.06	.47	.53	.06
.01	.08	.46	.54	.08
.01	.10	.45	.55	.10
.01	.12	.44	.56	.12
.02	.14	.43	.57	.14
.03	.16	.42	.58	.16
.03	.18	.41	.59	.18
.04	.20	.40	.60	.20
.05	.22	.39	.61	.22
.06	.24	.38	.62	.24
.07	.26	.37	.63	.26
.08	.28	.36	.64	.28
.09	.30	.35	.65	.30
.16	.40	.30	.70	.40
.25	.50	.25	.75	.50
.36	.60	.20	.80	.60
.49	.70	.15	.85	.70
.64	.80	.10	.90	.80
.81	.90	.05	.95	.90
1.00	1.00	.00	1.00	1.00

[a]The difference in success rates in a BESD is identical to r.

modest effect size that should prompt us to give up psychotherapy? From equation 6.15, we find the proportion-of-variance-accounted-for (r^2):

$$r^2 = \frac{\chi^2}{N} = \frac{4.2}{2,108} = .002$$

Thus, the propranolol study was discontinued for an effect accounting for one-fifth of 1 percent of the variance! To display this result as a BESD we take the square root of r^2 to obtain the r we use for the BESD. That r is about .04 which displays as shown in Table 6.8. As behavioral researchers we are not accustomed to thinking of r's of .04 as reflecting effect sizes of practical importance. If we were among the 4 per 100 who moved from one outcome to the other, we might well revise our view of the practical import of small effects!

Table 6.8. *The binomial effect size display for the discontinued propranolol study*

| | Treatment result | | |
Condition	Alive	Dead	Σ
Propranolol	52	48	100
Placebo	48	52	100
Σ	100	100	200

Concluding note on interpreting effect sizes

Rosenthal and Rubin (1982b) proposed that the reporting of effect sizes could be made more intuitive and more informative by using the BESD. It was their belief that the use of the BESD to display the increase in success rate due to treatment would more clearly convey the real-world importance of treatment effects than would the commonly used descriptions of effect size, especially those based on the proportion of variance accounted for.

One effect of the routine employment of a display procedure such as the BESD to index the practical meaning of our research results would be to give us more useful and realistic assessments of how well we are doing as researchers in the field of nonverbal communication in particular, and in the social and behavioral sciences more generally. Employment of the BESD has, in fact, shown that we are doing considerably better in our "softer" sciences than we thought we were, especially when the BESD is based on the results of (a) studies with small standard errors, and (b) meta-analytic summaries of series of studies.

7. The interpretation of interaction effects

Although most readers of this book will be familiar with analysis of variance procedures, the topic of the interpretation of interactions requires special attention for three reasons: (a) interaction effects are frequently obtained in research on nonverbal behavior, (b) interaction effects are very important in much research on nonverbal behavior, and (c) interaction effects are frequently misinterpreted in research on nonverbal behavior and, indeed, in behavioral research in general.

Referees and advisory editors for various journals in the behavioral sciences, and consultants in research methods, find the misinterpretation of interaction effects to be one of the most common of all methodological errors. The nature of the error is almost always the same: the effects of the interaction are not distinguished from the main effects. The cautionary note is best sounded in the warning: *If we're looking at the means we're not interpreting the interaction.*

An illustration
Suppose we have employed female and male encoders to encode various nonverbal stimuli to female and male decoders. Table 7.1 shows the resulting table of mean accuracy scores and the table of variance.

In the published report an investigator might accurately state that there was a significant effect of sex of encoder such that decoders decoding females performed better than those decoding males. The investigator might also state correctly that there was no significant effect of sex of decoder on performance. Finally, the investigator might say, *but it would be wrong,* that the significant interaction effect, displayed as in the top of Figure 7.1, demonstrated that males, but not females benefited from having a female encoder.

How has the investigator erred in referring the reader to this figure? The top of Figure 7.1 is a perfectly accurate display of the *means* of the four conditions, means which are comprised of two main effects plus an interaction.

Table 7.1. *Tables of means and of variance for a study of sex of encoders and sex of decoders*

Table of means			
	Decoders		
Encoders	Females	Males	Means
Females	4	10	7
Males	4	2	3
Means	4	6	5

Table of variance						
Source	SS	df	MS	F	r	p
Sex of encoder	16	1	16	4.00	.25	.05
Sex of decoder	4	1	4	1.00	.13	—
Interaction	16	1	16	4.00	.25	.05
Error term (MS error $\times$ $\frac{1}{16}$)	240	60	4			

However, plotting the means never plots the interaction (unless the main effects contributing to the means are exactly zero). An accurate display of the interaction appears at the bottom of Figure 7.1.

Here we see that the *interaction* shows that males benefit from having female encoders precisely to the same degree that females are harmed by having female encoders. The diagram of the interaction is X shaped; indeed, it is *always* true that in any 2 × 2 analysis of variance, the display of the interaction will be X shaped. This will become clearer as we proceed.

Defining interaction
Interaction effects are residual effects, or effects remaining in any analysis after lower order effects have been removed. In a two-way design (A × B), the interaction effects are the effects remaining after the row and column effects (the effects of A and B) have been removed. In a three-way design (A × B × C), and in higher order designs, there are four or more different interactions. In an A × B × C design there are three two-way interactions (A × B, A × C, B × C), each of which is the residual set of effects remaining after the removal of the two main effects designated by the letters naming the interaction; there is also a three-way interaction (A × B × C) which is the residual set of effects remaining after the removal of the three main effects

Figure showing overall results of the study of Table 7.1

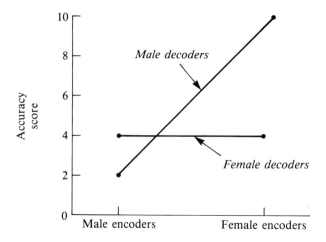

Figure showing interaction effects of the study of Table 7.1

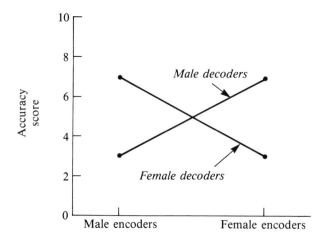

Figure 7.1. Comparison of figure showing overall effects with figure showing interaction effects exclusively

and the three two-way interactions. In an $A \times B \times C \times D$ or four-way design there are six two-way interactions ($A \times B$, $A \times C$, $A \times D$, $B \times C$, $B \times D$, $C \times D$), four three-way interactions ($A \times B \times C$, $A \times B \times D$, $A \times C \times D$, $B \times C \times D$), and one four-way interaction. In general, a *higher order interaction* is defined as the residual set of effects remaining after the main effects and all lower order interactions relevant to the higher order interaction have been removed. Thus the $A \times B \times C \times D$ interaction is defined as the set of effects remaining after the four main effects, the six two-way interactions, and the four three-way interactions have been subtracted from the total of all between-conditions effects.

Displaying the residuals

Before an interaction effect can be understood it must be identified and examined, that is, the residuals defining the interaction must be displayed. The logic is straightforward, but in a very high order interaction the computation can become burdensome and, regrettably, there are very few social science data analytic packages that routinely provide the residuals (a package that *does* is called Data-text; Armor & Couch, 1972). In a two-dimensional design, however, the computations are simple. Consider the results of our study of the effects of sex of encoder on females' and males' accuracy scores.

To find the interaction effects we must subtract the row and column effects from each condition of the study. *Row effects* are defined for each row as the mean of that row minus the grand mean. The *row effects* are $7 - 5 = 2$ for the female encoders and $3 - 5 = -2$ for the male encoders (see Subtable A of Table 7.2). To remove the row effect we subtract the row effect from every condition within that row. Subtracting 2 from the top row yields means of 6 and 4 (recall that subtracting a negative value is equivalent to adding a positive value). The table of means we started with, now with row effects removed (or "corrected-for"-row-effects), has been amended as shown in Subtable B of Table 7.2.

We must still remove the effects of columns. *Column effects* are defined for each column as the mean of that column minus the grand mean. The column effects are $4 - 5 = -1$ for the females and $6 - 5 = 1$ for the males. To remove the column effect we subtract it from every condition within that column. Subtracting -1 from the first column of our row-corrected table (Subtable B) just above, yields means of 3 and 7; subtracting 1 from the second column yields means of 7 and 3. The table of means we started with, now with both row and column effects removed, has been amended to Subtable C of Table 7.2. Once the row and column effects are all zero, we can be sure that what is left is only the set of residuals defining the interaction effect sometimes with, and sometimes without, the grand mean added.

It is these means that were shown in the bottom portion of Figure 7.1 displaying the correct interaction effects. However, these interaction effects are inflated by the presence of the grand mean, an inflation useful for display purposes earlier when we wanted to compare the results of the experiment

Table 7.2. *Computing and displaying interaction effects*

Subtable A: Original means

Encoders	Decoders		Means	Row effects
	Females	Males		
Females	4	10	7	2
Males	4	2	3	−2
Means	4	6	5[a]	
Column effects	−1	1		

Subtable B: Row effects removed

	Females	Males	Means	Row effects
Females	2	8	5	0
Males	6	4	5	0
Means	4	6	5[a]	
Column effects	−1	1		

Subtable C: Row and column effects removed

	Females	Males	Means	Row effects
Females	3	7	5	0
Males	7	3	5	0
Means	5	5	5[a]	
Column effects	0	0		

Subtable D: Row, column, and grand mean effects removed

	Females	Males	Means	Row effects
Females	−2	2	0	0
Males	2	−2	0	0
Means	0	0	0[a]	
Column effects	0	0		

[a]Grand mean.

defined as the condition means, with the interaction effect alone. In most situations, however, we prefer to display the interaction effects freed of the effect of the grand mean. To remove the grand mean from Subtable C of Table 7.2 we simply subtract it from every condition of the experiment. For our example that yields Subtable D of Table 7.2.

It should be noted that all four conditions show the same absolute value of the interaction effects, only the signs differ. That is always the case in a 2×2 analysis, and the signs on one of the diagonals are always different from the signs on the other diagonal if the interaction is not precisely zero. It is thus convenient to think of an interaction in a 2×2 table as the difference between the means of the two diagonals, just as it is convenient to think of the row or column effects as the differences between the row means or the column means.

Returning now to the top portion of Figure 7.1 we can see that it is an accurate display of the results of the experiment. It does show that females did not benefit from female encoders but that males did. That statement, however, is not a statement about the interaction effect per se but a statement made up in part of (a) a sex of encoder effect (the females are better), in part of (b) a sex of decoder effect (males score higher though not significantly so), and in part of (c) an interaction effect which we interpret as showing that female decoders are disadvantaged by female encoders as much as male decoders are helped by them, or, equivalently, but more instructively, that opposite-sex dyads perform better than do same-sex dyads.

More complex two-way interactions

So far we have considered only the simple case of interaction in a 2×2 design. In such a design we have seen that the residuals defining the interaction are all identical in absolute value with positive signs on one diagonal and negative signs on the other diagonal. In larger designs the situation is more complex. Because this is a chapter on interaction, our focus in the following example will be on the study of the interaction effects. This emphasis is not due to our regarding interaction effects as in any way more important than main effects. Rather, it is because interaction effects are so much more often misinterpreted than are main effects.

For our example we consider an experiment in which four different treatment procedures are administered to three different types of patients with results as shown in Table 7.3.

Patients of each of the three types were assigned at random to one of four treatment conditions: (1) a course of ten electroconvulsive treatments, (2) a course of three electroconvulsive treatments, (3) a combination of supportive psychotherapy and chemotherapy, and (4) supportive psychotherapy alone. In order to see the interaction of treatment × patient type both the row and column effects must be subtracted off. Usually it is desirable also to subtract off the grand mean and we begin by doing that. Since the grand mean is six, we simply subtract six from every one of the 3×4, or twelve, condition means, yielding Subtable A of Table 7.4.

Table 7.3. *Mean ratings of nonverbal equanimity in twelve conditions*

| Patient type | Treatment conditions | | | | |
	A_1 ECT (10)	A_2 ECT (3)	A_3 Support +drug	A_4 Support only	Mean
B_1 Psychotic depression	8	6	4	2	5
B_2 Neurotic depression	11	8	5	8	8
B_3 Paranoid reaction	2	4	6	8	5
Mean	7	6	5	6	6

Once the grand mean has been subtracted the new row means are the row effects and the new column means are the column effects. To remove the row effects simply subtract the effect of each row (row mean minus grand mean) from every condition within that row. Doing that for the present data yields Subtable B of Table 7.4. Subtracting the column effect from every condition mean within that column then yields Subtable C of Table 7.4.

Now that the grand mean, row effects, and column effects have been removed, we are left with the interaction effect shown in Subtable C of Table 7.4. The effects contributing most to the interaction are the effects furthest from zero and one way to approach the interpretation of the interaction is one residual at a time, starting with the largest absolute value. In this case the A_1B_3 condition shows the greatest residual (-4), suggesting that least improvement is shown by paranoid patients given a course of ten ECT treatments *disregarding row and column effects*. The next two largest residuals are the A_4B_1 and A_4B_3 conditions. The former suggests that support alone offered to psychotic depressive patients is relatively damaging (-3) while the latter suggests that support alone offered to paranoid patients is relatively quite beneficial (3). The term *relatively* is used here to emphasize that the effects shown by certain combinations of treatments and patients are large or small only in relation to other effects shown here *after the removal of the main effects of treatments and patients*.

We can be more systematic in our examination of the residuals by listing them in order of magnitude as shown in Table 7.5. Examining first the positive residuals suggests that paranoid patients may do better given support while depressive patients may do better given ECT. Examining the negative

Table 7.4. *Stepwise removal of grand mean, row, and column effects to expose residuals of Table 7.3*

Subtable A: Grand mean removed

	A_1	A_2	A_3	A_4	Mean
B_1	2	0	-2	-4	-1
B_2	5	2	-1	2	2
B_3	-4	-2	0	2	-1
Mean	1	0	-1	0	0

Subtable B: Grand mean and row effects removed

	A_1	A_2	A_3	A_4	Mean
B_1	3	1	-1	-3	0
B_2	3	0	-3	0	0
B_3	-3	-1	1	3	0
Mean	1	0	-1	0	0

Subtable C: Grand mean, row effects, and column effects removed

	A_1	A_2	A_3	A_4	Mean
B_1	2	1	0	-3	0
B_2	2	0	-2	0	0
B_3	-4	-1	2	3	0
Mean	0	0	0	0	0

Table 7.5. *Twelve conditions listed according to the algebraic value of their residuals*

Residual	Patient	Treatment
3	Paranoid	Support only
2	Psychotic depression	ECT 10
2	Neurotic depression	ECT 10
2	Paranoid	Support + drug
1	Psychotic depression	ECT 3
0	Psychotic depression	Support + drug
0	Neurotic depression	ECT 3
0	Neurotic depression	Support only
-1	Paranoid	ECT 3
-2	Neurotic depression	Support + drug
-3	Psychotic depression	Support only
-4	Paranoid	ECT 10

Table 7.6. *Table of twelve residuals (3 × 4) reduced to four residuals (2 × 2)*

	ECT $(A_1 + A_2)$	Support $(A_3 + A_4)$	Mean
Depressives $(B_1 + B_2)$	5	−5	0
Paranoids (B_3)	−5	5	0
Mean	0	0	0

residuals suggests that paranoid patients may do worse given ECT while depressive patients may do worse given support. It may be of value to simplify our design from four treatments to two by combining the two conditions receiving ECT and the two conditions receiving support. We can further simplify our design from three patient types to two by combining the two depressed groups. That yields a 2 × 2 table in each quarter of which we can record the sum of the residuals contributing to that quarter as shown in Table 7.6.

This simplification of the interaction to a 2 × 2 table represents one reasonable attempt to understand the patterning of the residuals defining the interaction. In a subsequent chapter dealing with contrasts, there will be more details about the simplification of complex interaction effects.

The complexity of an interaction depends in part on the *df* associated with the interaction, with *df* computed as the product of the *df* associated with each of its constituent elements. In the study we have just now been discussing, there were four treatment conditions so *df* = 3 for treatments, and three types of patients so *df* = 2 for patient type; therefore *df* for the treatment × patient type interaction = 3 × 2 = 6. Finding a pattern in these 6 *df*, such as the one shown just above as a 2 × 2 table, represents simplifying the 6 *df* interaction to a 1 *df* portion of that interaction.

An accurate description of the simplified structure of our interaction might be: depressed patients benefit from ECT to the same degree they are harmed by support while paranoid patients benefit from support to the same degree they are harmed by ECT. Note that we are describing the *interaction* effects or residuals and not necessarily the original condition means that are *not* merely a reflection of the interaction but of the row and column effects as well.

An alternative simplification of the 6 *df* interaction might involve keeping in mind the amount of ECT administered as well as whether ECT was administered. Thus we can display the three levels of ECT shown in Table 7.7.

Table 7.7. *Table of twelve residuals (3 × 4) reduced to six residuals (2 × 3)*

	(A_1) High (ECT 10)	(A_2) Low (ECT 3)	($A_3 + A_4$) No ECT	Mean
Depressives ($B_1 + B_2$)	4	1	−5	0
Paranoids (B_3)	−4	−1	5	0
Mean	0	0	0	0

Interpretation of this simplification might be that in going from none to some to more ECT, depressives are increasingly more benefited while paranoids are increasingly less benefited.

Three-way and higher order interactions

The principles of interpreting three-way and higher order interactions are straightforward extrapolations of the principles described here for two-way interactions. Three-way interactions are displayed by subtracting off the three main effects and the three two-way interactions leaving the residuals defining the three-way interactions. More details are given elsewhere (Rosenthal & Rosnow, 1984).

Further notes on interpretation

Organismic interactions. Although interactions are defined by, and therefore completely described by, a table of residuals, such a table is not usually of interest to the investigator without some additional interpretation. In an abstract discussion of interaction we can view a 2 × 3 table of residuals without labeling the rows and columns and without thinking about the scientific meaning of the interaction. Investigators of a substantive problem, however, must go further. They must try to make sense of the phenomenon. Consider a study of the effects of two drugs on patients' mood as judged from facial expressions with the following obtained interaction.

	Drug A	Drug B
Male	+1	−1
Female	−1	+1

We conclude that, at least for the interaction component of our results, drug A is relatively better for males while drug B is relatively better for females. The term "relatively" is used here to emphasize that the effects shown by certain combinations of drug and gender are large or small only in relation to other effects shown *after the removal of the main effects of drug and gender.*

It often happens in behavioral research that different treatment techniques are differentially effective for different subgroups. Such interactions, known as *organismic interactions,* reflect the fact that some types of interventions are especially effective for some but not other types of persons.

Synergistic effects.   Sometimes two or more treatments are applied simultaneously and *synergistic* effects occur such that receiving both treatments leads to better results than would have been predicted from a knowledge of the effects of each treatment taken alone. For example, in the following table it appears that treatment A alone or treatment B alone has no beneficial value but that the combination of treatments A and B is very beneficial:

		Treatment A	
		Present	*Absent*
Treatment B	*Present*	4	0
	Absent	0	0

Such a *positive synergistic* effect is probably best described in just that way, that is, that both treatments are required for any benefits to result. Note, however, that such a description is of the four means and not of the residuals. If we subtract the grand mean, row effects, and column effects we will find an interaction effect that tells quite a different story and that is identical in magnitude to the row effects and to the column effects. The interaction taken by itself will tell us that both or neither treatment are superior to either one treatment or the other.

It is often the case that when row, column, and interaction effects are all of comparable magnitudes, we would do well to interpret the results by examining the means apart from the row, column, and interaction effects preplanned by our design. In a subsequent chapter on contrasts, we shall see that if we had planned a study expecting the results shown just above it would have been poor data-analytic procedure to cast the data into a 2×2 factorial design, and analyze it without the use of a planned contrast.

Negative synergistic effects are also possible as shown here:

		Treatment A	
		Present	*Absent*
Treatment B	*Present*	0	4
	Absent	4	4

These results suggest that the treatments are harmful when taken together and not helpful when taken in isolation, since neither does better than the control group of no treatment. The results of this study, like those of the preceding one, are made up of row effects, column effects and interaction effects that are all identical in size. The residuals defining the interaction would suggest that receiving either treatment in isolation is better than receiving both treatments or neither treatment. As in the example of positive synergism, if we had anticipated results of this type, a 2×2 factorial design would not have been optimal; detailed discussion of this is to be found in a later chapter on contrasts. Before leaving the topic of negative synergism we should note that a possible basis for negative synergism is a ceiling effect as when the measuring instrument is simply unable to record benefits above a certain level. In that case the results might appear as follows:

		Treatment A	
		Present	*Absent*
Treatment B	*Present*	4	4
	Absent	4	0

Crossed-line interactions. Crossed-line interactions are interactions in which residuals for one group of subjects or sampling units show a relatively linear increase while residuals for another group of subjects show a relatively linear decrease. Actually, all 2×2 interactions are of this type since they are all characterized by an X shape; for example, one group improves in going from control to experimental condition while the other group gets worse in going from control to experimental condition.

As an illustration of a 2×3 interaction, consider three measures of sensitivity to nonverbal communication that have been administered to female and male students. The three measures are designed to measure sensitivity to the face, to the body, and to tone of voice, respectively. Of these three channels, the face is thought to be most easily controlled and tone is thought to be least easily controlled (Rosenthal & DePaulo, 1979a, 1979b). A fairly typical result in research of this type might yield the following accuracy scores:

	Channel			
	Face	*Body*	*Tone*	*Mean*
Female	6	4	2	4.0
Male	3	2	1	2.0
Mean	4.5	3.0	1.5	3.0

for which the table of effects would be as follows:

	Channel			
	Face	*Body*	*Tone*	*Mean*
Female	0.5	0.0	−0.5	1.0
Male	−0.5	0.0	0.5	−1.0
Mean	1.5	0.0	−1.5	0.0

The row effects show that females are better decoders of nonverbal cues than are males, a well-known result (Hall, 1979, 1984). The column effects show that face cues are easiest to decode and tone of voice cues are hardest to decode of these three types of cues, also a well-known result (Rosenthal et al., 1979). The interaction effects show that as the type of cue becomes more controllable by the encoder, the females' advantage over the males increases, a frequently obtained result (Rosenthal & DePaulo, 1979a, 1979b). A plot of these results would show an X-shaped figure (such as that shown near the beginning of this chapter) with one group increasing as the other group is decreasing. A convenient way to display crossed-line interactions is to plot the *difference* between the residuals for the two groups. In this case such a plot would show a linear increase in the superiority of women over men as the channels became more controllable:

| | Channel | | |
	Face	Body	Tone
Female	0.5	0.0	−0.5
Male	−0.5	0.0	0.5
Difference *(female advantage)*	1.0	0.0	−1.0

Crossed-quadratic interactions.   Sometimes the residuals of one group are ∪-shaped while the residuals of the other group are shaped like an inverted ∪ or ∩. This type of nonlinear shape, where the line changes direction once (going up and then down or vice versa) is called a *quadratic curve*. Curves changing direction twice (going up, down, and up again or vice versa) are called *cubic curves*. With each additional change in direction cubic curves become *quartic curves, quartic* curves become *quintic curves,* and so on.

As an illustration of a crossed-quadratic interaction, consider two groups of children tested under three conditions of arousal. The younger group of children seems less affected by arousal level than the older group, as shown in the following results:

| | | Arousal level | | | |
		Low	Medium	High	Mean
Age	*Younger*	3	6	3	4
	Older	5	11	5	7
	Mean	4.0	8.5	4.0	5.5

for which the table of effects would be as follows:

| | | Arousal level | | | |
		Low	Medium	High	Mean
Age	*Younger*	0.5	−1.0	0.5	−1.5
	Older	−0.5	1.0	−0.5	1.5
	Mean	−1.5	3.0	−1.5	0.0

The row effects show that the older children perform better than the younger children and the column effects show that medium arousal level is associated with better performance than is either low- or high-arousal level.

The residuals show crossed-quadratic curves with younger children showing a U-shaped performance curve relative to the older children who show an inverted U-shaped performance curve. Once again we must emphasize that these residuals refer exclusively to the interaction component of the results. Inspection of the condition means shows both groups of children producing an inverted U-shaped function. The older children simply show more of one relative to the younger children.

Simplifying complex tables of residuals

A general principle for the simplification of tables of residuals is to subtract one level of a factor from the other level of that factor for any two-level factor for which the difference between levels can be regarded as substantively meaningful. Following this procedure, a two-way interaction may be viewed as a change in a main effect due to the introduction of a second independent variable; a three-way interaction may be viewed as a change in a main effect due to the introduction of a two-way interaction, or as a change in a two-way interaction due to the introduction of a third independent variable.

Another general principle for the simplification of tables of residuals involves a process of concept formation for the diagonals of a table of residuals, usually a 2×2 table. If a suitable concept can be found to describe each diagonal of a 2×2 table of residuals, the interpretation of the interaction will be simplified to the interpretation of a main effect of diagonals. We will illustrate each of these two methods.

The method of meaningful differences.   We have already had a brief exposure to this method in our discussion of crossed-line interactions. In that example we subtracted the residuals for males from the residuals for females to create difference scores that represented the advantage of being female over male in the decoding of nonverbal cues. We then compared these female advantage scores for three types of measures of sensitivity to nonverbal cues and were thus able to interpret an interaction of test × sex as simply the main effect of test on the difference between the sexes. An even simpler example might be:

		A	B	A − B
Subjects	Type X	+1	−1	+2
	Type Y	−1	+1	−2

In this case two treatments, A and B, are each administered to two types of people, types X and Y. By taking the difference between treatments A and B we form a new measure, the advantage of treatment A over B. These advantage scores (A − B) can then be compared for persons of type X and Y.

In this example the advantage of treatment A over B is greater for type X than for type Y people because 2 is greater than -2. By subtracting B from A we have reduced a two-dimensional display of residuals to a one-dimensional display.

The method of meaningful diagonals.   In this method we simplify the table of residuals by imposing substantive meaning on the residuals located on the diagonals, usually of a 2×2 table. For example, we might be studying accuracy of decoding nonverbal cues as a function of the sex of the decoders and the sex of the encoders with interaction effects as follows:

		Sex of decoders	
		Female	Male
Sex of encoders	Female	+1	−1
	Male	−1	+1

The diagonal going from upper left to lower right might be conceptualized as the *same-sex dyad* diagonal, and the diagonal going from lower left to upper right might be conceptualized as the *opposite-sex dyad* diagonal. We could then state that the mean residual for same-sex dyads is greater $(+1)$ than that for opposite-sex dyads (-1). By employing a construct to describe the diagonals, we have reduced a two-dimensional display of residuals to a one-dimensional display as shown:

	Same-sex dyad	Opposite-sex dyad
	+1	−1
	+1	−1
Mean	+1	−1

Combined methods.   It is often possible to combine the two methods we have described to achieve a greater simplification of a fairly complex interaction. Consider the following three-way interaction in which male and female experimenters administered a nonverbal decoding task to male and female subjects, sometimes having been led to expect high achievement, sometimes having been led to expect low achievement from their subjects.

	Low expectations		High expectations	
	Female E	Male E	Female E	Male E
Female S	−1	+1	+1	−1
Male S	+1	−1	−1	+1

We begin the simplification process by applying the *Method of Meaningful differences.* In this case it makes most substantive sense to subtract the residuals for low expectations from the residuals for high expectations. These differences then represent expectancy effects, positive in sign when they are in the predicted direction (high > low) and negative in sign when they are in the opposite direction (high < low). The results of this first step are as shown:

	Female E	*Male E*
Female S	+2	−2
Male S	−2	+2

Now the three-way interaction of sex of experimenter, sex of subject, and expectancy has been simplified to a two-way interaction of sex of experimenter and sex of subject with the dependent variable of difference scores or expectancy effect scores. We can now apply the *Method of Meaningful Diagonals* to this two-way table and interpret the originally complex three-way interaction as showing that same-sex dyads show greater expectancy effects than do opposite-sex dyads.

A five-way interaction.   The same general procedures can often be applied to an even more complicated situation, a five-way interaction, as shown in the following case. This time we have female and male experimenters who are either black or white, administering a nonverbal decoding task, to male and female subjects who are either black or white, sometimes having been led to expect high, and sometimes low, performance. The design, then, is a race of $E \times$ sex of $E \times$ race of $S \times$ sex of $S \times$ expectancy of E factorial, each with two levels of each factor, a $2 \times 2 \times 2 \times 2 \times 2$ or 2^5 factorial design. The effects for the five-way interaction are shown in Table 7.8.

Our first step again is to eliminate one dimension of the design by subtracting the low expectancy residuals from the high expectancy residuals, yielding the expectancy effects of Table 7.9.

The entries of this table of difference scores can be viewed as a 2×2 interaction (race of $E \times$ race of S) of 2×2 interactions (sex of $E \times$ sex of S).

Table 7.8. *Table of thirty-two residuals defining a five-way interaction*

	Black *E*				White *E*			
	Male *E*		Female *E*		Male *E*		Female *E*	
(Expectancy)	High	Low	High	Low	High	Low	High	Low
Black S								
Male *S*	+1	−1	−1	+1	−1	+1	+1	−1
Female *S*	−1	+1	+1	−1	+1	−1	−1	+1
White S								
Male *S*	−1	+1	+1	−1	+1	−1	−1	+1
Female *S*	+1	−1	−1	+1	−1	+1	+1	−1

Table 7.9. *Table of sixteen expectancy effects (high – low)
computed from Table 7.8*

	Black *E*		White *E*	
	Male *E*	Female *E*	Male *E*	Female *E*
Black S				
Male *S*	+2	−2	−2	+2
Female *S*	−2	+2	+2	−2
White S				
Male *S*	−2	+2	+2	−2
Female *S*	+2	−2	−2	+2

The upper left and lower right 2×2 tables are identical to each other and opposite in signs to the 2×2 tables of the upper right and lower left. The first named diagonal describes the same-race dyads, the second named diagonal describes the opposite-race dyads. Within each of the four quadrants of the larger 2×2 table there are smaller 2×2 tables in which one diagonal describes same-sex dyads and in which the other diagonal describes opposite-sex dyads. Keeping that in mind leads us to our interpretation of the five-way interaction: Expectancy effects are greater for same-sex dyads that are also same-race dyads or different-sex dyads that are also different-race dyads than for dyads differing only on sex or only on race. We can redisplay this five-way interaction (or four-way interaction of difference scores) as a two-way interaction of two-way interactions of difference (i.e., expectancy effect) scores:

		Race of dyad	
		Same	Different
Sex of dyad	Same	+2	−2
	Different	−2	+2

Employing the principle illustrated in our earlier example, we made a single factor (same vs. different) of the race of $E \times$ race of S interaction, and a single factor (same vs. different) of the sex of $E \times$ sex of S interaction.

Such simplification of complex interactions is not always possible, though it is more likely when there is conceptual meaning to the diagonal cells of any 2×2 contained within a 2^n factorial design. In general, too, such simplification is more likely when there are fewer levels to the factors of the experiment and thus fewer *df* associated with the higher-order interaction that we are trying to understand. Some higher-order interactions will prove more intractable than others, but by careful examination of the residuals, by employing the methods of Meaningful Differences and Meaningful Diagonals, and by employing the contrast procedures discussed in detail in a later chapter, we can often make some progress.

A note on complexity.　Sometimes our research questions are complex and complex designs and analyses may be required. However, just because we know how to deal with complexity is no reason to value it for its own sake. If our questions are simple, simpler designs and simpler analyses are possible. Especially for the beginning researcher, there is considerable practical benefit to be derived from keeping the designs and analyses as simple as possible.

8. Contrasts: focused comparisons in the analysis of data

Focused **F** *tests*

Much of the business of research in nonverbal communication is carried out by means of analyses of variance which ordinarily culminate in one or more F tests that are often reported as "the results" of the research. The results, of course, are the entire table of means, the table of variance, the various tables of residuals, the effect size estimates, and much more. Here we focus only on the F tests themselves and how we can make them work harder for us. The rule of thumb is easy: Never (*almost* never) employ an F test in an analysis of variance, analysis of covariance, or multivariate analysis of variance that is unfocused, that is, that has more than a single df in the numerator of the F test when it is investigating some specific (or "fixed effect") set of questions. In most cases, unfocused F's address questions in which we are not really interested, questions of the form: are there likely to be some differences of some kinds among some of the groups in our study? That is the kind of question we ask when we examine, for example, the decoding ability of judges at five age levels and report the F for age levels with 4 df in the numerator. Such unfocused F tests often lead to the erroneous conclusion that there are no real differences when it is intuitively clear and statistically demonstrable that there really are.

The alternative to the unfocused F, the focused F, is an F of 1 df in the numerator. Some F's come that way, for example, comparing any two groups, and the rest can be made to speak to us in focused fashion via a contrast (Rosenthal & Rosnow, 1985; Snedecor & Cochran, 1967, 1980). In our example of comparing five age groups for nonverbal decoding ability, we might compute two contrasts; one for linear trend, and one for quadratic trend. The contrast for linear trend would tell us (with the possibility of an F four times as large as for the unfocused F test) whether decoding gets better or worse as people get older, a question of almost certain interest to the investigator. The contrast for quadratic trend would tell us whether the older and

Table 8.1. *Sensitivity to nonverbal cues at five ages*

Means						
			Ages			
8	9	10	11	12		
2.0	3.0	5.0	7.0	8.0		

Analysis of variance					
Source	SS	df	MS	F	p
Age levels	260	4	65	1.03	.40
Within ages	2,835	45	63		

younger groups tend to be more like each other than either is like the medium age groups. Not only do contrasts provide clearer answers to clearer questions, their consistent use often leads to improved experimental designs.

An example

An investigator is interested in the relationship between age and sensitivity to nonverbal cues. A standardized test of such sensitivity is administered to a total of fifty children – ten children at each of the following age levels: eight, nine, ten, eleven, and twelve. Table 8.1 shows the mean performance or sensitivity scores for each of the five age levels and the one-way analysis of variance of these data. Table 8.1 shows us that F for age levels = 1.03, $p = .40$, that is, that the differences among the five means are far from significant. Shall we conclude that, for this study, age was not significantly related to nonverbal sensitivity? If we did so we would be making a very grave, though very common, error.

Suppose we plot the means as shown in Figure 8.1. That plot does not appear consistent with the conclusion that age and performance are not related. Indeed, the correlation between levels of age and levels of sensitivity yield $r(3) = .992$, $p < .001$ (two-tailed).

How can we reconcile such clear and obvious results (the plot, the r, the p) with the results of the analysis of variance telling us that age did not matter? The answer is that the F above addresses a question that may be of relatively little interest to us. The question is diffuse and unfocused, that is, are there *any* differences among the five groups disregarding entirely the arrangement of the ages that constitute the levels of the independent variable? Thus, arranging the ages eight, nine, ten, eleven, twelve would yield the same F as

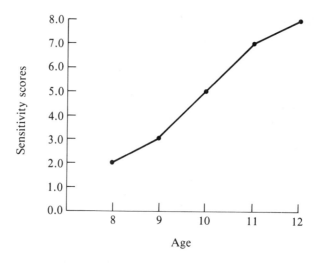

Figure 8.1. Mean sensitivity at five age levels.

arranging them twelve, eleven, ten, nine, eight, or ten, nine, eleven, twelve, eight. This diffuse question is unlikely to have been the one our investigator wanted to address. Far more likely he or she wanted to know whether performance increased with age or whether there was a *quadratic* (upright or inverted ∪; ∪ or ∩) trend.

The correlation we computed addressed the more focused question of whether performance increased linearly with age. In this example the *r* worked well, but note that we had only 3 *df* for testing the significance of that *r*. We shall want a more general, flexible, and powerful way of asking focused questions of our data. Once we learn how to do this there will be relatively few circumstances under which we will want to use unfocused, diffuse, or omnibus *F* tests. That, then, is the purpose of contrasts – to permit us to ask more focused questions of our data. What we get in return for the small amount of computation required to employ contrasts is very much greater statistical power and very much greater clarity of substantive interpretation of research results.

Definitions and procedures
Contrasts are comparisons, employing two or more groups, set up in such a way that the results obtained from the several conditions involved in the research are compared (or "contrasted") to the predictions based on theory, hypothesis, or hunch. These predictions are expressed as weights (called λ) and they can take on any convenient numerical value so long as the sum of

the weights ($\Sigma\lambda$) is zero for any given contrast. Contrasts are quite easy to compute within the context of the analysis of variance. The following formula (e.g., Snedecor & Cochran, 1967, p. 308) shows the computation of a contrast in terms of a sum of squares for the single df test being made. Because contrasts are based on only 1 df, the sum of squares is identical to the mean square and needs only to be divided by the appropriate mean square for error to yield an F test for the contrast.

$$MS \text{ contrast} = SS \text{ contrast} = \frac{L^2}{n\Sigma\lambda^2}$$

where L is the sum of all condition totals (T) each of which has been multiplied by the weight (λ) called for by the hypothesis, or:

$$L = \Sigma[T\lambda] = T_1\lambda_1 + T_2\lambda_2 + T_3\lambda_3 + \cdots + T_k\lambda_k$$

where k = number of conditions

n = number of observations in each condition, given equal n per condition[1]

λ = weights required by the hypothesis such that the sum of the weights equals zero.

We can apply this formula directly to the data of our example. The means were given as 2.0, 3.0, 5.0, 7.0, and 8.0, each mean based on an n of 10. To obtain the required values of T we multiply these means by n and get 20, 30, 50, 70, and 80. For each T we also need a λ based on our theory. If our prediction were that there would be a linear trend, that is, that there would be a regular increment of sensitivity for every regular increment of age, we might first think of using age level as our λ's and they would be eight, nine, ten, eleven, and twelve. However, the sum of these λ's is not zero as required, but fifty. Fortunately, that is easy to correct. We simply subtract the mean age level of ten (i.e., 50/5) from each of our λ's and thus obtain $(8-10)$, $(9-10)$, $(10-10)$, $(11-10)$, and $(12-10)$, or -2, -1, 0, $+1$, $+2$, a set of weights that does sum to zero. To save ourselves the effort of having to calculate these weights, Table 8.2 provides them for linear, quadratic, and cubic orthogonal trends, curves, or polynomials (after Snedecor & Cochran, 1967, p. 572). Later in this chapter these orthogonal polynomials will be described in more detail.

For our present example we have:

Age level	8	9	10	11	12	Σ
T	20	30	50	70	80	250
λ	-2	-1	0	$+1$	$+2$	0
$T\lambda$	-40	-30	0	70	160	160

[1] The situation of unequal n per condition will be discussed shortly.

Table 8.2. *Weights for orthogonal polynomial-based contrasts*

k^a	Polynomial[b]	\multicolumn{10}{c}{Ordered conditions}

k^a	Polynomial[b]	1	2	3	4	5	6	7	8	9	10
2	Linear	−1	+1								
3	Linear	−1	0	+1							
	Quadratic	+1	−2	+1							
4	Linear	−3	−1	+1	+3						
	Quadratic	+1	−1	−1	+1						
	Cubic	−1	+3	−3	+1						
5	Linear	−2	−1	0	+1	+2					
	Quadratic	+2	−1	−2	−1	+2					
	Cubic	−1	+2	0	−2	+1					
6	Linear	−5	−3	−1	+1	+3	+5				
	Quadratic	+5	−1	−4	−4	−1	+5				
	Cubic	−5	+7	+4	−4	−7	+5				
7	Linear	−3	−2	−1	0	+1	+2	+3			
	Quadratic	+5	0	−3	−4	−3	0	+5			
	Cubic	−1	+1	+1	0	−1	−1	+1			
8	Linear	−7	−5	−3	−1	+1	+3	+5	+7		
	Quadratic	+7	+1	−3	−5	−5	−3	+1	+7		
	Cubic	−7	+5	+7	+3	−3	−7	−5	+7		
9	Linear	−4	−3	−2	−1	0	+1	+2	+3	+4	
	Quadratic	+28	+7	−8	−17	−20	−17	−8	+7	+28	
	Cubic	−14	+7	+13	+9	0	−9	−13	−7	+14	
10	Linear	−9	−7	−5	−3	−1	+1	+3	+5	+7	+9
	Quadratic	+6	+2	−1	−3	−4	−4	−3	−1	+2	+6
	Cubic	−42	+14	+35	+31	+12	−12	−31	−35	−14	+42

[a]Number of conditions.
[b]Shape of trend.

For our formula for SS contrast we need L^2, n, and $\Sigma\lambda^2$. $L = \Sigma[T\lambda] = 160$, so $L^2 = (160)^2$; $n = 10$ as given earlier, and $\Sigma\lambda^2 = (-2)^2 + (-1)^2 + (0)^2 + (+1)^2 + (+2)^2 = 10$. So,

$$\frac{L^2}{n\Sigma\lambda^2} = \frac{(160)^2}{10(10)} = 256 = SS \text{ contrast} = MS \text{ contrast}$$

To compute the F test for this contrast we need only divide it by the mean square for error of our analysis of variance to find $F(1, 45) = 256/63 = 4.06$, $p = .05$. Since all F's employed to test contrasts have only 1 df in the numerator we can always take the square root of these F's to obtain the t test for the contrast, in case we want to make a one-tailed t test. In this example a one-tailed t test would be quite sensible, and $t(45) = 2.02$, $p = .025$, one-tailed.

It is characteristic of contrast sums of squares that they are identical whether we employ a given set of weights or their opposite, that is, the weights multiplied by -1. Thus, had we used the weights $+2, +1, 0, -1, -2$ instead of the weights $-2, -1, 0, +1, +2$ in the preceding example we would have obtained identical results, namely SS contrast $= 256$, and $F(1, 45) = 4.06$, $p = .05$. This p value, though one-tailed in the F distribution (in that it refers only to the right-hand portion of the F distribution) is two-tailed with respect to the hypothesis that sensitivity increases with age. If we take $[F]^{1/2} = t$ we must be very careful in making one-tailed t tests to be sure that the results do in fact bear out our prediction and not its opposite. A convenient device is to give t a positive sign when the result is in the predicted direction (e.g., sensitivity improves with age) and a negative sign when the result is in the opposite direction (e.g., sensitivity worsens with age).

To estimate the size of the effect of the linear relationship between performance and age we can employ the information that

$$r = \left[\frac{(df \text{ numerator})F}{(df \text{ numerator})F + df \text{ denominator}} \right]^{1/2} = \left[\frac{t^2}{t^2 + df} \right]^{1/2}$$

$$= \left[\frac{4.06}{4.06 + 45} \right]^{1/2} = .29$$

Thus, the correlation (r) between age level and average sensitivity level is of moderate size. An alternative computational formula for the effect size is

$$r = \left[\frac{SS \text{ contrast}}{SS \text{ contrast} + SS \text{ error}} \right]^{1/2} = \left[\frac{256}{256 + 2835} \right]^{1/2} = .29$$

What if we had divided the SS contrast by the total SS between age groups and taken the square root? We would have found $[256/260]^{1/2} = .992$, exactly the r we obtained earlier by direct computation of the correlation between age level and mean sensitivity level. This r, based on only 3 df, was valuable to us as an alerting device that we were about to make an error by forgetting to take account of the increasing nature of age. However, the r of .992 is a poor estimate of the relationship between *individual* children's age and sensitivity though it does a better job of estimating the correlation of age and sensitivity for the mean age and mean sensitivity of *groups* of children, with $n = 10$ per group. (Not only in this example but generally as well, it is often the case that correlations based on groups or other aggregated data are higher than those based on the original nonaggregated data.)

Additional examples

Testing for linear trend in age is a natural procedure for developmental researchers, but other contrasts may be preferred under some conditions. Suppose our investigator was confident only that twelve year olds would be superior to eight year olds. The investigator could have chosen weights (λ's) as follows:

Age level	8	9	10	11	12	Σ
T	20	30	50	70	80	250
λ	-1	0	0	0	$+1$	0
$T\lambda$	-20	0	0	0	$+80$	60

The SS contrast then would have been $L^2/n\Sigma\lambda^2 = (60)^2/10(2) = 180 = MS$ contrast which, when divided by the mean square for error of our earlier analysis of variance, yields $F(1, 45) = 180/63 = 2.86$, $t(45) = 1.69$, $p = .05$, one-tailed.

Comparing the twelve year olds to the eight year olds is something we knew how to do even before we knew about contrasts; we could simply compute the t test to compare those groups. Had we done so we would have found

$$t = \frac{M_1 - M_2}{[(1/n_1 + 1/n_2)MS \text{ error}]^{1/2}} = \frac{8.0 - 2.0}{[(1/10 + 1/10)63]^{1/2}} = 1.69, \quad df = 45$$

(the df associated with the mean square error), $p = .05$, one-tailed. Comparing the ordinary t test with the contrast t test shows them to be identical, as indeed they should be.

Suppose now that our hypothesis had been that both the eight and nine year olds would score significantly lower than the twelve year olds. We could then have chosen weights (λ's) as follows:

Age level	8	9	10	11	12	Σ
T	20	30	50	70	80	250
λ	-1	-1	0	0	$+2$	0
$T\lambda$	-20	-30	0	0	160	110

(Recall that our λ's must add to zero so that the $\lambda = +2$ of the twelve year olds is needed to balance the -1 and -1 of the eight and nine year olds.)

The SS contrast would have been $L^2/n\Sigma\lambda^2 = (110)^2/10(6) = 201.67 = MS$ contrast which, when divided by the mean square for error of our earlier analysis of variance, yields $F(1, 45) = 201.67/63 = 3.20$, $t(45) = 1.79$, $p = .04$, one-tailed.

Had we decided to compute a simple t test between the mean of the eight and nine year olds and the mean of the twelve year olds we could have done so as follows:

$$t = \frac{M_1 - M_2}{[(1/n_1 + 1/n_2)MS \text{ error}]^{1/2}} = \frac{8.0 - 2.5^a}{[(1/10 + 1/20^b)63]^{1/2}} = 1.79,$$

$df = 45$, $p = .04$, one-tailed

$^a(2.0 + 3.0)/2 = 2.5$ $^b n$ (eight year olds) $+ n$ (nine year olds) $= 20$

Once again the two methods of computing t yield identical results.

Unequal n per condition

So far in our discussion of contrasts we have assumed equal n per condition. When n's are not equal we employ an unweighted means approach (Rosenthal & Rosnow, 1984). Our basic formula for computing SS contrast is

$$\frac{L^2}{n\Sigma\lambda^2} \quad \text{which can be rewritten as} \quad \frac{(\Sigma T\lambda)^2}{n\Sigma\lambda^2}$$

To employ the unweighted means procedure we redefine the T and the n of the just-preceding formula so that n becomes the harmonic mean of the n's and T becomes the mean of the condition multiplied by the harmonic mean of the n's thus: Redefined $n = k/[\Sigma(1/n)] = n_h$ (harmonic mean n) where k is the number of conditions and $\Sigma(1/n)$ is the sum of the reciprocals of the n's, and Redefined $T = Mn_h$ where M is the mean of a condition and n_h is n as redefined above.

If we had a study of five conditions in which the n's were 10, 10, 10, 10, and 10, the arithmetic mean n and the harmonic mean n would both $= 10$. If the same fifty observations were allocated to conditions as 4, 6, 10, 14, 16, the arithmetic mean n would still be 10 but the harmonic mean n would be only 7.69, since

$$\frac{k}{\Sigma(1/n)} = \frac{5}{(1/4 + 1/6 + 1/10 + 1/14 + 1/16)} = 7.69$$

It would always be appropriate to employ the Redefined n and Redefined T, since they are required when n's are unequal and are identical to the original definitions of n and T when n's are equal, because

$$n_h = \frac{k}{\Sigma(1/n)} = \frac{k}{k(1/n)} = n \quad \text{when } n\text{'s are equal}$$

Orthogonal contrasts (and orthogonal polynomials)

When we consider a set of research results based on k conditions it is possible to compute up to $k-1$ contrasts, each of which is uncorrelated with, or *orthogonal* to, every other contrast. Contrasts are orthogonal to each other when the correlation between them is zero, and the correlation between them will be zero when the sum of the products of the analogous weights or λ's is zero. Thus the following two sets of contrast weights are orthogonal:

		Condition			
Contrast	A	B	C	D	Σ
λ_1 set	-3	-1	$+1$	$+3$	0
λ_2 set	$+1$	-1	-1	$+1$	0
Product $\lambda_1\lambda_2$	-3	$+1$	-1	$+3$	0

The set of contrast weights λ_1 can be seen to represent four points on a straight line, while the set λ_2 can be seen to represent four points on a

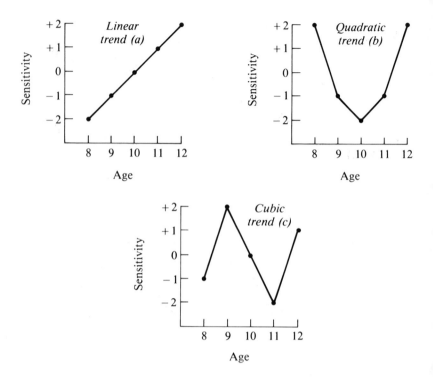

Figure 8.2. Examples of linear, quadratic, and cubic trends.

U-shaped function. The third row, labeled $\lambda_1\lambda_2$, shows the products of these linear and quadratic weights which add up to zero and are thus orthogonal ($-3, +1, -1, +3$, when added, yield zero).

A particularly useful set of orthogonal contrasts based on the coefficients of orthogonal polynomials (curves or trends) should be considered whenever the k conditions of the study can be arranged from the smallest to the largest levels of the independent variable as is the case when age levels, dosage levels, learning trials, or other ordered levels comprise the independent variable. Table 8.2 shows us that when there are three levels or conditions (represented as $k = 3$), the weights defining a linear trend are $-1, 0, +1$ while the orthogonal weights defining the quadratic trend are $+1, -2, +1$. No matter how many levels of k there may be, the linear trend λ's always show a consistent gain (or loss), while the quadratic trend λ's always show a change in direction from down to up in a U curve (or up to down in a ∩ curve). Cubic trends, which can be assessed when there are four or more conditions, show two changes of direction from up to down to up (or down to up to down).

The three displays of Figure 8.2 show the results of three hypothetical studies that were (a) perfectly linear, (b) perfectly quadratic, and (c) perfectly

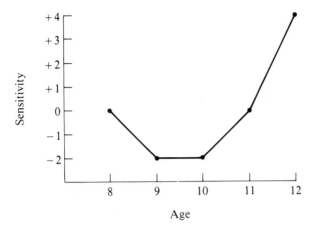

Figure 8.3. Curve showing both linear and quadratic components.

cubic. These three displays show idealized results. In most real-life applications we find combinations of linear and nonlinear results. For example, the results in Figure 8.3 show a curve that has both strong linear and strong quadratic components.

We have noted that it is possible to compute up to $k-1$ orthogonal contrasts among a set of k means or totals. Thus if we had four conditions we could compute three orthogonal contrasts, each based on a different polynomial or trend, the linear, quadratic, and cubic. The sums of squares of these three contrasts would add up to the total sum of squares among the four conditions. However, although there are only $k-1$ orthogonal contrasts in a given set such as those based on orthogonal polynomials, there is an infinite number of *sets* of contrasts that could be computed, each of which is made up of $k-1$ orthogonal contrasts. The *sets* of contrasts, however, would not be orthogonal to one another. For example, in the following contrasts, Set I is comprised of mutually orthogonal contrasts, as is Set II, but none of the three contrasts in Set I is orthogonal to any of the contrasts of Set II.

	Contrast Set I					*Contrast Set II*			
	A	B	C	D		A	B	C	D
λ_1	-3	-1	$+1$	$+3$	λ_1	-1	-1	-1	$+3$
λ_2	$+1$	-1	-1	$+1$	λ_2	-1	-1	$+2$	0
λ_3	-1	$+3$	-3	$+1$	λ_3	-1	$+1$	0	0

Nonorthogonal contrasts
Although there is some advantage to employing orthogonal contrasts, in that each contrast addresses a fresh and nonoverlapping question, there is no

Table 8.3. *Mean performance score at four age levels*[a]

	Age levels				
	6	8	10	12	Σ
Means	4.0	4.0	5.0	7.0	20
Hypothesis I λ's	−3	−1	+1	+3	0
Hypothesis II λ's	−1	−1	−1	+3	0

$$SS_I = \frac{L^2}{n\Sigma\lambda^2} = \frac{(\Sigma T\lambda)^2}{n\Sigma\lambda^2} = \frac{[40(-3)+40(-1)+50(+1)+70(+3)]^2}{10[(+3)^2+(+1)^2+(-1)^2+(-3)^2]} = 50$$

$$SS_{II} = \frac{L^2}{n\Sigma\lambda^2} = \frac{(\Sigma T\lambda)^2}{n\Sigma\lambda^2} = \frac{[40(-1)+40(-1)+50(-1)+70(+3)]^2}{10[(-1)^2+(-1)^2+(-1)^2+(+3)^2]} = 53.3$$

$$SS \text{ between conditions} = \frac{(40)^2}{10} + \frac{(40)^2}{10} + \frac{(50)^2}{10} + \frac{(70)^2}{10} - \frac{(200)^2}{40} = 60$$

[a] $n = 10$ at each age level.

a priori reason not to employ correlated (or nonorthogonal) contrasts. An especially valuable use of these contrasts is in the comparison of certain plausible rival hypotheses. Suppose we tested children at age levels six, eight, ten, and twelve. One plausible developmental prediction (which we call hypothesis I) is for a constant rate of improvement with age while a rival hypothesis (II) predicts only that twelve year olds will differ from all younger children. Table 8.3 shows the results of this research, the contrast weights used to test each hypothesis, the sums of squares associated with each contrast and the sums of squares between all conditions $(df = 3)$.

Both the contrasts do a good job of fitting the data, with SS_I taking up 50/60 (or 83 percent) of the between-conditions SS and SS_{II} taking up 53.3/60 (or 89 percent) of the between-conditions SS. Hypothesis II did a bit better than hypothesis I but probably not enough better to make us give up hypothesis I. That both hypotheses did well should not surprise us too much since the correlation between the weights representing the two hypotheses was quite substantial $(r = .77)$. There might even have been a third hypothesis that predicted that six and twelve year olds would differ most but that eight and ten year olds would not differ from one another. Such a prediction would have been expressed by hypothesis III λ's of −1, 0, 0, +1. Hypothesis III would have been correlated .95 with hypothesis I and .82 with hypothesis II. The SS contrast for this set of weights would be 45, accounting for 75 percent of the total variance among conditions.

Table 8.4. *Improvement found in the nonverbal behavior of depressed patients in four treatment programs*

Means

	Treatment programs				
	Nonhospitalization		Hospitalization		
Patient age	Psychotherapy program A	Companionship program B	Traditional program C	Milieu therapy D	Σ
Old	5[a]	7	2	2	16
Middle age	9	7	4	8	28
Young	7	7	0	2	16
Σ	21	21	6	12	60

Analysis of variance

Source	SS	df	MS	F	p
Treatment	5.40	3	1.80	36.00	very small
Age	2.40	2	1.20	24.00	very small
Interaction	1.60	6	.27	5.34	.001
Within	5.40	108	.05		

[a] Data are sums of ten improvement scores.

Contrasts in two-factor studies

So far we have considered contrasts only for one-way analyses of variance. We turn our attention now to the decomposition of the main effects and interactions of two-way analyses of variance into appropriate and informative contrasts. Table 8.4 shows the results of a hypothetical experiment on the effects of various treatments on improvement in the nonverbal behaviors observed in depressed patients. There were four levels of the treatment factor and three levels of the age factor. There were forty patients each in the older, middle-aged, and younger samples and ten of these patients were randomly assigned to each of the four treatment conditions. Two of the treatment groups were hospitalized and two were not. Within the former conditions one group was treated traditionally while the other received milieu (environmental) therapy. Within the latter conditions one group was given psychotherapy while the other was given a new companionship program. Table 8.4 shows the *sums* of the ten observations for each of the twelve combinations of treatment and age, and the traditional two-way analysis of variance of these data, an analysis we regard as merely preliminary.

Table 8.5. *Treatment totals, contrast weights, and contrast* SS *for the study of Table 8.4*

	Treatment programs				
	Nonhospitalization		Hospitalization		
	Psycho-therapy	Compan-ionship	Tradi-tional	Milieu	Σ
Totals (T)	21	21	6	12	60
n	30	30	30	30	120
Nonhospitalization vs. hospitalization: λ_1	$+1$	$+1$	-1	-1	0
Psychotherapy vs. companionship: λ_2	$+1$	-1	0	0	0
Traditional vs. milieu: λ_3	0	0	-1	$+1$	0
Totals $\times \lambda_1$	21	21	-6	-12	24
Totals $\times \lambda_2$	21	-21	0	0	0
Totals $\times \lambda_3$	0	0	-6	$+12$	6

Contrast SS_1
(nonhospitalization vs. hospitalization) $= \dfrac{(24)^2}{30(4)} = 4.8$

Contrast SS_2
(psychotherapy vs. companionship) $= \dfrac{(0)^2}{30(2)} = 0.0$

Contrast SS_3
(traditional vs. milieu) $= \dfrac{(6)^2}{30(2)} = 0.6$

We begin by computing a set of orthogonal contrasts among the four levels of treatments. There are three questions we wish to address by means of these contrasts: (1) Does hospitalization make a difference? (2) Given nonhospitalization, does psychotherapy differ from the companionship program? and (3) Given hospitalization, does traditional treatment differ from milieu therapy? Table 8.5 shows the treatment totals (taken from Table 8.4), the weights assigned for each of our three orthogonal contrasts, and the product of the totals × the weights $(T\lambda)$. Note that the weights are assigned according to the particular questions to be answered. For λ_1, the weights are consistent with question 1, which contrasts hospitalization (traditional and milieu) with nonhospitalization (psychotherapy and companionship). For λ_2, the weights are consistent with question 2, which contrasts only the two nonhospitalization treatments, therefore assigning zero weights to the irrelevant treatments. For λ_3, which addresses question 3, this is reversed, with the zero weights now assigned to the nonhospitalization treatments.

The right-hand column of Table 8.5 provides the sums of the preceding four column entries. The first value (60) is the grand sum of all scores for the study. The next three values reassure us that we have met the requirement that contrast weights must sum to zero. The final three values (24, 0, and 6) are the sums of $T\lambda$ products, or the L's we require to compute contrasts. Since contrast SS's are given by $L^2/n\Sigma\lambda^2$ our three contrast SS's are as shown at the bottom of Table 8.5. Adding these three SS's yields 5.4 which is equal to the total between treatments SS based on 3 df as shown in the table of variance at the bottom of Table 8.4. Special note should be made of the fact that n is always the number of cases upon which the total (T) is based. In the present contrasts each T is based on thirty observations (ten at each of three age levels). Had the number of observations in the $4 \times 3 = 12$ conditions been unequal, we would have redefined T for each of the twelve conditions as the mean score for that condition multiplied by the harmonic mean of the n's of the twelve conditions. In that case the treatment sums would have become the sum of the three redefined values of T since each treatment total is made up of three conditions, one at each age level. The n for that treatment total would then become three times the harmonic mean n. We postpone interpretation of our contrasts until we come to our final table of variance.

We turn next to the decomposition of the patients' age factor into two orthogonal contrasts. In this case, since age is an ordered variable (rather than categorical or nominal) we turn again to our table of orthogonal polynomials (Table 8.2) to find the weights for a linear and quadratic trend. We see that for a three-level factor the weights for linear and quadratic trends are $-1, 0, +1$, and $+1, -2, +1$, respectively. The linear trend addresses the question of whether older patients benefit more (or less) from the average treatment than younger patients. The quadratic trend addresses the question of whether middle-aged patients benefit more (or less) from the average treatment than do (the average of) the older and younger patients. Table 8.6 shows the age effect totals of Table 8.4, the n for each age level, the weights assigned for each of our two orthogonal polynomial contrasts, the product of the totals $\times$ the weights ($T\lambda$), and the computation of the SS's for the linear and quadratic trends. Adding these two SS yields 2.4 which is equal to the total between age SS based on 2 df and shown in Table 8.4. We postpone interpretation of our contrasts until we come to our final table of variance.

Crossing contrasts

Having decomposed the main effects of treatments and of age we turn our attention now to the decomposition of the interaction effects. Many kinds of contrasts could be employed to decompose the interaction. One that is frequently used in two-factor studies addresses the question of whether the contrasts of one main effect are altered (modified or moderated) by the contrasts

Table 8.6. *Age effect totals, contrast weights, and contrast SS for the study of Table 8.4*

Patient age	Totals	n	Linear (λ_1)	Quadratic (λ_2)	Totals $\times \lambda_1$	Totals $\times \lambda_2$
Old	16	40	+1	+1	16	16
Middle age	28	40	0	−2	0	−56
Young	16	40	−1	+1	−16	16
Σ	60	120	0	0	0	−24

$$\text{Contrast } SS_1 = \frac{L^2}{n\Sigma\lambda^2} = \frac{[16(+1)+28(0)+16(-1)]^2}{40[(+1)^2+(0)^2+(-1)^2]} = \frac{(0)^2}{40(2)} = 0.0$$
(linear trend)

$$\text{Contrast } SS_2 = \frac{L^2}{n\Sigma\lambda^2} = \frac{[16(+1)+28(-2)+16(+1)]^2}{40[(+1)^2+(-2)^2+(+1)^2]} = \frac{(-24)^2}{40(6)} = 2.4$$
(quadratic trend)

of the other main effect. For example, we might ask whether the predicted effect of hospitalization varies as a function of linear trend in age, for example, so that younger patients benefit more than older ones from nonhospitalization. Constructing the contrast weights for these crossed (interaction) contrasts is accomplished by multiplying the contrast weight (λ) defining the column effect contrast (treatments in this example) by the contrast weight (λ) defining the row effect contrast (patient age in this example) as shown in Table 8.7. To obtain the entries of column 1 we multiply the heading λ of column 1 (psychotherapy) by each of the three row λ's (patient age). In this case multiplying +1 by +1, 0, −1 in turn yields +1, 0, −1. Results for column 2 (companionship) are identical. For column 3 (traditional) we multiply −1 by +1, 0, −1 and obtain −1, 0, +1; the same result is obtained for column 4 (milieu).

Since we had three treatment effect contrasts and two age effect contrasts we can obtain six crossed interaction contrasts by crossing each treatment contrast by each age contrast. These six contrasts are:

1. Hospitalization versus nonhospitalization × Linear trend in age
2. Psychotherapy versus companionship × Linear trend in age
3. Traditional versus milieu therapy × Linear trend in age
4. Hospitalization versus nonhospitalization × Quadratic trend in age
5. Psychotherapy versus companionship × Quadratic trend in age
6. Traditional versus milieu therapy × Quadratic trend in age

Table 8.8 shows the construction of the weights for these crossed (interaction) contrasts, and Table 8.9 shows the computation of the sums of squares for two of these contrasts; numbers (1) and (4) above. The sums of squares

Table 8.7. *Construction of crossed (interaction) contrast weights by multiplying column × row contrast weights*

| | | Treatment programs | | | | |
| | | Nonhospitalization | | Hospitalization | | |
Patient age	Age contrast (λ)	Psychotherapy	Companionship	Traditional	Milieu	Σ^a
	Treatment contrast (λ):	+1	+1	−1	−1	
Old	+1	+1	+1	−1	−1	0
Middle	0	0	0	0	0	0
Young	−1	−1	−1	+1	+1	0
	Σ^a	0	0	0	0	0

[a]Note that the row and column sums must be zero for contrast weights that are exclusively part of interaction effects.

Table 8.8. *Construction of crossed (interaction) contrast weights by multiplying column and row contrast weights: six contrasts*

		Treatment programs			
		Nonhospitalization		Hospitalization	
Patient age	Age contrast (λ)	Psychotherapy	Companionship	Traditional	Milieu
	Treatment contrast (λ):	+1	+1	−1	−1
Old	+1	+1	+1	−1	−1
Middle	0	0	0	0	0
Young	−1	−1	−1	+1	+1
	Treatment contrast (λ):	+1	−1	0	0
Old	+1	+1	−1	0	0
Middle	0	0	0	0	0
Young	−1	−1	+1	0	0
	Treatment contrast (λ):	0	0	−1	+1
Old	+1	0	0	−1	+1
Middle	0	0	0	0	0
Young	−1	0	0	+1	−1
	Treatment contrast (λ):	+1	+1	−1	−1
Old	+1	+1	+1	−1	−1
Middle	−2	−2	−2	+2	+2
Young	+1	+1	+1	−1	−1

		Treatment contrast (λ):			
Old	+1	+1	−1	0	0
Middle	−2	+1	−1	0	0
Young	+1	−2	+2	0	0

		Treatment contrast (λ):			
Old	+1	0	0	−1	+1
Middle	−2	0	0	+2	−2
Young	+1	0	0	−1	+1

Table 8.9. *Computation of sums of squares for contrasts (1) and (4) of Table 8.8*

A. *Subtable of condition totals (from Table 8.4; n = 10 per condition)*

	Treatment programs			
	Nonhospitalization		Hospitalization	
Patient age	Psychotherapy	Companionship	Traditional	Milieu
Old	5	7	2	2
Middle	9	7	4	8
Young	7	7	0	2

B. *Subtable of residuals defining interaction[a]*

	Treatment programs			
	Nonhospitalization		Hospitalization	
Patient age	Psychotherapy	Companionship	Traditional	Milieu
Old	−1	1	1	−1
Middle	0	−2	0	2
Young	1	1	−1	−1

C. *Subtable of contrast computations*

$$\text{Contrast } SS = \frac{L^2}{n\Sigma\lambda^2}$$

$$\text{Contrast } SS \, (1) = \frac{[-1(+1)+1(+1)+1(-1)+-1(-1)+0(0)+-2(0)+0(0)+}{10[(+1)^2+(+1)^2+(-1)^2+(-1)^2+(0)^2+(0)^2+(0)^2+}$$

$$\frac{2(0)+1(-1)+1(-1)+-1(+1)+-1(+1)]^2}{(0)^2+(-1)^2+(-1)^2+(+1)^2+(+1)^2]} = \frac{(-4)^2}{10(8)} = 0.2$$

$$\text{Contrast } SS \, (4) = \frac{[-1(+1)+1(+1)+1(-1)+-1(-1)+0(-2)+-2(-2)+0(+2)+}{10[(+1)^2+(+1)^2+(-1)^2+(-1)^2+(-2)^2+(-2)^2+(+2)^2+}$$

$$\frac{2(+2)+1(+1)+1(+1)+-1(-1)+-1(-1)]^2}{(+2)^2+(+1)^2+(+1)^2+(-1)^2+(-1)^2]} = \frac{(12)^2}{10(24)} = 0.6$$

[a]Computed from the just-preceding subtable of totals (A) by subtracting the grand mean, column effects, and row effects as shown in Chapter 7 and as reviewed, in part, later in this chapter. Each of the residuals shown is still a sum of ten observations but after subtraction of row, column, and grand mean (total) effects.

of the remaining contrasts, which were similarly computed, are reported in Table 8.10.

   Table 8.10 shows the two-factor analysis of variance (of Table 8.4) now fully decomposed so that we have a contrast for each of the 3 *df* for treat-

Table 8.10. *Two-factor analysis of variance decomposed such that all between-condition* df*'s are specified*

	SS	df	MS	F	p	r
Source						
Treatment	(5.4)	(3)	(1.8)	(36)	(.001)	–
Hospitalization vs. nonhospitalization (H)	4.8	1	4.8	96	.001	.69
Psychotherapy vs. companionship (P)	0.0	1	0.0	00	–	.00
Traditional vs. milieu (T)	0.6	1	0.6	12	.001	.32
Age	(2.4)	(2)	(1.2)	(24)	(.001)	–
Linear trend (L)	0.0	1	0.0	0	–	.00
Quadratic trend (Q)	2.4	1	2.4	48	.001	.55
Treatment × age	(1.6)	(6)	(0.267)	(5.34)	(.001)	–
HL	0.2	1	0.2	4	.05	.19
PL	0.1	1	0.1	2	.20	.13
TL	0.1	1	0.1	2	.20	.13
HQ	0.6	1	0.6	12	.001	.32
PQ	0.3	1	0.3	6	.02	.23
TQ	0.3	1	0.3	6	.02	.23
Within	5.4	108	.05			

ments, for each of the 2 *df* for age levels, and for each of the 6 *df* for the treatments × age levels interactions. The last column gives the magnitudes of each effect in terms of *r*, and we shall interpret our results in order of their effect size. It should be noted that to learn the direction of each of these effects we must examine the means and/or the residuals defining main effects and interactions. The table of variance does not yield that information.

(H) Hospitalization: better outcomes accrue to the nonhospitalized than to the hospitalized.

(Q) Quadratic trend: better outcomes accrue to the middle-aged than to the average of the young and old.

(T) Traditional: if hospitalized, better outcomes accrue to those receiving milieu therapy rather than traditional treatment.

(HQ) Hospitalization × Quadratic: hospitalization is relatively more effective for the middle-aged than for the young and old (averaged) but nonhospitalization is relatively more effective for the young and old (averaged).

(PQ) Psychotherapy × Quadratic: if not hospitalized, psychotherapy is more effective for the middle-aged than for the young and old (averaged) but the companionship program is relatively more effective for the young and old (averaged).

Interpretation of the remaining contrasts (including TQ which is as large as PQ) is left to the reader.

It will be noted that the interpretation of contrasts based on main effects is considerably easier than the interpretation of contrasts based on interaction effects (crossed contrasts in our example). When we consider the quadratic trend in age level, for example, we have only to look at the row totals (or means if the *n*'s were unequal) to see immediately that the benefit scores of the middle-aged are higher than those of the average of the young and old (see Table 8.4). However, inspection does not so immediately reveal the nature of the crossed contrasts. For example, when we consider the crossed contrast of Hospitalization × Quadratic trend in age (which we know from Table 8.10 to be significant statistically and of at least moderate size), what is it we should look for, for example, in Table 8.4 to tell us what it means?

We cannot use the condition totals directly to tell us about this interaction contrast or any other interaction contrast. That is because the condition totals (or means) are made up partially of the grand mean, partially of the column effects, partially of the row effects, and partially of the interaction effects. The preceding chapter dealing with interaction effects gives more detail on this, but here it is enough to note that if we want a clear look at an interaction effect we must remove the column and row effects; removal of the grand mean is optional for purposes of interpretation. Table 8.4 shows the column totals we want to remove before the interaction can be interpreted. These totals are 21, 21, 6, and 12. The mean of these column totals is 15 so we can reexpress the column totals as residuals or deviations from this mean (i.e., as 6, 6, −9, and −3).

"Removing" column effects means setting our residual column effects equal to zero. We can do this by subtracting 6 units from the first two columns (2 units from each of the three conditions of those columns), adding 9 units to the third column (3 units to each of the three conditions of that column), and adding 3 units to the fourth column (1 unit to each of the three conditions of that column). When we do this we change the entries of Table 8.4 to those shown in Table 8.11.

The row totals we want to remove next are shown in Table 8.11 as 16, 28, 16. The mean of these row totals is 20 so the row totals are reexpressed as deviations or residuals from this mean as −4, +8, and −4. To remove the row effects we add 4 units to the first and third rows (1 to each of the four conditions of that row) and subtract 8 units from the second row (2 from each of the four conditions of that row). When we have done this, Table 8.11 is transformed into Table 8.12.

Table 8.11. *Data of Table 8.4 after removal of column effects*

	Treatment programs				
	Nonhospitalization		Hospitalization		
Patient age	Psychotherapy	Companionship	Traditional	Milieu	Σ
Old	3	5	5	3	16
Middle	7	5	7	9	28
Young	5	5	3	3	16
Σ	15	15	15	15	60

Table 8.12. *Data of Table 8.11 after removal of row effects*

	Treatment programs				
	Nonhospitalization		Hospitalization		
Patient age	Psychotherapy	Companionship	Traditional	Milieu	Σ
Old	4	6	6	4	20
Middle	5	3	5	7	20
Young	6	6	4	4	20
Σ	15	15	15	15	60

The Hospitalization × Quadratic interaction contrast tells us that hospitalization effects differ for the middle-aged versus the average of the young and old. Another way to phrase this is to say that the quadratic trend in age differs as a function of the hospitalization condition. For the present data we can now see that the middle-aged are relatively better off hospitalized (compared to the young and old averaged) and relatively worse off not hospitalized (compared to the young and old averaged). Because the weights for this contrast are the same for columns 1 and 2 and for columns 3 and 4 we can simplify Table 8.12 by combining the conditions for which the contrast weights are identical. This is done in Table 8.13.

Table 8.13 shows clearly that middle-aged patients are relatively better off hospitalized while the young and old (averaged) are relatively better off not hospitalized. It also shows that hospitalization and nonhospitalization lead to oppositely directed linear trends (the Hospitalization × Linear trend contrast of earlier tables). Younger patients do worse when hospitalized, better when not hospitalized, a contrast that was significant at $p < .05$, $F(1, 108) = 4.00$, $r = .19$.

Table 8.13. *Data of Table 8.12 combining columns of identical contrast weights*

Patient age	Treatment programs		
	Nonhospitalization	Hospitalization	Σ
Old	10	10	20
Middle	8	12	20
Young	12	8	20
Σ	30	30	60

9. Contrasts in repeated-measures designs

So far we have considered contrasts only in the situation of "between subjects" designs. That is, every element to which we assigned a weight, prediction, or λ was comprised of different sampling units. But it happens frequently in the conduct of judgment studies that we measure our sampling units more than once, as in studies of sensitivity to nonverbal cues in various channels of nonverbal communication, or in studies of learning, or in developmental studies of changes over time. Indeed, sound principles of experimental design lead us frequently to employ within-subject or repeated-measures designs in order to increase experimental precision and, therefore, statistical power (Rosenthal & Rosnow, 1984, Chapter 22). Our need for employing contrasts is just as great within repeated-measures designs as in between-subjects designs. Consider the following study: Four subjects each are measured on three occasions one week apart on a test of nonverbal decoding skill. The entries of Table 9.1 are the observations of nonverbal skill scores obtained on three occasions by each of the four subjects.

The preliminary analysis of variance of Table 9.1 tells us that nonverbal skill performance varies from occasion to occasion, but that was not our question. Our primary question was whether there was a steady increase in performance over time, that is, a linear trend with weights of $-1, 0, +1$. Our secondary question was whether there was a tendency for scores first to improve and then to fall back to the original level, that is, a quadratic trend with weights of $-1, +2, -1$.

Accordingly, we simply apply our standard procedure for computing contrasts to the column totals of our table of results:

	Occasions		
	(sums of four scores)		
Column totals:	20	32	20
n *of observations:*	4	4	4
Linear λ:	-1	0	$+1$
Quadratic λ:	-1	$+2$	-1

$$\frac{L^2}{n\Sigma\lambda^2} \text{ for linear trend} = \frac{(-20+0+20)^2}{4(2)} = 0$$

Table 9.1. *Results of a study of nonverbal skill measured on three occasions for each of four subjects*

Scores

Subjects	Occasions			
	1	2	3	Σ
A	8	12	10	30
B	7	11	9	27
C	3	5	1	9
D	2	4	0	6
Σ	20	32	20	72

Analysis of variance

Source	SS	df	MS	F	p
Between subjects	150	3	50.00	—	—
Within subjects	(32)	(8)			
Occasions	24	2	12.00	9.00	.02
Occasions × subjects	8	6	1.33		

Table 9.2. *Expanded analysis of variance of Table 9.1*

Source	SS	df	MS	F	p
Between subjects	150	3	50.00	—	—
Within subjects	(32)	(8)			
(Occasions	24	2	12.00	9.00	.02)
Linear trend	0	1	0	—	—
Quadratic trend	24	1	24.00	18.00	.006
Occasions × subjects	8	6	1.33		

Table 9.3. *Data of Table 9.1 corrected for grand mean*

Subjects	Occasions				
	1	2	3	Σ	$\bar{X}$
A	2	6	4	12	4
B	1	5	3	9	3
C	−3	−1	−5	−9	−3
D	−4	−2	−6	−12	−4
Σ	−4	8	−4	0	0
$\bar{X}$	−1	2	−1	0	0

$$\frac{L^2}{n\Sigma\lambda^2} \text{ for quadratic trend} = \frac{(-20+64-20)^2}{4(6)} = \frac{(24)^2}{24} = 24$$

These two contrasts show that the total variation among the column totals was entirely due to the quadratic trend. We can now rewrite the table of variance subdividing the occasions effect into the two contrast effects as shown in Table 9.2.

Each of our contrasts was tested against the same error term against which we tested the overall effect of occasions. Under most circumstances that is probably the wisest choice of error term for each contrast. It is not, however, the only choice we have. We can also construct a specific error term for each contrast. Just as the error term for the occasions effect is the crossing of the occasions effect by the subjects effect, so, too, is the unique error term for each contrast constructed by crossing that contrast by the subject effect.

It will be best to begin by having a look at the overall interaction of occasions × subjects, which is the set of residuals remaining after we have removed the grand mean, row effects, and column effects. Our original data of Table 9.1 after subtracting off the grand mean becomes as shown in Table 9.3. Next we subtract off the row effects from each entry of each row which gives us the data of Table 9.4. Now we subtract off the column effects so that only the interaction effects, or residuals, remain. These residuals are shown in Table 9.5.

Table 9.5 shows the residuals defining the occasions × subjects interaction. The sum of squares for these residuals is easily computed as $\Sigma^{12}X^2 = 8$, the value obtained earlier for our table of variance (Table 9.1) by the usual method of subtraction (i.e., Total SS minus Subjects SS minus Occasions SS). This interaction sum of squares must now be decomposed into two independent portions, one representing the linear trend × subjects interaction and the other representing the quadratic trend × subjects interaction.

Table 9.4. *Data of Table 9.1 corrected for grand mean and row effects*

| Subjects | Occasions | | | | |
	1	2	3	Σ	$\bar{X}$
A	−2	2	0	0	0
B	−2	2	0	0	0
C	0	2	−2	0	0
D	0	2	−2	0	0
Σ	−4	8	−4	0	0
$\bar{X}$	−1	2	−1	0	0

Table 9.5. *Data of Table 9.1 corrected for grand mean, row effects, and column effects*

Subjects	Occasions			
	1	2	3	Σ
A	-1	0	1	0
B	-1	0	1	0
C	1	0	-1	0
D	1	0	-1	0
Σ	0	0	0	0

Table 9.6. *Raw and standardized contrast scores for four subjects*

Subjects	Linear contrast		Quadratic contrast	
	L	$L^2/\Sigma\lambda^2$	L	$L^2/\Sigma\lambda^2$
A	2	2	0	0
B	2	2	0	0
C	-2	2	0	0
D	-2	2	0	0
Σ	0	8	0	0

We proceed by computing for each subject a standardized "score" for each contrast. This *standardized contrast score* is defined as $L^2/\Sigma\lambda^2$ for each subject, where L is the sum of each of the subject's residual scores after it has been multiplied by the appropriate λ or contrast weight. Thus for subject A, her scores (residuals) of -1, 0, $+1$ are multiplied by the linear weights of -1, 0, $+1$ respectively, to form the L for the linear contrast; they are multiplied by -1, $+2$, -1 to form the L for the quadratic contrast. Subject A's L score for the linear contrast, therefore, is $(-1)(-1) + (0)(0) + (1)(1) = 2$. Her standardized contrast score is $L^2/\Sigma\lambda^2 = 2^2/2 = 2$. Subject A's L score for the quadratic contrast is $(-1)(-1) + (0)(+2) + (1)(-1) = 0$. Her standardized contrast score is $L^2/\Sigma\lambda^2 = 0^2/6 = 0$. Table 9.6 shows the L (raw contrast score) and $L^2/\Sigma\lambda^2$ (standardized contrast score) for each subject for both the linear and quadratic contrasts.

The sum of squares for the linear trend × subjects interaction is simply the sum of all of the subjects' standardized contrast scores. In this case, that sum of squares equals eight. The analogous sum of squares for the quadratic

Table 9.7. *Expanded analysis of variance of Table 9.1 with decomposed error terms*

Source	SS	df	MS	F	p
Between subjects	150	3	50.00	—	—
Within subjects	(32)	(8)			
Occasions	24	2	12.00	9.00	.02
[a]Occasions × subjects	8	6	1.33		
Linear trend	0	1	0		
[a]Linear × subjects	8	3	2.67		
Quadratic trend	24	1	24.00	∞	0
[a]Quadratic × subjects	0	3	0		

[a]Appropriate error term for the just-preceding effect.

trend × subjects interaction is equal to zero. The sum of these two sums of squares is eight which is just what the table of residuals requires. That is, the linear × subjects plus the quadratic × subjects sums of squares, each with 3 df, must be equal to the overall occasions × subjects interaction with 6 df. Table 9.7 shows the final table of variance of the data of Table 9.1 with the interaction decomposed into two sources of variance.

Table 9.7 shows that all of the variation between occasions is due to the quadratic trend, while none of the variation in the interaction between occasions and subjects is due to the quadratic trend × subjects component of the total interaction. This yields an unusually large F for the quadratic effect, one tending toward infinity (∞). It seems better practice normally to pool these specialized error terms, especially when each is based on few df. Therefore, in the present example we might prefer to compute $F(1, 6)$ for quadratic trend as $24/1.33 = 18$, $p = .006$, rather than as $24/0$.

Contrast scores for individuals

So far in our consideration of contrasts on repeated measures we have been interested only in contrasts on groups of subjects; for example, the large quadratic trend effect shown in our original data of Table 9.1 applied to the sum of the four subjects measured on three occasions. Sometimes, however, we would like to be able to say for each subject (or whatever the sampling unit might be, e.g., groups, countries, school systems, etc.), the degree to which that subject shows any particular contrast. Such would be the case if we wanted to correlate some other attribute (e.g., age, sex, personality score, etc.) with the degree to which the planned contrast characterized each subject.

A few pages back we encountered the procedure of computing L scores as a step in computing standardized contrast scores in the process of computing specific error terms for contrasts in repeated measures. In that situation, since we were trying to decompose an occasions × subjects interaction, we operated only on the residual scores remaining to each subject after we had subtracted off the grand mean, row effects, and column effects. Now, however, since we want to compute contrast scores in the column effects (occasions) we want to operate on the original data. The results we obtain will be the same whether we subtract from the original data the grand mean and row effects (subject effects) or not. Thus, we could operate directly on our original data, or on the data from which the grand mean has been removed, or on the data from which the grand mean and the row effects have both been removed. We compute the raw contrast score L by multiplying each of the subject's scores by the appropriate λ or contrast weight. Thus, for subject A of our original data table, her scores of 8, 12, 10 are multiplied by the linear weights of -1, 0, $+1$, respectively, to form the L score for the linear contrast. Her scores are multiplied by -1, $+2$, -1 to form the L score for the quadratic contrast, or by any other weights (summing to zero) representing any other contrast.

Subject A's L score for the linear contrast, based on the data of Table 9.1 (original raw scores), therefore, is $8(-1) + 12(0) + 10(+1) = 2$. Subject A's L score for the quadratic contrast, based on the original data, is $8(-1) + 12(+2) + 10(-1) = 6$. Had we based subject A's linear and quadratic L scores on the "de-meaned" data, these L scores would have been $2(-1) + 6(0) + 4(+1) = 2$, and $2(-1) + 6(+2) + 4(-1) = 6$ respectively, exactly the same as the L scores based on the original data. Had we based subject A's linear and quadratic L scores on the data with both the grand mean and the row effects removed, these L scores would have been $-2(-1) + 2(0) + 0(+1) = 2$, and $-2(-1) + 2(+2) + 0(-1) = 6$, again, exactly the same as the L scores based on the original data.

Once we know how to compute L (contrast) scores for any hypothesis, such as that for linear trend or quadratic trend (or any other set of contrast weights), we can directly test the question of whether the subjects as a group show that particular trend to a significant extent. If the null hypothesis were true, for example, that there were no linear trend in the population, we would expect, on the average, that positive linear trends by some subjects would be offset by negative linear trends by other subjects so that there would be no net linear trend. Thus, under the hypothesis of no linear trend we expect the mean L (contrast) score for linear trend to be zero. We can, therefore, test the hypothesis of linear trend by a simple t test of the L scores against the value of zero expected if the null hypothesis were true; thus

$$t = \frac{\bar{L} - 0}{[S^2/N]^{1/2}}$$

where $\bar{L}$ is the mean of the L scores, S^2 is computed from the L scores, and N is the number of L scores.

For the original data of Table 9.1 the L scores are 2, 2, -2, -2, computed as follows:

Subject A	$8(-1) + 12(0) + 10(1) = 2$
Subject B	$7(-1) + 11(0) + 9(1) = 2$
Subject C	$3(-1) + 5(0) + 1(1) = -2$
Subject D	$2(-1) + 4(0) + 0(1) = -2$

Therefore, $\bar{L} = 0$,

$$S^2 = \Sigma(L - \bar{L})^2/(N-1) = [(2-0)^2 + (2-0)^2 + (-2-0)^2 + (-2-0)^2]/3$$
$$= 16/3 = 5.33, \quad N = 4,$$

so that

$$t = \frac{0-0}{[5.33/4]^{1/2}} = \frac{0}{1.15} = 0$$

Since $t^2 = F$, we can equally well compute an F test of the hypothesis of linear trend for these subjects, and since $t = 0$, $t^2 = F = 0$ as well. Examination of Table 9.7 shows that the mean square for linear trend is zero and F is, therefore, also zero.

As a further illustration of the use of L scores to test hypotheses, we show the t test of the hypothesis of a quadratic trend for the same four subjects. The L scores are obtained as follows:

Subject A	$8(-1) + 12(2) + 10(-1) = 6$
Subject B	$7(-1) + 11(2) + 9(-1) = 6$
Subject C	$3(-1) + 5(2) + 1(-1) = 6$
Subject D	$2(-1) + 4(2) + 0(-1) = 6$

Therefore, $\bar{L} = 6$,

$$S^2 = \Sigma(L - \bar{L})^2/(N-1) = [(6-6)^2 + (6-6)^2 + (6-6)^2 + (6-6)^2]/3$$
$$= 0/3 = 0, \quad N = 4$$

so that

$$t = \frac{6-0}{[0/4]^{1/2}} = \infty$$

We note that since $S^2 = 0$, $t = \infty$ and, therefore, since $F = t^2$, F is also ∞ as shown for the quadratic trend effect of Table 9.7.

Table 9.8. *Results of a study of three subjects measured on four occasions*

Scores

	Occasions				
Subjects	1	2	3	4	Σ
A	−1	+3	−3	+1	0
B	−3	−1	+1	+3	0
C	−1	+1	+1	−1	0
Σ	−5	+3	−1	+3	0

Analysis of variance

Source	SS	df	MS	F	p
Between subjects	0	2	0	—	—
Within subjects	(44)	(9)			
Occasions	14.67	3	4.89	1.00	—
[a]Occasions × subjects	29.33	6	4.89		
Linear trend	6.67	1	6.67	1.00	—
[a]Linear × subjects	13.33	2	6.67		
Quadratic trend	1.33	1	1.33	1.00	—
[a]Quadratic × subjects	2.67	2	1.33		
Cubic trend	6.67	1	6.67	1.00	
[a]Cubic × subjects	13.33	2	6.67		

[a]Appropriate error term for the just-preceding effect.

It will generally be the case that the simple t test of the mean L score against the zero value expected if the null hypothesis were true will yield the same result (in the sense of $t^2 = F$) as the F test of the same contrast when the mean square for the contrast (e.g., linear, quadratic, any other) is tested against the specific error term for that contrast. If, however, we have employed a pooled or aggregated error term for our F test, that will no longer be true, although the results will still tend to be quite similar. We should also note that the S^2 computed for the t test will not generally be the same as the S^2 computed for the F test but will be larger than the latter by a factor of $\Sigma\lambda^2$. That is, the S^2 computed for the t test differs from the error MS for that particular contrast by a factor of the sum of the squared contrast weights.

We use the data of Table 9.8 to illustrate this and to serve as a review.

Table 9.9. *Raw and standardized contrast scores for three subjects based on residuals shown below*

Scores

Subjects	Linear		Quadratic		Cubic	
	L	$L^2/\Sigma\lambda^2$	L	$L^2/\Sigma\lambda^2$	L	$L^2/\Sigma\lambda^2$
A	−6.67	2.22	−1.33	0.44	13.33	8.89
B	13.33	8.89	−1.33	0.44	−6.67	2.22
C	−6.67	2.22	2.67	1.78	−6.67	2.22
Σ	0	13.33	0	2.67	0	13.33

Residuals

Subjects	Occasions				
	1	2	3	4	Σ
A	0.67	2.00	−2.67	0.00	0
B	−1.33	−2.00	1.33	2.00	0
C	0.67	0.00	1.33	−2.00	0
Σ	0	0	0	0	0

As a review of how we obtained this table of variance we need the contrast weights or λ's for the linear, quadratic, and cubic trends, given that there are four occasions. These weights are −3, −1, +1, +3; −1, +1, +1, −1; and −1, +3, −3, +1 respectively (see Table 8.2). Table 9.9 shows the raw and standardized contrast scores for these three subjects for all three contrasts, and gives the residuals of the original data of this example.

The scores of Table 9.9 were obtained by computing the L scores as well as the standardized contrast scores for each subject's raw scores, as shown earlier for the data of our previous example (residuals). The sums of the standardized contrast scores are the sums of squares for the linear × subjects, quadratic × subjects, and cubic × subjects error terms of our analysis of variance. This analysis also shows that the F's for the linear, quadratic, and cubic trends are all equal to 1.00. We now want to show that we could directly compute a t test to test each of these contrasts if we preferred.

We begin by returning to the original data for three subjects, since to compute t we shall want to operate on a set of L scores based on the original data (with or without subtracting off the grand mean, here equal to zero, and with or without subtracting off the row effects, here also equal to zero). For these data, the L scores for linear trend for the three subjects are 0, 20, and 0.

Each L score is the sum of the products of the subject's scores multiplied by the contrast weight or λ, for example, $(-1)(-3)+(3)(-1)+(-3)(+1)+(1)(+3)=0$. For these three L scores the mean or $\bar{L}=6.67$, $S^2=133.33$, $N=3$, so that

$$t = \frac{\bar{L}-0}{[S^2/N]^{1/2}} = \frac{6.67}{[133.33/3]^{1/2}} = 1.00$$

Since $t^2=F$, we see that this method of computing contrasts yields results identical to those of the method of the analysis of variance shown earlier. Note, however, that the mean square for t, or S^2, is 133.33 which is $\Sigma\lambda^2$ or twenty times larger than the mean square error for the F of our table of variance (6.67).

For these data the L scores for quadratic trend for the three subjects are 0, 0, and 4. Each score is the sum of the products of the subject's scores multiplied by the contrast weight or λ, for example, $(-1)(-1)+(3)(+1)+(-3)(+1)+(1)(-1)=0$, $\bar{L}=1.33$, $S^2=5.33$, $N=3$, so that

$$t = \frac{1.33-0}{[5.33/3]^{1/2}} = 1.00$$

Once again $t=1=t^2=F$ showing that the method of t yields results identical to those based on the analysis of variance.

The L scores for the cubic trend for these three subjects are 20, 0, and 0. Once again, these L scores are computed as a sum of products, for example, $(-1)(-1)+(3)(+3)+(-3)(-3)+(1)(+1)=20$, $\bar{L}=6.67$, $S^2=133.33$, $N=3$, so that

$$t = \frac{6.67-0}{[133.33/3]^{1/2}} = 1.00$$

Again, the method of t yields results identical to those of the analysis of variance procdure.

Effect size estimation
Whenever reporting the results of a contrast some indication of effect size should also be given. When the contrasts are trend effects perhaps the most natural effect size indicator is r. We can compute r in several ways:

$$r = \left[\frac{SS \text{ trend}}{(SS \text{ trend} + SS \text{ error for trend})} \right]^{1/2}$$

$$r = \left[\frac{F}{F + df \text{ error for trend}} \right]^{1/2}$$

$$r = \left[\frac{t^2}{t^2 + df} \right]^{1/2}$$

For all three of the t tests above, and for all the F's associated with each of these t's, $r = .58$. The df associated with each t, or with the denominator of each F, was 2. Suppose, however, that we had decided to use as our error terms in the analysis of variance not the unique error term but a pooled error term, on the assumption that the three error terms of 6.67, 1.33, and 6.67 differed from one another only by virtue of sampling variation. The pooled error term would then be $(13.33 + 2.67 + 13.33)/(2 + 2 + 2) = 4.89$. Our F's would now change from $F = 1.00$ for all three trend contrasts to F linear $= 1.36$; F quadratic $= 0.27$; and F cubic $= 1.36$. When looking up the significance level of these F's we would enter the appropriate table of F values with 1 df for the numerator (*all* contrasts have $df = 1$ for the numerator of F) and with 6 df for the denominator, because we now have a more stable estimated error term, that is, one that is several degrees of freedom closer to the population value of the error term. However, and here it is easy to go astray, we should *not* use the pooled df in the formulas for computing r from F or t, but rather the df of the specifically computed error terms (e.g., linear × subjects). The formulas for computing r from F or t require that the df reflect the size of the experiment (i.e., the number of subjects minus the number of different between-subjects conditions) not the df for the estimate of the MS error. Often, of course, these two values will be the same. However, in repeated-measures studies having three or more levels of the repeated-measures variable, the df's for various error terms (repeated measures × subjects interactions) will be larger than the df for specific error terms (e.g., linear trend × subjects interaction) by a factor equal to the number of levels of the repeated-measures factor minus one. The use of the df of the pooled error term can lead to estimates of effect size (e.g., r) that are much too low.

For our example of three subjects observed on four occasions, the three F's for contrasts (each computed on the basis of its specific error term) were all equal to 1.00, and for each, $r = .58$. When we employed a pooled error term, our three F's became 1.36, 0.27, and 1.36 each, with 1 and 6 df for the purpose of looking up the p value associated with each F. Using those df to compute r (an improper procedure) would give r's of .43, .21, and .43, respectively. However, using the proper df of 2 (rather than 6) for the denominator of F, or for t, would give r's of .64, .34, and .64.

Similarly, when using sums of squares to compute r ($r = [SS$ trend$/(SS$ trend $+ SS$ error for trend)$]^{1/2}$) the SS for error for trend should either be the specific error term for that trend (e.g., linear × subjects interaction) or, if based on a pooled error term, it should be redefined as MS pooled error × df

for specific error term, so that $r = \{SS \text{ trend}/(SS \text{ trend} + [df \text{ specific error term}]MS \text{ pooled error term})\}^{1/2}$.

Before leaving the topic of effect size estimation, we add a note of clarification as to why df for pooled error terms are appropriate to employ for purposes of looking up p values associated with test statistics but not for computing effect sizes. Imagine an experiment in which we compare a new with an old treatment procedure but we have available only four subjects. We assign two to each treatment procedure at random and find $t(2) = 2$, $F(1, 2) = 4$, and $r = .82$, a very large effect size. Now imagine that we actually knew the *population* variance of the dependent variable we had employed. The *value* of t (or F) would not be affected, but now we would use a different row in our table of t (or F) to look up our significance levels, since now we have a t with $df = \infty$ rather than $df = 2$.

The *size of the effect,* however, should not be affected by whatever part of the table we employ to find the p value associated with t (or F). Yet if we employed as our df for t (or for the error term of F) a very large number (like ∞) the actual r of .82 would be reduced to zero, an obviously absurd result.

Homogeneity of covariances

A very important bonus accrues to us from our systematic use of contrasts in the case of repeated-measures analyses. In such analyses it is assumed that the various levels of the repeated measurements are all related to one another to a similar degree. For example, if we measure a group of subjects ten times on some task, the ordinary use of the omnibus F test with 9 df in the numerator requires that the tenth measurement correlates about as highly with the first as with the ninth, an assumption that may often not be met (Judd & Kenny, 1981; Winer, 1971).

The bonus from the use of contrasts is that contrast effects, when tested against their specific contrast × subjects error terms (or against a pooled error term of relatively homogeneous components), do not require meeting such an assumption. Indeed, as we have seen, such contrasts are identical to t tests on subjects' contrast scores and there can be no covariance for just a single set of scores.

Mixed sources of variance

We have had a detailed look at carving contrasts out of repeated measures. It is frequently the case, however, that repeated-measures designs occur in a context of mixed between-subjects and within-subjects factors. To anticipate the discussion a bit, this poses no new problem so long as the contrasts of interest are entirely part of a between-subjects factor or entirely part of a

Table 9.10. *Results of a study of two groups of subjects measured on three occasions*

Scores

Subjects		Occasions 1	2	3	Σ
Females	A	8	12	10	30
	B	7	11	9	27
Males	C	3	5	1	9
	D	2	4	0	6
	Σ	20	32	20	72

Analysis of variance

Source	SS	df	MS	F	p
Between subjects	(150)	(3)	(50.00)		
Gender	147	1	147.00	98.00	.01
[a]Subjects (within gender)	3	2	1.50		
Within subjects	(32)	(8)			
Occasions	24	2	12.00	∞	1/∞
Occasions × gender	8	2	4.00	∞	1/∞
[b]Occasions × subjects	0	4	0		
Linear trend	0	1	0	–	–
Linear × gender	8	1	8.00	∞	1/∞
[b]Linear × subjects	0	2	0		
Quadratic trend	24	1	24.00	∞	1/∞
Quadratic × gender	0	1	0	–	–
[b]Quadratic × subjects	0	2	0		

[a]Appropriate error term for the just-preceding effect.
[b]Appropriate error term for the just-preceding two effects.

single within-subjects factor. It does pose a problem, however, when the contrast of interest involves a between *and* a within factor, or two or more within-subjects factors having different error terms.

For our illustration we return to the data of Table 9.1, but with the added information that Subjects A and B were female while Subjects C and D were male. Table 9.10 shows these data and the full model analysis of variance of these data. This table is analogous to Table 9.7 showing the expanded analysis of variance with decomposed error terms except that we have added several sources of variance associated with our new factor of gender: gender, occasions × gender, linear trend × gender, and quadratic trend × gender. The latter two terms are contrasts carved out of the occasions × gender source of variance. There is nothing new about the contrast for gender; it was computed with weights (λ's) of +1 for females and −1 for males and tested against subjects within gender. The linear and quadratic contrasts were taken from the occasions effect, and the linear × gender and quadratic × gender contrasts were taken from the occasions × gender source of variance. All contrasts were tested against their own specific error terms. The weights for the linear × gender contrast were:

$$
\begin{array}{ccc}
-1 & 0 & +1 \\
+1 & 0 & -1
\end{array}
$$

applied to the table of residuals:

	Occasions			
	1	*2*	*3*	Σ
Females ($n=2$)	−2	0	+2	0
Males ($n=2$)	+2	0	−2	0
Σ ($n=4$)	0	0	0	0

so that $L^2/n\Sigma\lambda^2 = 8^2/2(4) = 8$, since $L = -2(-1) + 0(0) + 2(+1) + 2(+1) + 0(0) + -2(-1) = 8$.

The weights for the quadratic × gender contrast were

$$
\begin{array}{ccc}
-1 & +2 & -1 \\
+1 & -2 & +1
\end{array}
$$

So far, there is nothing new or complicated about employing contrasts in mixed-source designs. That is because we have only considered contrasts that had straightforward error terms. But suppose it were hypothesized that women tested on the first occasion would score higher than men tested on the third occasion. For this hypothesis our weights (λ's) are as follows:

	Occasions				
	1	*2*	*3*	Σ	*Mean*
Females	+1	0	0	+1	+.33
Males	0	0	−1	−1	−.33
Σ	+1	0	−1	.00	.00
Mean	+.50	.00	−.50	.00	.00

Examination of the column totals or means shows that our contrast involves a prediction of a linear trend in occasions. The row totals show that our contrast also involves a prediction of a gender effect. The residuals show that our contrast also involves a prediction of an occasions × gender interaction, specifically a quadratic trend × gender interaction. We can show the quadratic trend × gender interaction that is implied by our contrast weights just given, simply by subtracting off the row and column effects implied by our contrast. Thus when subtracting off the row means for the preceding table, we have:

	Occasions				
	1	*2*	*3*	Σ^a	*Mean*
Females	.67	−.33	−.33	0	0
Males	.33	.33	−.67	0	0
Σ	1.00	.00	−1.00	0	0
Mean	.50	.00	−.50	0	0

^{a}Rounded.

Then, subtracting off the column means yields:

	Occasions				
	1	*2*	*3*	Σ^a	*Mean*
Females	.17	−.33	.17	0	0
Males	−.17	.33	−.17	0	0
Σ	0	0	0	0	0
Mean	0	0	0	0	0

^{a}Rounded.

Inspection of the residuals now shows that we are predicting a relative ∪ shape for females and an inverted ∪ shape (or ∩) for males. This quadratic trend × gender interaction, like all interaction effects, is unrelated to the row and column effects.

We *could* test for significance all the effects we had implicated in our contrast, but that would be a very low-power procedure under most circumstances, essentially dissipating the strength of our prediction over three other contrasts. It would be better to test our hypothesis with just a single contrast. Rewriting Table 9.10 yields the following table of totals:

	Occasions			
	1	*2*	*3*	Σ
Females (*n* = 2)	15	23	19	57
Males (*n* = 2)	5	9	1	15
Σ (*n* = 4)	20	32	20	72

The contrast sum of squares, $L^2/n\Sigma\lambda^2$, is, therefore, $[15(+1)+0+0+0+0+1(-1) = 14]^2/2(2) = 49$. Now we have the numerator for our F, but where shall we find the denominator? We have seen from our analysis of the column effects, row effects, and interaction effects that all are involved in our prediction so that the error terms for these three effects are *all* candidates for our choice of error term (i.e., subjects within gender; linear × subjects; and quadratic × subjects). The general approach to this problem involves four steps:

1. Diagnosis of effects involved
   A. Select all effects of the analysis due to the contrast
   B. Select all error terms for these effects
2. Aggregation where possible
   A. Total aggregation
   B. Partial aggregation
3. Consensus of high- and low-power tests
   A. Both yield significant results
   B. Neither yield significant results
4. Reporting of inconsistent tests

1. Diagnosis of effects

Once we have decided on our contrast, we diagnose any effects our contrast may have on any of the terms of our analysis model. In our example we saw that our contrast had effects on one between-subjects main effect, one within-subjects main effect, and one within-subjects interaction effect. If we cannot be sure of these effects by inspection we compute an analysis of variance directly on our contrast weights (λ's) and note any nonzero effects.

After we have diagnosed these nonzero effects we find the appropriate error term for each of them. It is these error terms we shall consider for aggregation.

2. Aggregation procedures

The basic idea in aggregation is to decide when to combine two or more error terms because (1) no prior theory suggests strongly that they should be different in their population values and (2) our estimates appear not too different, say within a factor of two of each other (Green & Tukey, 1960).

Suppose, for example, that in a study of the type we have been discussing we find the following SS's, df, and MS's for our three error terms:

Source	SS	df	MS		
Subjects within gender	200	2	100		aggregated =
Linear × subjects	160	2	80	aggregated = $\dfrac{160+120}{2+2}=70$	$\dfrac{200+160+120}{2+2+2}=80$
Quadratic × subjects	120	2	60		

We would begin at the bottom and work our way up, first trying to aggregate the repeated measures error terms of 80 and 60.[1] Since $80/60 = 1.33$,

[1] We begin at the bottom assuming that we have listed our sources of variance such that more complex terms will be listed below simpler terms. This is the usual format for listing sources of variance and is standard for most computer packages.

far less than 2.0, we aggregate these terms by adding their sums of squares and dividing this grand sum by the sum of the df's of the two terms. With equal df we arrive at a pooled error term for within subjects of 70. Next we consider for aggregation the between-subjects term of $MS = 100$ with our newly aggregated $MS = 70$. This, too, seems aggregable since $100/70 = 1.43$, considerably less than 2.0. Again we add the sums of squares of the candidates for aggregation and divide by the sum of their df's. This was an example of total aggregation where all relevant error terms could be aggregated. The data of the analysis of variance table of this chapter are probably aggregable even though the MS for between-subjects error differs from the MS for within error by a factor greater than 2.0. That is because the df for each error term are so small that we would greatly doubt that an error term could really be zero, and because a ratio of a larger to a smaller MS could reach ten, twenty, or thirty before we would have very strong reason to believe the MS's to differ in the population.

Partial aggregation occurs when some of the terms, usually some of the repeated-measures (within-subjects) mean squares, can be aggregated with one another but others (often a between-subjects term) cannot be. In that case we go on to step 3 in just the same way we would if no aggregation had been possible.

3. Consensus tests

Where total aggregation is possible we have an easy answer to our question of which error term to employ for our contrast mean square. However, where no aggregation is possible, or where aggregation is only partial, no easy answer is available and we turn to consensus tests.

The basic idea of consensus tests is to employ as the denominator of our contrast mean square first the largest of the error terms involved in the contrast, and then the smallest. Employing the largest of the error terms yields an F for our contrast that we know to be too small; employing the smallest of the error terms yields an F that we know to be too large. However, if both F's lead to the conclusion that there probably is a relationship in the population between our independent and dependent variable (for example, if both F's are significant at our favorite alpha level) there is little problem in our having been unable to specify clearly a single error term.

Similarly, when the use of the largest and the smallest relevant error terms both lead to the same conclusion – that there is probably no appreciable relationship between our independent and dependent variable (for example, if both F's are smaller than required for our favorite alpha level) – there is also little problem in our having been unable to specify clearly a single error term.

4. Inconsistent tests

If the use of both the largest and smallest relevant error terms lead us to the same conclusions, there is no great problem from our having two or more candidates for a relevant error term for our contrast. However, it may happen instead that the use of our largest error term leads to a nonsignificant F while the use of our smallest error term leads to a significant F. In that case we shall have to give both F's along with the report that our results are ambiguous with respect to significance testing. If we find it essential to come up with a rough estimate of a single F, we can aggregate all the relevant error terms despite their heterogeneity and compute the F based on this new error term. However, we would employ the df for the denominator of our F test associated with the error term having the fewest df (Rosenthal & Rubin, 1980). This F may be only a poor estimate of the one we would like to be able to compute. Perhaps we can take some comfort from knowing that this estimate will at least be better than the two extreme F's we computed first, those based on the largest and smallest error terms.

Effect size estimation

Whichever of the above procedures we have followed to obtain the F test for our contrast, some estimate of effect size should be reported for every significance test reported. The same procedures can be used that were described earlier but with the reminder that the df used in computing an effect size, say r, should be the df of the contrast-specific error term, *not* the df of the pooled error term. The appropriate df, then, will generally be the number of subjects minus the number of different between-subject conditions.

PART III
The meta-analysis of judgment studies

10. Comparing and combining judgment studies

Even after a thorough and well-done analysis of the results of our judgment study, we are not quite finished. We will need to put the results of our study into the context of other studies addressing the same questions. We will want to know whether our results are consistent with, or different from, the results of other studies; those conducted by us and those conducted by others. In this chapter we present some of the basic quantitative procedures for comparing our results with other results and for combining our results with other results. The procedures that will be described, the so-called meta-analytic procedures, will prove valuable even when we have not conducted any judgment studies of our own. Any review of the literature will profit from the application of meta-analytic procedures, a fact becoming rapidly clear to investigators wanting to review bodies of literature. In 1976, for example, there were six meta-analytic publications; in 1982 there were 120 (Lamb & Whitla, 1983). The early 1980s also saw the emergence of a series of textbooks describing in varying degrees of detail the history, theory, problems, and procedures of meta-analysis (Cooper, 1984; Glass, McGaw, & Smith, 1981; Hedges & Olkin, 1985; Hunter, Schmidt, & Jackson, 1982; Light & Pillemer, 1984; Mullen & Rosenthal, 1985; Rosenthal, 1980, 1984).

A framework for meta-analytic procedures

Before we describe computational procedures it will be useful to consider a general framework for putting into perspective a variety of meta-analytic procedures. Table 10.1 provides a summary of four types of meta-analytic procedures that are applicable to the special case where just two studies are to be evaluated. It is useful to list the two-study case separately because there are some especially convenient computational procedures for this situation. The two columns of Table 10.1 show that there are two major ways to evaluate the results of research studies – in terms of their statistical significance

179

Table 10.1. *Four types of meta-analytic procedures applicable to a set of two studies*

	Results defined in terms of:	
Analytic process	Significance testing	Effect size estimation
Comparing studies	A	B
Combining studies	C	D

(e.g., *p* levels) and in terms of their effect sizes (e.g., the difference between means divided by the common standard deviation σ or S, indices employed by Cohen [1969, 1977] and by Glass [1976a, 1976b, 1980], or the Pearson *r*). The two rows of Table 10.1 show that there are two major analytic processes applied to the set of studies to be evaluated, comparing and combining. The cell labeled A in Table 10.1 represents the procedure that evaluates whether the significance level of one study differs significantly from the significance level of the other study. The cell labeled B represents the procedure that evaluates whether the effect size (e.g., *d* or *r*) of one study differs significantly from the effect size of the other study. Cells C and D represent the procedures that are used to estimate the overall level of significance and the average size of the effect, respectively. Illustrations of these procedures will be given below.

Table 10.2 provides a more general summary of six types of meta-analytic procedures that are applicable to the case where three or more studies are to be evaluated. The columns are as in Table 10.1 but the row labeled "Comparing studies" in Table 10.1 has now been subdivided into two rows – one for the case of diffuse tests and one for the case of focused tests.

When studies are compared as to their significance levels (Cell A) or their effect sizes (Cell B) by diffuse tests, we learn whether they differ significantly among themselves with respect to significance levels or effect sizes respectively, but we do not learn how they differ or whether they differ according to any systematic basis. When studies are compared as to their significance levels (Cell C) or their effect sizes (Cell D) by focused tests, or contrasts, we learn whether the studies differ significantly among themselves in a theoretically predictable or meaningful way. Thus, important tests of hypotheses can be made by the use of focused tests. Cells E and F of Table 10.2 are simply analogues of Cells C and D of Table 10.1 representing procedures used to estimate overall level of significance and average size of the effect, respectively.

Table 10.2. *Six types of meta-analytic procedures applicable to a set of three or more studies*

	Results defined in terms of:	
Analytic process	Significance testing	Effect size estimation
Comparing studies: diffuse tests	A	B
Comparing studies: focused tests	C	D
Combining studies	E	F

Meta-analytic procedures: two independent studies

Even when we have been quite rigorous and sophisticated in the interpretation of the results of a single study, we are often prone to err in the interpretation of two or more studies. For example, Smith may report a significant effect of some social intervention only to have Jones publish a rebuttal demonstrating that Smith was wrong in her claim. A closer look at both their results may show the following:

Smith's Study: $t(78) = 2.21$, $p < .05$, $d = .50$, $r = .24$.

Jones's Study: $t(18) = 1.06$, $p > .30$, $d = .50$, $r = .24$.

Smith's results were more significant than Jones's to be sure, but the studies were in perfect agreement as to their estimated sizes of effect defined by either d or r. A comparison of their respective significance levels reveals furthermore, that these p's are not significantly different ($p = .42$). Clearly, Jones was quite wrong in claiming that he had failed to replicate Smith's results. We shall begin this section by considering some procedures for comparing quantitatively the results of two independent studies, that is, studies conducted with different research participants. The examples we shall be examining in this chapter are in most cases hypothetical, constructed specifically to illustrate a wide range of situations that occur when working on meta-analytic problems.

Comparing studies

Significance testing. Ordinarily when we compare the results of two studies we are more interested in comparing their effect sizes than their p values.

However, sometimes we cannot do any better than comparing their p values, and here is how we do it (Rosenthal & Rubin, 1979a): For each of the two test statistics we obtain a reasonably exact one-tailed p level. All of the procedures described in this chapter require that p levels be recorded as *one-tailed*. Thus $t(100) = 1.98$ is recorded as $p = .025$, not $p = .05$. Then, as an illustration of being "reasonably exact," if we obtain $t(30) = 3.03$ we give p as .0025, not as "$< .05$." Extended tables of the t distribution are helpful here (e.g., Federighi, 1959; Rosenthal & Rosnow, 1984). For each p, we find Z, the standard normal deviate corresponding to the p value. Since both p's must be one-tailed, the corresponding Z's will have the same sign if both studies show effects in the same direction, but different signs if the results are in the opposite direction. The difference between the two Z's when divided by $[2]^{1/2}$, yields a new Z that corresponds to the p value that the difference between the Z's could be so large, or larger, if the two Z's did not really differ. Recapping,

$$\frac{Z_1 - Z_2}{[2]^{1/2}} \text{ is distributed as } Z. \tag{10.1}$$

Example 1. Studies A and B yield results in opposite directions and neither is "significant." One p is .06, one-tailed, the other is .12, one-tailed but in the opposite tail. The Z's corresponding to these p's are found in a table of the normal curve to be $+1.56$ and -1.18 (note the opposite signs to indicate results in opposite directions). Then, from the preceding equation (10.1) we have

$$\frac{Z_1 - Z_2}{[2]^{1/2}} = \frac{(1.56) - (-1.18)}{1.41} = 1.94$$

as the Z of the difference between the two p values or their corresponding Z's. The p value associated with a Z of 1.94 is .026 one-tailed or .052 two-tailed. The two p values thus may be seen to differ significantly, suggesting that we may want to draw different inferences from the results of the two studies.

Example 2. Studies A and B yield results in the same direction and both are significant. One p is .04, the other is .000025. The Z's corresponding to these p's are 1.75 and 4.06 (since both Z's are in the same tail they have the same sign). From equation 10.1 we have

$$\frac{Z_1 - Z_2}{[2]^{1/2}} = \frac{(4.06) - (1.75)}{1.41} = 1.64$$

as our obtained Z of the difference. The p associated with that Z is .050 one-tailed or .100 two-tailed, so we may want to conclude that the two p values differ significantly, or nearly so. It should be emphasized, however, that finding one Z greater than another does not tell us whether that Z was greater because the size of the effect was greater, the size of the study (e.g., N) was greater, or both.

Example 3. Studies A and B yield results in the same direction, but one is "significant" ($p = .05$) and the other is not ($p = .06$). This illustrates the worst-case scenario for inferential errors where investigators might conclude that the two results are "inconsistent" because one is significant and the other is not. Regrettably, this example is not merely theoretical. Just such errors have been made and documented (Nelson, Rosenthal, & Rosnow, 1986; Rosenthal & Gaito, 1963, 1964). The Z's corresponding to these p's are 1.64 and 1.55. From equation 10.1 we have

$$\frac{Z_1 - Z_2}{[2]^{1/2}} = \frac{(1.64) - (1.55)}{1.41} = .06$$

as our obtained Z of the difference between a p value of .05 and .06. The p value associated with this difference is .476 one-tailed or .952 two-tailed. This example shows clearly just how nonsignificant the difference between significant and nonsignificant results can be.

Effect size estimation. When we ask whether two studies are telling the same story, what we usually mean is whether the results (in terms of the estimated effect size) are reasonably consistent with each other or whether they are significantly heterogeneous. The present chapter will emphasize r as the effect size indicator, but analogous procedures are available for comparing such other effect size indicators as Hedges's (1981) g or differences between proportions, d' (Hedges, 1982b; Hsu, 1980; Rosenthal & Rubin, 1982a). These will be described and illustrated shortly.

For each of the two studies to be compared we compute the effect size r and find for each of these r's the associated Fisher z_r defined as

$$\tfrac{1}{2} \log_e[(1+r)/(1-r)]$$

Tables to convert our obtained r's to Fisher z_r's are available in most introductory textbooks of statistics. Then, when N_1 and N_2 represent the number of sampling units (e.g., subjects) in each of our two studies, the quantity

$$\frac{z_{r_1} - z_{r_2}}{[1/(N_1 - 3) + 1/(N_2 - 3)]^{1/2}} \quad \text{is distributed as } Z \qquad (10.2)$$

(Snedecor & Cochran, 1967, 1980).

Example 4.   Studies A and B yield results in opposite directions with effect sizes of $r = .60$ ($N = 15$) and $r = -.20$ ($N = 100$), respectively. The Fisher z_r's corresponding to these r's are .69 and $-.20$, respectively (note the opposite signs of the z_r's to correspond to the opposite signs of the r's). Then, from the preceding equation (10.2) we have

$$\frac{z_{r_1} - z_{r_2}}{[1/(N_1 - 3) + 1/(N_2 - 3)]^{1/2}} = \frac{(.69) - (-.20)}{[1/12 + 1/97]^{1/2}} = 2.91$$

as the Z of the difference between the two effect sizes. The p value associated with a Z of 2.91 is .002 one-tailed or .004 two-tailed. These two effect sizes, then, differ significantly.

Example 5.   Studies A and B yield results in the same direction with effect sizes of $r = .70$ ($N = 20$) and $r = .25$ ($N = 95$), respectively. The Fisher z_r's corresponding to these r's are .87 and .26, respectively. From equation 10.2 we have

$$\frac{(.87) - (.26)}{[1/17 + 1/92]^{1/2}} = 2.31$$

as our obtained Z of the difference. The p associated with that Z is .01 one-tailed or .02 two-tailed. Here is an example of two studies that agree there is a significant positive relationship between variables X and Y, but disagree significantly in their estimates of the size of the relationship.

Example 6.   Studies A and B yield effect size estimates of $r = .00$ ($N = 17$) and $r = .30$ ($N = 45$), respectively. The Fisher z_r's corresponding to these r's are .00 and .31, respectively. From equation 10.2 we have

$$\frac{(.00) - (.31)}{[1/14 + 1/42]^{1/2}} = -1.00$$

as our obtained Z of the difference between our two effect size estimates. The p associated with that Z is .16 one-tailed or .32 two-tailed. Here we have an example of two effect sizes, one zero ($r = .00$), the other ($r = .30$) significantly different from zero ($t(43) = 2.06$, $p < .025$ one-tailed), but which do not differ significantly from one another. This illustrates well how careful we must be in concluding that results of two studies are heterogeneous just because one is significant and the other is not or because one has a zero estimated effect size and the other does not (Rosenthal & Rosnow, 1984a).

Other effect size estimates.   Although r is our preferred effect size estimate in this chapter, analogous procedures are available for such other effect size estimates as $(M_1 - M_2)/S$ (Hedges's g) or the difference between proportions, d'. We begin with the case of Hedges's g.

For each of the two studies to be compared, we compute the effect size $(M_1 - M_2)/S$ (Hedges's g) and the quantity $1/w$ which is the estimated variance of g. We obtain w as follows (Rosenthal & Rubin, 1982a):

$$w = \frac{2(n_1 n_2)(n_1 + n_2 - 2)}{(n_1 + n_2)[t^2 + 2(n_1 + n_2 - 2)]} \tag{10.3}$$

When we have w we can test the significance of the difference between any two independent g's by means of a Z test since

$$\frac{g_A - g_B}{[1/w_A + 1/w_B]^{1/2}} \quad \text{is distributed as } Z \tag{10.4}$$

as shown in somewhat different form in Rosenthal and Rubin (1982a). Note the similarity in structure between equations 10.4 and 10.2. In both cases the differences in effect size are divided by the square root of the sums of the variances of the individual effect sizes.

Example 7. Studies A and B yield results in the same direction with effect sizes of $g = 1.86$ ($t = 4.16$; $N = 20$) and $g = .51$ ($t = 2.49$; $N = 95$), respectively. Assuming that the two conditions being compared within each study are comprised of sample sizes of ten and ten in Study A and forty-seven and forty-eight in Study B, we first find w for each study:

$$w_A = \frac{2(n_1 n_2)(n_1 + n_2 - 2)}{(n_1 + n_2)[t^2 + 2(n_1 + n_2 - 2)]}$$

$$= \frac{2(10)(10)(10 + 10 - 2)}{(10 + 10)[(4.16)^2 + 2(10 + 10 - 2)]} = 3.38$$

$$w_B = \frac{2(n_1 n_2)(n_1 + n_2 - 2)}{(n_1 + n_2)[t^2 + 2(n_1 + n_2 - 2)]}$$

$$= \frac{2(47)(48)(47 + 48 - 2)}{(47 + 48)[(2.49)^2 + 2(47 + 48 - 2)]} = 22.98$$

Therefore, from equation 10.4:

$$\frac{g_A - g_B}{[1/w_A + 1/w_B]^{1/2}} = \frac{1.86 - .51}{[1/3.38 + 1/22.98]^{1/2}} = 2.32$$

as our obtained Z of the difference. The p associated with that Z is .01 one-tailed or .02 two-tailed. Here is an example of two studies that agree there is a significant effect of the independent variable, but disagree significantly in their estimates of the size of the effect.

Suppose that in the present example we had found Studies A and B but that no effect sizes had been computed – only t tests. If our preference were to work with r as our effect size estimate, we could get r from equation 6.16. Recall that t's and N's for these studies were 4.16 ($N=20$) and 2.49 ($N=95$), respectively; then we can get the two r's:

$$r_A = \left[\frac{t^2}{t^2 + df} \right]^{1/2} = \left[\frac{(4.16)^2}{(4.16)^2 + 18} \right]^{1/2} = .70$$

$$r_B = \left[\frac{t^2}{t^2 + df} \right]^{1/2} = \left[\frac{(2.49)^2}{(2.49)^2 + 93} \right]^{1/2} = .25$$

We could compare these r's easily; in fact we did so in Example 5. The Z we obtained there was 2.31, very close to the Z we obtained when comparing g's ($Z = 2.32$).

Now suppose we had remembered how to get r from t but had forgotten how to compare two r's. If we recalled how to compare two g's, we could convert our r's to g's by means of the following (Rosenthal, 1984, equation 2.27):

$$g = \frac{r}{[1 - r^2]^{1/2}} \times \left[\frac{df(n_1 + n_2)}{n_1 n_2} \right]^{1/2}$$

For the present example:

$$g_A = \frac{.70}{[1 - (.70)^2]^{1/2}} \times \left[\frac{18(10 + 10)}{(10)(10)} \right]^{1/2} = 1.86$$

$$g_B = \frac{.25}{[1 - (.25)^2]^{1/2}} \times \left[\frac{93(47 + 48)}{(47)(48)} \right]^{1/2} = .51$$

Of course, we could also have computed g directly from t by means of equation 6.4:

$$g_A = t \left[\frac{1}{n_1} + \frac{1}{n_2} \right]^{1/2} = 4.16 \left[\frac{1}{10} + \frac{1}{10} \right]^{1/2} = 1.86$$

$$g_B = t \left[\frac{1}{n_1} + \frac{1}{n_2} \right]^{1/2} = 2.49 \left[\frac{1}{47} + \frac{1}{48} \right]^{1/2} = .51$$

Finally, if we should have Cohen's d available $[(M_1 - M_2)/\sigma]$ and wanted to get g, we could do so as follows:

$$g = \frac{d}{[(n_1 + n_2)/(n_1 + n_2 - 2)]^{1/2}} \tag{10.5}$$

If our effect size estimate were the difference between proportions (d'), our procedure would be analogous to that when our effect size estimate was

Hedges's g. Again, we need the estimated variance of the effect size estimate, $1/w$. In this application we estimate w by equation 10.6 which works well unless n_1 or n_2 is very small and p_1 or p_2 is very close to zero or one. If n_1 or n_2 is very small, a conservative procedure is to replace $p(1-p)$ by its maximal possible value of .25 (i.e., when $p = (1-p) = .50$ we find $p(1-p)$ to be at a maximum and equal to .25):

$$w = \frac{n_1 n_2}{n_2 p_1(1-p_1) + n_1 p_2(1-p_2)} \tag{10.6}$$

In meta-analytic work, however, we are sometimes unable to obtain the values of n_1 and n_2. Accordingly, we employ an approximation to w that depends only on the total study size N and the effect size estimate d' (Rosenthal & Rubin, 1982a):

$$w = \frac{N}{1 - d'^2} \tag{10.7}$$

This approximation to equation 10.6 holds exactly when p_1 and p_2 are the same amount above and below .5 and when $n_1 = n_2$.

When we have w we can test the significance of the difference between any two independent d''s by means of a Z test since

$$\frac{d'_A - d'_B}{[1/w_A + 1/w_B]^{1/2}} \text{ is distributed as } Z \tag{10.8}$$

as shown in somewhat different form in Rosenthal and Rubin (1982a). Just as was the case when effect size estimates were r and g (equations 10.2 and 10.4), the differences in effect size are divided by the square root of the sums of the variances of the individual effect sizes.

Example 8. Studies A and B yield results in the same direction with effect sizes of $d' = .70$ ($N = 20$) and $d' = .25$ ($N = 95$), respectively. Assuming that the two conditions being compared within each study are comprised of sample sizes of ten and ten in Study A and forty-seven and forty-eight in Study B, we find w first from equation 10.6. Then, as a further illustration, we also employ the approximation equation 10.7:

$$w_{A_1} = \frac{n_1 n_2}{n_2 p_1(1-p_1) + n_1 p_2(1-p_2)} = \frac{(10)(10)}{(10).85(.15) + (10).15(.85)} = 39.22$$

$$w_{B_1} = \frac{n_1 n_2}{n_2 p_1(1-p_1) + n_1 p_2(1-p_2)}$$

$$= \frac{(47)(48)}{(48).375(.625) + (47).625(.375)} = 101.32$$

$$w_{A_2} = \frac{N}{1-d'^2} = \frac{20}{1-(.70)^2} = 39.22, \text{ agreeing perfectly with the result above } (w_{A_1}).$$

$$w_{B_2} = \frac{N}{1-d'^2} = \frac{95}{1-(.25)^2} = 101.33, \text{ disagreeing only in the second decimal place with the result above } (w_{B_1}) \text{ because this approximation } (w_{B_2}) \text{ assumed } n_1 = n_2 = 47.5 \text{ rather than } n_1 = 47 \text{ and } n_2 = 48 \text{ as in the result above } (w_{B_1}).$$

Now, we can test the difference between our two effect sizes from equation 10.8:

$$\frac{d'_A - d'_B}{[1/w_{A_1} + 1/w_{B_1}]^{1/2}} = \frac{.70 - .25}{[1/39.22 + 1/101.32]^{1/2}} = 2.39$$

as our obtained Z of the difference. The p associated with that Z is .0084 one-tailed or .017 two-tailed. This example, Example 8, was selected to reflect the same underlying effect size as Example 7 and Example 5. The three Z's found by our three methods agreed very well with one another with Z's of 2.39, 2.32, and 2.31, respectively.

Combining studies

Significance testing.   After comparing the results of any two independent studies, it is an easy matter also to combine the p levels of the two studies. Thus, we get an overall estimate of the probability that the two p levels might have been obtained if the null hypothesis of no relationship between X and Y were true. Many methods for combining the results of two or more studies are available; they will be described later and have been summarized elsewhere (Rosenthal, 1978, 1980). Here it is necessary to give only the simplest and most versatile of the procedures, the method of adding Z's called the *Stouffer method* by Mosteller and Bush (1954). This method, just like the method of comparing p values, asks us first to obtain accurate p levels for each of our two studies and then to find the Z corresponding to each of these p levels. Both p's must be given in one-tailed form, and the corresponding Z's will have the same sign if both studies show effects in the same direction. They will have different signs if the results are in the opposite direction. The sum of the two Z's when divided by $[2]^{1/2}$, yields a new Z. This new Z corresponds to the p value that the results of the two studies combined (or results even further out in the same tail) could have occurred if the null hypothesis of no relationship between X and Y were true. Recapping,

$$\frac{Z_1 + Z_2}{[2]^{1/2}} \text{ is distributed as } Z \qquad (10.9)$$

Should we want to do so, we could weight each Z by its df, its estimated quality, or any other desired weights (Mosteller & Bush, 1954; Rosenthal, 1978, 1980).

The general procedure for weighting Z's is to (a) multiply each Z by any desired weight (assigned before inspection of the data), (b) add the weighted Z's, and (c) divide the sum of the weighted Z's by the square root of the sum of the squared weights as follows:

$$\text{Weighted } Z = \frac{w_1 Z_1 + w_2 Z_2}{[w_1^2 + w_2^2]^{1/2}} \tag{10.10}$$

Example 11 will illustrate the application of this procedure.

Example 9.   Studies A and B yield results in opposite directions and both are significant. One p is .05, one-tailed, the other is .0000001, one-tailed but in the opposite tail. The Z's corresponding to these p's are found in a table of normal deviates to be -1.64 and 5.20, respectively (note the opposite signs to indicate results in opposite directions). Then from equation 10.9 we have

$$\frac{Z_1 + Z_2}{[2]^{1/2}} = \frac{(-1.64) + (5.20)}{1.41} = 2.52$$

as the Z of the combined results of Studies A and B. The p value associated with a Z of 2.52 is .006 one-tailed or .012 two-tailed. Thus, the combined p supports the result of the more significant of the two results. If these were actual results we would want to be very cautious in interpreting our combined p both because the two p's were significant in opposite directions and because the two p's were so very significantly different from each other. We would try to discover what differences between Studies A and B might have led to results so significantly different.

Example 10.   Studies A and B yield results in the same direction, but neither is significant. One p is .11, the other is .09 and their associated Z's are 1.23 and 1.34, respectively. From equation 10.9 we have

$$\frac{(1.23) + (1.34)}{1.41} = 1.82$$

as our combined Z. The p associated with that Z is .034 one-tailed or .068 two-tailed.

Example 11.   Studies A and B are those of Example 9 but now we have found from a panel of experts that Study A earns a weight (w_1) of 3.4 on assessed internal validity while Study B earns only a weight (w_2) of 0.9. The

Z's for Studies A and B had been -1.64 and 5.20 respectively. Therefore, employing equation 10.10 we find:

$$\frac{(3.4)(-1.64)+(0.9)(5.20)}{[(3.4)^2+(0.9)^2]^{1/2}} = \frac{-0.896}{3.517} = -0.25$$

as the Z of the combined results of Studies A and B. The p value associated with this Z is .40 one-tailed or .80 two-tailed. Note that weighting has led to a nonsignificant result in this example. In Example 9 where there was no weighting (or, more accurately, equal weighting with $w_1 = w_2 = 1$), the p value was significant at $p = .012$ two-tailed.

If the weighting had been by df rather than research quality, and if df for Studies A and B had been 36 and 144 respectively, the weighted Z would have been:

$$\frac{(36)(-1.64)+(144)(5.20)}{[(36)^2+(144)^2]^{1/2}} = \frac{689.76}{148.43} = 4.65$$

This result shows the combined Z ($p < .000002$ one-tailed) to have been moved strongly in the direction of the Z with the larger df because of the substantial difference in df between the two studies. Note that when weighting Z's by df we have decided to have the size of the study play a very large role in determining the combined p. The role is very large because the size of the study has already entered into the determination of each Z and is, therefore, entering a second time into the weighting process.

Effect size estimation.   When we want to combine the results of two studies, we are at least as interested in the combined estimate of the effect size as we are in the combined probability. Just as was the case when we compared two effect size estimates, we shall consider r as our primary effect size estimate in the combining of effect sizes. However, we note that many other estimates are possible (e.g., Cohen's d, Hedges's g, or Glass's Δ, or differences between proportions, d').

For each of the two studies to be combined, we compute r and the associated Fisher z_r and have

$$\frac{z_{r_1}+z_{r_2}}{2} = \bar{z}_r \tag{10.11}$$

as the Fisher z_r corresponding to our mean r. We use an r to z_r or z_r to r table to look up the r associated with our mean $\bar{z}_r$. Tables are handier than computing r from z_r from the following: $r = (e^{2z_r}-1)/(e^{2z_r}+1)$. Should we want to do so we could weight each z_r by its df, that is, $N-3$ (Snedecor & Cochran, 1967, 1980), by its estimated research quality, or by any other weights assigned before inspection of the data.

The weighted mean z_r is obtained as follows:

$$\text{weighted mean } z_r = \frac{w_1 z_{r_1} + w_2 z_{r_2}}{w_1 + w_2} \tag{10.12}$$

Example 14 will illustrate the application of this procedure.

Example 12. Studies A and B yield results in opposite directions, one $r =$ .80, the other $r = -.30$. The Fisher z_r's corresponding to these r's are 1.10 and -0.31, respectively. From equation 10.10 we have

$$\frac{z_{r_1} + z_{r_2}}{2} = \frac{(1.10) + (-0.31)}{2} = .395$$

as the mean Fisher z_r. From our z_r to r table we find a z_r of .395 associated with an r of .38.

Example 13. Studies A and B yield results in the same direction, one $r =$ .95, the other $r = .25$. The Fisher z_r's corresponding to these r's are 1.83 and .26, respectively. From equation 10.11 we have

$$\frac{1.83 + .26}{2} = 1.045$$

as the mean Fisher z_r. From our z_r to r table we find a z_r of 1.045 to be associated with an r of .78. Note that if we had averaged the two r's without first transforming them to Fisher z_r's we would have found the mean r to be $(.95 + .25)/2 = .60$, substantially smaller than .78. This illustrates that the use of Fisher's z_r gives heavier weight to r's that are further from zero in either direction.

Example 14. Studies A and B are those of Example 6 but now we have decided to weight the studies by their df (i.e., $N-3$ in this application). Therefore, equation 10.12 can be rewritten to indicate that we are using df as weights as follows:

$$\text{weighted } \bar{z}_r = \frac{df_1 z_{r_1} + df_2 z_{r_2}}{df_1 + df_2} \tag{10.13}$$

In Example 6 we had r's of .00 and .30 based on N's of 17 and 45, respectively. The Fisher z_r's corresponding to our two r's are .00 and .31. Therefore, we find our weighted $\bar{z}_r$ to be:

$$\frac{(17-3).00 + (45-3).31}{(17-3) + (45-3)} = \frac{13.02}{56} = .232$$

which corresponds to an r of .23.

Finally, it should be noted that before combining tests of significance, and/or effect size estimates, it is very useful first to test the significance of the difference between the two p values or, what is preferable if they are available, the two effect sizes. If the results of the studies *do* differ we should be most cautious about combining their p values or effect sizes – especially when their results are in opposite directions.

Other effect size estimates. All that has been said about the combining of r's applies in principle also to the combining of other effect size estimates. Thus, we can average Hedges's g, or Cohen's d, or Glass's Δ, or the difference between proportions, d', or any other effect size estimate, with or without weighting. The difference in practice is that when we combine r's we typically transform them to Fisher's z_r's before combining, while with most other effect size estimates we do not transform them before combining them.

Meta-analytic procedures: any number of independent studies

Although we can do quite a lot in the way of comparing and combining the results of sets of studies with just the procedures given so far, it does happen often that we have three or more studies of the same relationship that we want to compare and/or combine. The purpose of this section is to present generalizations of the procedures given in the last section so that we can compare and combine the results of any number of independent studies. Again, the examples are hypothetical, constructed to illustrate a wide range of situations occuring in meta-analytic work in any domain. Often, of course, the number of studies entering into our analyses will be larger than the number required to illustrate the various meta-analytic procedures.

Comparing studies: diffuse tests

Significance testing. Given three or more p levels to compare we first find the standard normal deviate, Z, corresponding to each p level. All p levels must be one-tailed, and the corresponding Z's will have the same sign if all studies show effects in the same direction, but different signs if the results are not all in the same direction. The statistical significance of the heterogeneity of the Z's can be obtained from a χ^2 computed as follows (Rosenthal & Rubin, 1979a):

$$\Sigma(Z_j - \bar{Z})^2 \text{ is distributed as } \chi^2 \text{ with } K-1 \ df \qquad (10.14)$$

In this equation Z_j is the Z for any one study, $\bar{Z}$ is the mean of all the Z's obtained, and K is the number of studies being combined.

Example 15. Studies A, B, C, and D yield one-tailed p values of .15, .05, .01, and .001, respectively. Study C, however, shows results opposite in direction from those of studies A, B, and D. From a normal table we find the Z's corresponding to the four p levels to be 1.04, 1.64, -2.33, and 3.09. (Note the negative sign for the Z associated with the result in the opposite direction.) Then, from the preceding equation (10.14) we have

$$\Sigma(Z_j - \bar{Z})^2 = [(1.04) - (0.86)]^2 + [(1.64) - (0.86)]^2$$
$$+ [(-2.33) - (0.86)]^2 + [(3.09) - (0.86)]^2 = 15.79$$

as our χ^2 value which for $K - 1 = 4 - 1 = 3 \ df$ is significant at $p = .0013$. The four p values we compared, then, are clearly significantly heterogeneous.

Effect size estimation.   Here we want to assess the statistical heterogeneity of three or more effect size estimates. We again emphasize r as the effect size estimator, but analogous procedures are available for comparing such other effect size estimators as Hedges's (1981) g or differences between proportions (Hedges, 1982b; Hsu, 1980; Rosenthal & Rubin, 1982a). These will be described and illustrated shortly.

For each of the three or more studies to be compared we compute the effect size r, its associated Fisher z_r, and $N - 3$, where N is the number of sampling units on which each r is based. Then, the statistical significance of the heterogeneity of the r's can be obtained from a χ^2 (Snedecor & Cochran, 1967, 1980) because:

$$\Sigma(N_j - 3)(z_{r_j} - \bar{z}_r)^2 \text{ is distributed as } \chi^2 \text{ with } K - 1 \ df \qquad (10.15)$$

In this equation z_{r_j} is the Fisher z_r corresponding to any r, and $\bar{z}_r$ is the weighted mean z_r, that is,

$$\bar{z}_r = \frac{\Sigma(N_j - 3)z_{r_j}}{\Sigma(N_j - 3)} \qquad (10.16)$$

Example 16.   Studies A, B, C, and D yield effect sizes of $r = .70$ ($N = 30$), $r = .45$ ($N = 45$), $r = .10$ ($N = 20$) and $r = -.15$ ($N = 25$), respectively. The Fisher z_r's corresponding to these r's are found from tables of Fisher z_r to be .87, .48, .10, and $-.15$, respectively. The weighted mean z_r is found from the previous equation (10.16) to be

$$\frac{[27(.87) + 42(.48) + .17(.10) + 22(-.15)]}{[27 + 42 + 17 + 22]} = \frac{42.05}{108} = .39$$

Then, from the equation for χ^2 (equation 10.15), we have

$$\Sigma(N_j-3)(z_{r_j}-\bar{z}_r)^2 = 27(.87-.39)^2+42(.48-.39)^2+.17(.10-.39)^2$$
$$+22(-.15-.39)^2 = 14.41$$

as our χ^2 value which for $K-1=3$ df is significant at $p=.0024$. The four effect sizes we compared, then, are clearly significantly heterogeneous.

Other effect size estimates.   Although r is our preferred effect size estimate in this chapter, analogous procedures are available for such other effect size estimates as $(M_1-M_2)/S$ (Hedges's g) or the difference between proportions (d'). We begin with the case of Hedges's g.

For each of the studies in the set we compute Hedges's g $[(M_1-M_2)/S]$ and the reciprocal (w) of the estimated variance of g $(1/w)$. We saw in equation 10.3 how to compute w (Rosenthal & Rubin, 1982a):

$$w = \frac{2(n_1 n_2)(n_1+n_2-2)}{(n_1+n_2)[t^2+2(n_1+n_2-2)]} \tag{10.3}$$

Once we have w we can test the heterogeneity of the set of g's because Hedges (1982b) and Rosenthal and Rubin (1982a) have shown that:

$\Sigma w_j(g_j-\bar{g})^2$ is distributed approximately as χ^2 with $K-1$ df (10.17)

The quantity $\bar{g}$ is the weighted mean g defined as:

$$\bar{g} = \frac{\Sigma w_j g_j}{\Sigma w_j} \tag{10.18}$$

Note the similarity in structure between equations 10.17 and 10.15 and between 10.18 and 10.16. Equation 10.17 will be an adequate approximation in most circumstances but it will lose some accuracy when sample sizes are very small and t statistics are large.

Example 17.   Studies A, B, C, and D yield effect sizes of $g=1.89$ $(N=30)$, $g=.99$ $(N=45)$, $g=.19$ $(N=20)$ and $g=-.29$ $(N=25)$, respectively. To employ equations 10.17 and 10.18 we will need to compute w for each effect size. Equation 10.3 showing how to compute w requires knowing the sample sizes of the two groups being compared in each study $(n_1$ and $n_2)$ as well as the results of the t test. If the t tests were not available we could compute our own from equations 6.4 or 6.5, for example:

$$t = \frac{g}{[1/n_1+1/n_2]^{1/2}} \tag{10.19}$$

If the n_1 and n_2 values are not reported but N (i.e., n_1+n_2) is known and if it is reasonable to assume approximately equal sample sizes, we can replace n_1 and n_2 by $N/2$. In that case equation 10.19 simplifies to:

Table 10.3. *Work table for comparing four effect sizes* (g)

Study	N	g^a	t^b	t^2	w^c	wg
A	30	1.89	5.18	26.79	5.07	9.58
B	45	.99	3.32	11.03	9.97	9.87
C	20	.19	.42	.18	4.98	.95
D	25	−.29	−.72	.53	6.18	−1.79
Σ	120	2.78	8.20	38.53	26.20	18.61

^{a}Obtainable from: $g = 2t/N^{1/2}$ (from equation 10.20).
^{b}Obtainable from: $t = gN^{1/2}/2$ (equation 10.20).
^{c}Obtainable from: $w = N(N-2)/2(t^2+2N-4)$ (equation 10.21).

$$t = g \times \frac{[N]^{1/2}}{2} \qquad (10.20)$$

and equation 10.3 simplifies to:

$$w = \frac{N(N-2)}{2(t^2+2N-4)} \qquad (10.21)$$

Since in the present example we were not given n_1, n_2, or t for studies A, B, C, and D, we employ equation 10.20 to obtain t and equation 10.21 to obtain w for each study. Table 10.3 shows the results of these computations which are shown in detail only for Study A for which $N = 30$ and $g = 1.89$. From equation 10.20 we find:

$$t = g \times \frac{[N]^{1/2}}{2} = 1.89 \times \frac{[30]^{1/2}}{2} = 5.18$$

From equation 10.21 we find:

$$w = \frac{N(N-2)}{2(t^2+2N-4)} = \frac{30(28)}{2(5.18^2+2(30)-4)} = 5.07$$

Before we can employ equation 10.17, our χ^2 test for heterogeneity, we must find $\bar{g}$, the weighted mean g (see equation 10.18), which can be found from the appropriate entries in the row of sums of Table 10.3:

$$\bar{g} = \frac{\Sigma w_j g_j}{\Sigma w_j} = \frac{18.61}{26.20} = .71$$

Now, we can employ equation 10.17 to compute χ^2:

$$\Sigma w_j(g_j - \bar{g})^2 = 5.07(1.89 - .71)^2 + 9.97(.99 - .71)^2 + 4.98(.19 - .71)^2$$
$$+ 6.18(-.29 - .71)^2 = 15.37$$

a χ^2 value which, for $K-1=3\ df$, is significant at $p=.0015$. The four effect sizes we compared, then, are clearly significantly heterogeneous.

The four effect sizes of this example were chosen to be the equivalents in units of g to the effect sizes of Example 16 which were in units of r. The $\chi^2(3)$ based on g was somewhat larger (by 7 percent) than the $\chi^2(3)$ based on r and the p of .0015 is slightly more significant than that for Example 16 (.0024). The agreement is close enough for practical purposes but we should not expect perfect agreement. Incidentally, if we have available a set of r's and want to convert them to g's, still assuming approximately equal sample sizes within each condition, we can employ the following:

$$g = \frac{2r}{[1-r^2]^{1/2}} \times \left[\frac{N-2}{N}\right]^{1/2} \tag{10.22}$$

Should we want to convert g's to r's we can employ the following:

$$r = \left[\frac{g^2N}{g^2N+4(N-2)}\right]^{1/2} \tag{10.23}$$

If our effect size estimate were the difference between proportions (d'), our procedure would be analogous to that when our effect size estimate was Hedges's g. For each of the studies in the set we compute d' and the reciprocal (w) of the estimated variance of d' ($1/w$). The basic estimate of w is provided by equation 10.6 which works well unless n_1 or n_2 is very small and p_1 or p_2 is very close to zero or one. If n_1 or n_2 is very small, a conservative procedure is to replace $p(1-p)$ by its maximal possible value of .25. We give equation 10.6 again:

$$w = \frac{n_1 n_2}{n_2 p_1(1-p_1)+n_1 p_2(1-p_2)} \tag{10.6}$$

The approximation to this expression that depends only on the total study size (N) and the effect size estimate d' was given earlier as equation 10.7:

$$w = \frac{N}{1-d'^2} \tag{10.7}$$

This approximation to equation 10.6 holds exactly when p_1 and p_2 are the same amount above and below .5 and when $n_1 = n_2$.

Once we have w we can test the heterogeneity of the set of d''s by means of equation 10.17 (Rosenthal & Rubin, 1982a) but substituting d' for g:

$\Sigma w_j(d'-\bar{d}')^2$ is distributed approximately as χ^2 with $K-1\ df$ (10.24)

The quantity $\bar{d}'$ is the weighted mean d' defined as:

Table 10.4. *Work table for comparing four effect sizes* (d')

Study	N	d'	d'^2	1−d'^2	w^a	wd'
A	30	.70	.4900	.5100	58.82	41.174
B	45	.45	.2025	.7975	56.43	25.394
C	20	.10	.0100	.9900	20.20	2.020
D	25	−.15	.0225	.9775	25.58	−3.837
Σ	120	1.10	.7250	3.2750	161.03	64.751

[a]Obtainable from: $w = N/(1-d'^2)$ (equation 10.7).

$$\bar{d}' = \frac{\Sigma w_j d'_j}{\Sigma w_j} \tag{10.25}$$

a quantity defined analogously to $\bar{g}$ (see equation 10.18).

Example 18. Studies A, B, C, and D yield effect sizes of $d' = .70, .45, .10,$ and $-.15$, respectively. Table 10.4 shows the results of the computations of w for each of the studies. To illustrate these computations for Study A we employ equation 10.7 as follows:

$$w = \frac{N}{1-d'^2} = \frac{30}{1-(.70)^2} = 58.82$$

Before we can employ equation 10.24, our χ^2 test for heterogeneity, we must find $\bar{d}'$, the weighted mean d' (equation 10.25), which can be found from the appropriate entries in the row of sums of Table 10.4:

$$\bar{d}' = \frac{\Sigma w_j d'_j}{\Sigma w_j} = \frac{64.751}{161.03} = .40$$

Then, employing equation 10.24 we find:

$$\Sigma w_j (d' - \bar{d}')^2 = 58.82(.70 - .40)^2 + 56.43(.45 - .40)^2$$
$$+ 20.20(.10 - .40)^2 + 25.58(-.15 - .40)^2 = 14.99$$

a χ^2 value which, for $K-1 = 3$ df is significant at $p = .0018$. The four effect sizes are significantly heterogeneous.

The four effect sizes of this example were chosen to be the equivalents in units of d' to the effect sizes of Example 16 (r) and Example 17 (g). Table 10.5 summarizes the data for the three effect size estimates of Examples 16, 17, and 18. While the three $\chi^2(3)$ values are not identical, they are quite similar to one another as are the three significance levels. Table 10.5 also

Table 10.5. *Tests for the heterogeneity of effect sizes defined as* r, g, *and* d'

	Effect sizes		
	r	*g*	*d'*
Study A	.70	1.89	.70
Study B	.45	.99	.45
Study C	.10	.19	.10
Study D	−.15	−.29	−.15
Median	.28	.59	.28
Unweighted mean	.31[a]	.70	.28
Weighted mean	.37[a]	.71	.40
$\chi^2(3)$	14.41[a]	15.37	14.99
p	.0024	.0015	.0018

[a]Based on Fisher's z_r transformation.

suggests that the metric *r* is quite similar to the metric *d'*. Indeed, as we saw in Chapter 6 in our discussion of the BESD, when the proportions being compared are the same amount above and below .5 and when $n_1 = n_2$, *r* computed from such a 2×2 table does indeed equal *d'*.

Comparing studies: focused tests

Significance testing.   Although we know how to answer the diffuse question of the significance of the differences among a collection of significance levels, we are often able to ask a more focused and more useful question. For example, given a set of *p* levels for studies of teacher expectancy effects, we might want to know whether results from younger children show greater degrees of statistical significance than do results from older children (Rosenthal & Rubin, 1978a). Normally, our greater interest would be in the relationship between our weights derived from theory and our obtained effect sizes. Sometimes, however, the effect size estimates, along with their sample sizes, are not available. More rarely, we may be intrinsically interested in the relationship between our weights and the obtained levels of significance.

As was the case for diffuse tests, we begin by finding the standard normal deviate, *Z*, corresponding to each *p* level. All *p* levels must be one-tailed, and the corresponding *Z*'s will have the same sign if all studies show effects in the same direction, but different signs if the results are not all in the same direction. The statistical significance of the contrast testing any specific hypothesis about the set of *p* levels can be obtained from a *Z* computed as follows (Rosenthal & Rubin, 1979a):

$$\frac{\Sigma \lambda_j Z_j}{[\Sigma \lambda_j^2]^{1/2}} \text{ is distributed as } Z \qquad (10.26)$$

In this equation λ_j is the theoretically derived prediction or contrast weight for any one study, chosen such that the sum of the λ_j's will be zero, and Z_j is the Z for any one study.

Example 19. Studies A, B, C, and D yield one-tailed p values of $1/10^7$, .0001, .21, and .007, respectively, all with results in the same direction. From a normal table we find the Z's corresponding to the four p levels to be 5.20, 3.72, .81, and 2.45. Suppose that Studies A, B, C, and D had involved differing amounts of peer tutor contact such that Studies A, B, C, and D had involved 8, 6, 4, and 2 hours of contact per month, respectively. We might, therefore, ask whether there was a linear relationship between number of hours of contact and statistical significance of the result favoring peer tutoring. The weights of a linear contrast involving four studies are 3, 1, -1, and -3. Therefore, from the preceding equation we have

$$\frac{\Sigma \lambda_j Z_j}{[\Sigma \lambda_j^2]^{1/2}} = \frac{(3)5.20 + (1)3.72 + (-1).81 + (-3)2.45}{[(3)^2 + (1)^2 + (-1)^2 + (-3)^2]^{1/2}} = \frac{11.16}{[20]^{1/2}} = 2.50$$

as our Z value, which is significant at $p = .006$, one-tailed. The four p values, then, tend to grow linearly more significant as the number of hours of contact time increases.

Effect size estimation. Here we want to ask a more focused question of a set of effect sizes. For example, given a set of effect sizes for studies of peer tutoring, we might want to know whether these effects are increasing or decreasing linearly with the number of hours of contact per month. We again emphasize r as the effect size estimator, but analogous procedures are available for comparing such other effect size estimators as Hedges's (1981) g or differences between proportions (d') (Rosenthal & Rubin, 1982a). These will be described and illustrated shortly.

As was the case for diffuse tests, we begin by computing the effect size r, its associated Fisher z_r, and $N-3$, where N is the number of sampling units on which each r is based. The statistical significance of the contrast, testing any specific hypothesis about the set of effect sizes, can be obtained from a Z computed as follows (Rosenthal & Rubin, 1982a):

$$\frac{\Sigma \lambda_j z_{r_j}}{[\Sigma (\lambda_j^2 / w_j)]^{1/2}} \text{ is distributed as } Z \qquad (10.27)$$

In this equation, λ_j is the contrast weight determined from some theory for any one study, chosen such that the sum of the λ_j's will be zero. The z_{r_j} is the Fisher z_r for any one study and w_j is the inverse of the variance of the effect size for each study. For Fisher z_r transformations of the effect size r, the variance is $1/(N_j-3)$ so $w_j = N_j - 3$.

Example 20.   Studies A, B, C, and D yield effect sizes of $r = .89, .76, .23,$ and $.59$, respectively, all with $N = 12$. The Fisher z_r's corresponding to these r's are found from tables of Fisher z_r to be 1.42, 1.00, .23, and .68, respectively. Suppose that Studies A, B, C, and D had involved differing amounts of peer tutor contact such that Studies A, B, C, and D had involved 8, 6, 4, and 2 hours of contact per month, respectively. We might, therefore, ask whether there was a linear relationship between number of hours of contact and size of effect favoring peer tutoring. As in Example 19, the appropriate weights, or λ's, are 3, 1, -1, and -3. Therefore, from the preceding equation we have

$$\frac{\Sigma \lambda_j z_{r_j}}{[\Sigma(\lambda_j^2/w_j)]^{1/2}} = \frac{(3)1.42+(1)1.00+(-1).23+(-3).68}{[(3)^2/9+(1)^2/9+(-1)^2/9+(-3)^2/9]^{1/2}}$$

$$= \frac{2.99}{[2.222]^{1/2}} = 2.01$$

as our Z value which is significant at $p = .022$ one-tailed. The four effect sizes, therefore, tend to grow linearly larger as the number of hours of contact time increases. Interpretation of this relationship must be very cautious. After all, studies were not assigned at random to the four conditions of contact hours. It is generally the case that variables moderating the magnitude of effects found should not be interpreted as giving strong evidence for any causal relationships. Moderator relationships can, however, be very valuable in suggesting the possibility of causal relationships, possibilities that can then be studied experimentally or as nearly experimentally as possible.

Other effect size estimates.   Although r is our preferred effect size estimate in this chapter, analogous procedures are available for such other effect size estimates as $(M_1 - M_2)/S$ (Hedges's g) or the difference between proportions (d'). We begin with the case of Hedges's g.

Once again we compute the reciprocal (w) of the estimated variance of g ($1/w$) for each study. We employ equation 10.3 when the individual sample sizes (n_1 and n_2) are known and unequal and equation 10.21 when they are unknown or when they are equal. These equations are as follows:

$$w = \frac{2(n_1 n_2)(n_1+n_2-2)}{(n_1+n_2)[t^2+2(n_1+n_2-2)]} \tag{10.3}$$

$$w = \frac{N(N-2)}{2(t^2+2N-4)} \tag{10.21}$$

Table 10.6. *Work table for computing contrasts among effect sizes* (g)

Study	N	g^a	t^b	t^2	λ^c	λ^2	λg	w^d	λ^2/w
A	12	3.56	6.17	38.02	3	9	10.68	1.03	8.74
B	12	2.13	3.69	13.61	1	1	2.13	1.79	.56
C	12	.43	.74	.55	−1	1	− .43	2.92	.34
D	12	1.33	2.30	5.31	−3	9	−3.99	2.37	3.80
Σ	48	7.45	12.90	57.49	0	20	8.39	8.11	13.44

[a] Obtainable from: $g = 2t/N^{1/2}$ (from equation 10.20).
[b] Obtainable from: $t = gN^{1/2}/2$ (equation 10.20).
[c] Determined by theory but with $\Sigma\lambda = 0$.
[d] Obtainable from $w = N(N-2)/2(t^2+2N-4)$ (equation 10.21).

We employ the computed w's to test the significance of any contrast we may wish to investigate. The quantity:

$$\frac{\Sigma\lambda_j g_j}{[\Sigma(\lambda_j^2/w_j)]^{1/2}} \text{ is distributed approximately as } Z \qquad (10.28)$$

an equation that is identical in structure to equation (10.27) (Rosenthal & Rubin, 1982a). In this application w_j is defined as in equations 10.3 or 10.21 and λ_j is the contrast weight we assign to the jth study on the basis of our theory. The only restriction is that the sum of the λ_j's must be zero (Rosenthal & Rosnow, 1984, 1985).

Example 21. Studies A, B, C, and D yield effect sizes of $g = 3.56, 2.13, .43,$ and 1.33, respectively, all with $N = 12$. As in Example 20, we assume 8, 6, 4, and 2 hours of peer tutoring per month were employed in Studies A, B, C, and D, respectively. We ask whether there was a linear relationship between number of hours of contact and size of effect favoring peer tutoring. As in Example 20, the appropriate weights, or λ's, are 3, 1, −1, and −3.

Table 10.6 lists the ingredients required to compute our test of significance (Z) for the contrast, and reminds us of the formulas that can be used to obtain the various quantities. Now we can apply equation 10.28 to find:

$$\frac{\Sigma\lambda_j g_j}{[\Sigma(\lambda_j^2/w_j)]^{1/2}} = \frac{8.39}{[13.44]^{1/2}} = 2.29$$

as our Z value which is significant at $p = .011$, one-tailed.

The four effect sizes of this example were chosen to be the equivalents in units of g to the effect sizes of Example 20 which were in units of r. The Z based on g is somewhat larger (by 14 percent) than the Z based on r (2.01) and the p of .011 is somewhat more significant than that for Example 20 ($p =$ .022). The agreement, therefore, is hardly perfect but it is close enough for practical purposes.

If a meta-analyst has a favorite effect size estimate, he or she need have no fear that a different meta-analyst employing a different effect size estimate would reach a dramatically different conclusion. However, what should *not* be done is to (a) employ a variety of effect size estimates, (b) perform the various meta-analytic procedures on all of them and (c) report only those results most pleasing to the meta-analyst. There is nothing wrong with employing multiple effect size estimates, but *all* analyses conducted should also be reported. General and special equations showing the relationships between g and r are given as equations 10.22 and 10.23.

If our effect size estimate were the difference between proportions (d'), our procedure would be analogous to that when our effect size estimate was Hedges's g. Once again we compute the reciprocal (w) of the estimated variance of d' ($1/w$) for each study. We employ equation 10.6 when the individual sample sizes n_1 and n_2 are known and unequal and equation 10.7 when they are unknown or when they are equal. The equations are as follows:

$$w = \frac{n_1 n_2}{n_2 p_1(1-p_1) + n_1 p_2(1-p_2)} \tag{10.6}$$

$$w = \frac{N}{1 - d'^2} \tag{10.7}$$

Once we have w we can test any contrast by means of equation 10.28 (Rosenthal & Rubin, 1982a) but substituting d' for g:

$$\frac{\Sigma \lambda_j d'_j}{[\Sigma(\lambda_j^2/w_j)]^{1/2}} \text{ is distributed approximately as } Z \tag{10.29}$$

In this application w_j is defined as in equations 10.6 or 10.7 and λ_j is as defined above.

Example 22.   Studies A, B, C, and D yield effect sizes of $d' = .89, .76, .23,$ and .59, respectively, all with $N = 12$. As in Example 21, we assume 8, 6, 4, and 2 hours of peer tutoring per month were employed in Studies A, B, C, and D, respectively. Again we want to test the linear contrast with λ's of 3, 1, -1, and -3. Table 10.7 lists the ingredients required to compute our test of significance (Z) for the contrast. Now we can apply equation 10.29 to find:

$$\frac{\Sigma \lambda_j d'_j}{[\Sigma(\lambda_j^2/w_j)]^{1/2}} = \frac{1.43}{[.7592]^{1/2}} = 1.64$$

as our Z value which is significant at $p = .050$ one-tailed.

Table 10.7. *Work table for computing contrasts among effect sizes* (d')

Study	N	d'	d'²	1−d'²	λ[a]	λ²	λd'	w_j[b]	λ²/w
A	12	.89	.79	.21	3	9	2.67	57.14	.1575
B	12	.76	.58	.42	1	1	.76	28.57	.0350
C	12	.23	.05	.95	−1	1	− .23	12.63	.0792
D	12	.59	.35	.65	−3	9	−1.77	18.46	.4875
Σ	48	2.47	1.77	2.23	0	20	1.43	116.80	.7592

[a] Determined by theory but with $\Sigma\lambda = 0$.
[b] Obtainable from: $w = N/(1-d'^2)$ (equation 10.7).

Table 10.8. *Tests for linear contrasts in effect sizes defined as* r, g, *and* d'

	Effect sizes		
	r	g	d'
Study A	.89	3.56	.89
Study B	.76	2.13	.76
Study C	.23	.43	.23
Study D	.59	1.33	.59
Median	.68	1.73	.68
Mean	.68[a]	1.86	.62
Z (linear contrast)	2.01[a]	2.29	1.64
p	.022	.011	.050

[a] Based on Fisher's z_r transformation.

The four effect sizes of this example were chosen to be equivalent in units of d' to the effect sizes of Example 20 (r) and Example 21 (g). Table 10.8 summarizes the data for the three effect size estimates of Examples 20, 21, and 22. The three Z tests of significance of the linear contrast are somewhat variable, with the Z for the effect size estimator g being about 14 percent larger than that for r and the Z for the effect size estimator d' being about 18 percent smaller than that for r. However, the range of significance levels is not dramatic with the most significant result at $p = .011$ and the least significant at $p = .050$.

Before leaving the topic of focused tests, it should be noted that their use is more efficient than the more common procedure of counting each effect size or significance level as a single observation (e.g., Eagly & Carli, 1981; Hall, 1980, 1984; Rosenthal & Rubin, 1978a; Smith, Glass, and Miller, 1980).

In that procedure we might, for example, compute a correlation between Fisher z_r values and the λ's of Example 20 to test the hypothesis of greater effect size being associated with greater contact time. Although that r is substantial (.77), it does not even approach significance because of the small number of df upon which the r is based. The procedures employing focused tests, or contrasts, employ much more of the information available and, therefore, are less likely to lead to Type II errors.

Combining studies

Significance testing. After comparing the results of any set of three or more studies it is an easy matter also to combine the p levels of the set of studies to get an overall estimate of the probability that the set of p levels might have been obtained if the null hypothesis of no relationship between X and Y were true. Of the various methods available that will be described in the next chapter, we present here only the generalized version of the method presented earlier in our discussion of combining the results of two groups.

This method requires only that we obtain Z for each of our p levels, all of which should be given as one-tailed. Z's disagreeing in direction from the bulk of the findings are given negative signs. Then, the sum of the Z's divided by the square root of the number (K) of studies yields a new statistic distributed as Z. Recapping,

$$\frac{\Sigma Z_j}{[K]^{1/2}} \text{ is distributed as } Z \tag{10.30}$$

Should we want to do so, we could weight each of the Z's by its df, its estimated quality, or any other desired weights (Mosteller & Bush, 1954; Rosenthal, 1978, 1980).

The general procedure for weighting Z's is to (a) multiply each Z by any desired weight (assigned before inspection of the data), (b) add the weighted Z's, and (c) divide the sum of the weighted Z's by the square root of the sum of the squared weights as follows:

$$\text{Weighted } Z = \frac{\Sigma w_j Z_j}{[\Sigma w_j^2]^{1/2}} \tag{10.31}$$

Example 24 will illustrate the application of this procedure.

Example 23. Studies A, B, C, and D yield one-tailed p values of .15, .05, .01, and .001, respectively. Study C, however, shows results opposite in direction from the results of the remaining studies. The four Z's associated with these four p's, then, are 1.04, 1.64, -2.33, and 3.09. From equation 10.30 we have

$$\frac{\Sigma Z_j}{[K]^{1/2}} = \frac{(1.04)+(1.64)+(-2.33)+(3.09)}{[4]^{1/2}} = 1.72$$

as our new Z value which has an associated p value of .043 one-tailed, or .086 two-tailed. We would normally employ the one-tailed p value if we had correctly predicted the bulk of the findings but would employ the two-tailed p value if we had not. The combined p that we obtained in this example supports the results of the majority of the individual studies. However, even if these p values (.043 and .086) were more significant, we would want to be very cautious about drawing any simple overall conclusion because of the very great heterogeneity of the four p values we were combining. Example 15, which employed the same p values, showed that this heterogeneity was significant at $p = .0013$. It should be emphasized again, however, that this great heterogeneity of p values could be due to heterogeneity of effect sizes, heterogeneity of sample sizes, or both. To find out about the sources of heterogeneity, we would have to look carefully at the effect sizes and sample sizes of each of the studies involved.

Example 24. Studies A, B, C, and D are those of Example 23 just above, but now we have decided to weight each study by the mean rating of internal validity assigned it by a panel of methodologists. These weights (w) were 2.4, 2.2, 3.1, and 3.8 for Studies A, B, C, and D, respectively. Employing equation 10.31 we find:

$$\text{Weighted } Z = \frac{\Sigma w_j Z_j}{[\Sigma w_j^2]^{1/2}}$$

$$= \frac{(2.4)(1.04)+(2.2)(1.64)+(3.1)(-2.33)+(3.8)(3.09)}{[(2.4)^2+(2.2)^2+(3.1)^2+(3.8)^2]^{1/2}}$$

$$= \frac{10.623}{[34.65]^{1/2}} = 1.80$$

as the Z of the weighted combined results of Studies A, B, C, and D. The p value associated with this Z is .036 one-tailed or .072 two-tailed. In this example weighting by quality of research did not lead to a very different result than was obtained when weighting was not employed (Example 23); in both cases $p \cong .04$, one-tailed. Actually, it might be more accurate to say for Example 23 that weighting was equal with all w's $= 1$ than to say that no weighting was employed.

Effect size estimation. When we combine the results of three or more studies we are at least as interested in the combined estimate of the effect size as we are in the combined probability. We follow here our earlier procedure of considering r as our primary effect size estimator while recognizing that many other estimates are possible. For each of the three or more studies to be combined we compute r and the associated Fisher z_r and have

$$\frac{\Sigma z_r}{K} = \bar{z}_r \tag{10.32}$$

as the Fisher $\bar{z}_r$ corresponding to our mean r (where K refers to the number of studies combined). We use a table of Fisher z_r to find the r associated with our mean z_r. Should we want to give greater weight to larger studies we could weight each z_r by its df, that is, $N-3$ (Snedecor & Cochran, 1967, 1980), by its estimated research quality, or by any other weights assigned before inspection of the data.

The weighted mean z_r is obtained as follows:

$$\text{Weighted } \bar{z}_r = \frac{\Sigma w_j z_{r_j}}{\Sigma w_j} \tag{10.33}$$

Example 26 will illustrate the application of this procedure.

Example 25.   Studies A, B, C, and D yield effect sizes of $r = .70, .45, .10,$ and $-.15$, respectively. The Fisher z_r values corresponding to these r's are .87, .48, .10, and $-.15$, respectively. Then, from equation 10.32 we have

$$\frac{\Sigma z_r}{K} = \frac{(.87)+(.48)+(.10)+(-.15)}{4} = .32$$

as our mean Fisher z_r. From our table of Fisher z_r values we find a z_r of .32 to correspond to an r of .31. Just as in our earlier example of combined p levels, however, we would want to be very cautious in our interpretation of this combined effect size. If the r's we have just averaged were based on substantial sample sizes, as was the case in Example 16, they would be significantly heterogeneous. Therefore, averaging without special thought and comment would be inappropriate.

Example 26.   Studies A, B, C, and D are those of Example 25 but now we have decided to weight each study by a mean rating of ecological validity assigned to it by several experts. These weights were 1.7, 1.6, 3.1, and 2.5 for Studies A, B, C, and D, respectively. Employing equation 10.33 we find:

$$\text{Weighted } Z = \frac{\Sigma w_j z_{r_j}}{\Sigma w_j} = \frac{(1.7)(.87)+(1.6)(.48)+(3.1)(.10)+(2.5)(-.15)}{1.7+1.6+3.1+2.5}$$

$$= \frac{2.182}{8.90} = .24$$

as our mean Fisher z_r, which corresponds to an r of .24. In this example weighting by quality of research led to a somewhat smaller estimate of combined effect size than did equal weighting (.24 versus .31).

Other effect size estimates.   Any other effect size, for example, Cohen's d, Hedges's g, Glass's Δ, the difference between proportions (d'), and so forth can be combined with or without weighting just as we have shown for r. The only difference is that when we combine r's we typically transform them to Fisher's z_r's before combining, while for most other effect size estimates we combine them directly without prior transformation.

11. Combining probabilities

General procedures

In the preceding chapter, some basic procedures that can be used to compare and to combine levels of significance and effect size estimates were presented. In addition to the basic procedures presented, there are various alternative methods available for combining probability levels that are especially useful under particular circumstances.

In this section on general procedures we summarize the major methods for combining the probabilities obtained from two or more studies testing essentially the same directional hypothesis. Although it is possible to do so, no consideration is given here to questions of combining results from studies in which the direction of the results cannot be made immediately apparent, as would be the case for F tests (employed in analysis of variance) with $df > 1$ for the numerator or for chi-square tests (of independence in contingency tables) with $df > 1$. Although the present section is intended to be self-contained, it is not intended to serve as a summary of all the useful ideas on the topic at hand that are contained in the literature referenced. The seminal work of Mosteller and Bush (1954) is especially recommended. For a review of the relevant literature see Rosenthal (1978a).

The basic methods

Table 11.1 presents the results of a set of five illustrative studies. The first column of information about the studies lists the results of the t test. The sign preceding t gives the direction of the results; a positive sign means the difference is consistent with the bulk of the results, a negative sign means the difference is inconsistent. The second column records the df upon which each t was based.

The third column gives the one-tailed p associated with each t. It should be noted that one-tail p's are always less than .50 when the results are in the consistent direction, but they are always greater than .50 when the results

Table 11.1. *Summary of seven methods for combining probabilities of independent experiments*

Study	t	df	One-tail p	Effect size r	Z	$-2 \log_e p$
1	+1.19	40	.12	.18	+1.17	4.24
2	+2.39	60	.01	.29	+2.33	9.21
3	-0.60	10	.72	-.19	-0.58	0.66
4	+1.52	30	.07	.27	+1.48	5.32
5	+0.98	20	.17	.21	+0.95	3.54
Σ	+5.48	160	1.09	+.76	+5.35	22.97
Mean	+1.10	32	.22	+.15	+1.07	4.59
Median	+1.19	30	.12	+.21	+1.17	4.24

1. *Method of adding logs*

$$\chi^2(df=2N) = \Sigma - 2\log_e p = 22.97, \quad p = .011 \text{ one-tail} \tag{11.1}$$

2. *Method of adding probabilities* (applicable when Σp near unity or less)

$$P = \frac{(\Sigma p)^N}{N!} = \frac{(1.09)^5}{5!} = .013 \text{ one-tail} \tag{11.2}$$

3. *Method of adding t's*

$$Z = \frac{\Sigma t}{\{\Sigma[df/(df-2)]\}^{1/2}} = \frac{5.48}{[40/38+60/58+10/8+30/28+20/18]^{1/2}}$$

$$= \frac{5.48}{[5.5197]^{1/2}} = 2.33, \quad p = .01 \text{ one-tail} \tag{11.3}$$

4. *Method of adding Z's*

$$Z = \frac{\Sigma Z}{N^{1/2}} = \frac{5.35}{5^{1/2}} = 2.39, \quad p = .009 \text{ one-tail} \tag{11.4}$$

5. *Method of adding weighted Z's*

$$Z = \frac{T}{\sigma_T} = \frac{df_1 Z_1 + df_2 Z_2 + \cdots + df_n Z_n}{[df_1^2 + df_2^2 + \cdots + df_n^2]^{1/2}}$$

$$= \frac{(40)(+1.17)+(60)(+2.33)+\cdots+(20)(+0.95)}{[(40)^2+(60)^2+\cdots+(20)^2]^{1/2}}$$

$$= \frac{244.2}{[6,600]^{1/2}} = 3.01, \quad p = .0013 \tag{11.5}$$

6. *Method of testing mean p*

$$Z = (.50 - \bar{p})[12N]^{1/2}$$
$$= (.50 - .22)[12(5)]^{1/2} = 2.17, \quad p = .015 \text{ one-tail} \tag{11.6}$$

7. *Method of testing mean Z*

$$t = \frac{\Sigma Z/N}{[S_{(Z)}^2/N]^{1/2}} = \frac{+1.07}{[.22513]^{1/2}} = 2.26, \quad df = 4, \quad p < .05 \text{ one-tail} \tag{11.7}$$

or

$$F = \frac{(\Sigma Z)^2}{(N)S_{(Z)}^2} = 5.09, \quad df = 1,4, \quad p < .05 \text{ one-tail}$$

are not consistent. For example, study 3 with a t of $-.60$ is tabulated with a one-tail p of .72. If the t had been in the consistent direction, that is, $+.60$, the one-tail p would have been .28. It is important to note that it is the direction of difference which is found to occur on the average that is assigned the $+$ sign, and hence the lower one-tail p. The basic computations and results are identical whether we were very clever and predicted the net direction of effect or not clever at all and got it quite wrong. At the very end of our calculations, we can double the final overall level of significance if we want to make an allowance for not having predicted the net direction of effect.

The fourth column of the table gives the size of the effect defined in terms of the Pearson r.

The fifth column gives the standard normal deviate, or Z associated with each p value. The final column of our table lists the natural logarithms of the one-tail p's (of the third column of information) multiplied by -2. Each is a quantity distributed as χ^2 with 2 df and is an ingredient of the first method of combining p levels to be presented in this section (Fisher, 1932, 1938).

1. Adding logs. The last column of our table is really a list of χ^2 values. The sum of independent χ^2's is also distributed as χ^2 with df equal to the sum of the df's of the χ^2's added. Therefore, we need only add the five χ^2's of our table and look up this new χ^2 with $5 \times 2 = 10$ df. The results are given just below the row of medians of our table; $\chi^2 = 22.97$, which is associated with a p of .011, one-tail, when $df = 10$.

The method of adding logs, sometimes called the *Fisher method,* though frequently cited, suffers from the disadvantage that it can yield results that are inconsistent with such simple overall tests as the *sign* test of the null hypothesis of a 50:50 split (Siegel, 1956). Thus, for a large number of studies, if the vast majority showed results in one direction, we could easily reject the null hypothesis by the sign test even if the consistent p values were not very much below .50. However, under these situations the Fisher method would not yield an overall significant p (Mosteller & Bush, 1954). Another problem with the Fisher method is that if two studies with equally and strongly significant results in opposite directions are obtained, the Fisher method supports the significance of either outcome! Thus p's of .001 for $A > B$ and .001 for $B > A$ combine to a $p < .01$ for $A > B$ or $B > A$ (Adcock, 1960). Despite these limitations, the Fisher method remains the best known and most discussed of all the methods of combining independent probabilities (see Rosenthal [1978] for a review of the literature). Because of its limitations, however, routine use does not appear indicated.

2. Adding probabilities. A powerful method has been described by Edgington (1972a) in which the combined probability emerges when the sum of the observed *p* levels is raised to the power equivalent to the number of studies being combined (N) and divided by $N!$. Essentially, this formula gives the area of a right triangle when the results of two studies are being combined, the volume of a pyramid when the results of three studies are combined, and the *n*-dimensional generalization of this volume when more studies are involved. Our table shows the results to be equivalent to those obtained by the Fisher method for this set of data. The basic *Edgington method* is useful and ingenious but is limited to small sets of studies, since it requires that the sum of the *p* levels not exceed unity by very much. When the sum of the *p* levels does exceed unity, the overall *p* obtained tends to be too conservative unless special corrections are introduced.

3. Adding t's. A method that has none of the disadvantages of the preceding two methods was described by Winer (1971). Based on the result that the variance of the *t* distribution for any given *df* is $df/(df-2)$, it requires adding the obtained *t* values and dividing that sum by the square root of the sum of the *df*'s associated with the *t*'s after each *df* has been divided by $df-2$.

The result of the calculation is itself approximately a standard normal deviate that is associated with a particular probability level when each of the *t*'s is based on *df* of 10 or so. When applied to the data of our table, the *Winer method* yields $p = .01$, one-tail, a result very close to the earlier two results. The limitation of this method is that it cannot be employed at all when the size of the samples for which *t* is computed becomes less than three, because that would involve dividing by zero or by a negative value. In addition, the method may not give such good approximations to the normal with $df < 10$ for each *t*.

4. Adding Z's. Perhaps the simplest of all, the *Stouffer method* described in the last chapter (Mosteller & Bush, 1954) asks us only to add the standard normal deviates (or *Z*'s) associated with the *p*'s obtained, and divide by the square root of the number of studies being combined (Adcock, 1960; Cochran, 1954; Stouffer, Suchman, DeVinney, Star, & Williams, 1949, p. 45). Each *Z* was a standard normal deviate under the null hypothesis. The variance of the sum of independent normal deviates is the sum of their variances. Here, this sum is equal to the number of studies, since each study has unit variance. Our table shows results for the Stouffer method that are very close to those obtained by the method of adding *t*'s ($Z = 2.39$ vs. $Z = 2.33$).

5. Adding weighted Z's. Mosteller and Bush (1954) have suggested a technique that permits us to weight each standard normal deviate by the size of the sample on which it is based (or by its *df*), or by any other desirable positive weighting such as the elegance, internal validity, or real-life representativeness (ecological validity) of the individual study. The method, which was illustrated in the last chapter, requires us to add the products of our weights and Z's, and to divide this sum by the square root of the sum of the squared weights. Our table shows the results of the application of the weighted Stouffer method with df employed as weights. We note that the result is the lowest overall p we have seen. This is due to the fact that, for the example, the lowest p levels are given the heaviest weighting because they are associated with the largest sample sizes and df. Lancaster (1961) has noted that when weighting is employed, the Z method is preferable to weighting applied to the Fisher method for reasons of computational convenience and because the final sum obtained is again a normal variable. Finally, for the very special case of just two studies, Zelen and Joel (1959) describe the choice of weights to minimize type II errors.

6. Testing the mean p.   Edgington (1972b) has proposed a normal curve method to be used when there are four or more studies to be combined. The mean of the p's to be combined is subtracted from .50, and this quantity is multiplied by the square root of $12N$, where N is the number of studies to be combined. (The presence of a twelve derives from the fact that the variance of the population of p values is one-twelfth, when the null hypothesis of no treatment effects is true.)

7. Testing the mean Z.   In this modification of the Stouffer method, Mosteller and Bush (1954) first convert p levels to Z values. They then compute a t test on the mean Z value obtained with the df for t equal to the number of Z values available minus one. Mosteller and Bush, however, advise against this procedure when there are fewer than five studies to be combined. That suggestion grows out of the low power of the t test when based on few observations. Our table illustrates this low power by showing that this method yields the largest combined p of any of the methods reviewed.

Additional methods

1. Counting.   When the number of studies to be combined grows large, a number of counting methods can be employed (Brozek & Tiede, 1952; Jones & Fiske, 1953; Wilkinson, 1951). The number of p values below .50 can be called +, the number of p values above .50 can be called −, and a sign test can be performed. If twelve of fifteen results are consistent in either direction, the sign test tells us that results so rare "occur by chance" only 3.6 percent of the time. This procedure, and the closely related one that follows, have been employed by Hall (1979).

Table 11.2. *Counting method for assessing overall significance of a relationship (χ^2 method)*

Counts	Studies reaching $p \le .05$	Studies not reaching $p \le .05$	Σ
Obtained	12	108	120
Expected (if null hypothesis true)	6^a	114^b	120

Note:

$$\chi^2(1) = \Sigma \frac{(O-E)^2}{E} = \frac{(12-6)^2}{6} + \frac{(108-114)^2}{114} = 6.32, \quad p = .012 \qquad (11.8)$$

or, since $Z = [\chi^2(1)]^{1/2}$,

$$Z = [6.32]^{1/2} = 2.51, \quad p = .006, \text{ one-tail} \qquad (11.9)$$

[a]Computed from $.05(N) = .05(120) = 6$.
[b]Computed from $.95(N) = .95(120) = 114$.

The χ^2 statistic may also be useful in comparing the number of studies expected to reach a given level of significance, under the null hypothesis, with the number actually reaching that level (Rosenthal, 1969, 1976; Rosenthal & Rosnow, 1975a, 1975b; Rosenthal & Rubin, 1978a). In this application there are two cells in our table of counts, one for the number reaching some critical level of p, the other for the number not reaching that critical level of p. When there are 100 or more studies available, we can set our critical p level at .05. Our expected frequency for that cell is $.05N$ while our expected frequency for the other cell is $.95N$. For example, suppose that 12 of 120 studies show results at $p \le .05$ in the same direction. Then our expected frequencies for the two cells are $.05(120)$ and $.95(120)$ respectively, as shown in Table 11.2.

It is not necessary to set our critical value of p at .05. We could as well use .10 or .01. However, it is advisable to keep the expected frequency of our smaller cell at five or above. Therefore, we would not use a critical value of .01 unless we had at least 500 studies altogether. To keep our smaller expected frequency at five or more we would use a critical level of .10 if we had fifty studies, a critical level of .20 if we had twenty-five studies, and so forth. More generally, when there are fewer than 100 studies but more than nine, we enter in one cell an expected frequency of 5 and in the other an expected frequency of $N-5$. The observed frequency for the first cell, then, is the number of studies reaching a $p < 5/N$. The observed frequency for the second cell is the number of studies with $p > 5/N$. The resulting χ^2 can then be entered into a table of critical χ^2 values. Alternatively, the square root of χ^2 can be computed to yield Z, the standard normal deviate. Although clear-cut results on the issue are not available, it appears likely that the counting methods are not as powerful as other methods described here.

2. Blocking.   The last method, adapted from the procedure given by Snedecor and Cochran (1967; see also Cochran & Cox, 1957) requires that we reconstruct the means, sample sizes, and mean square within conditions for each of our studies. We then combine the data into an overall analysis of variance in which treatment condition is the main effect of primary interest and in which studies are regarded as a blocking variable. If required because of differences among the studies in their means and variances, the dependent variables of the studies can be put onto a common scale (e.g., zero mean and unit variance).

When studies are assumed to be a fixed factor, as they sometimes are (Cochran & Cox, 1957), or when the MS for treatments × studies is small relative to the MS within, the treatment effect is tested against the pooled MS within (Cochran & Cox, 1957). When the studies are regarded as a random factor and when the MS for treatments × studies is substantial relative to the MS within (say, $F > 2$), the treatments × studies effect is the appropriate error term for the treatment effect. Regardless of whether studies are viewed as fixed or random factors, the main effect of studies and the interaction of treatments × studies are tested against the MS within.

Substantial main effects of studies may or may not be of much interest, but substantial treatments × studies interaction effects will usually be of considerable interest. It will be instructive to study the residuals defining the interaction closely for clues as to the nature of the possible moderating variables affecting the operation of the treatment effect. Analysis of the residuals might show, for example, that it is the better (or more poorly) designed studies that show greater predicted effects. The blocking method is sometimes not applicable because authors have not reported sufficient data in their papers.

Table 11.3 illustrates this last method as applied to the set of five studies we have been using as our example (see Table 11.1). An unweighted means analysis of variance was computed and the results fell within the range of results obtained by our earlier described methods. The only real disadvantage of this approach is that it may involve considerably more work than some of the other methods. This will be especially true when the number of studies grows from just a few to dozens, scores, or hundreds. The computations for the unweighted means analysis of variance are shown next.

2.a. Computations: unweighted means.   The details of the unweighted means analysis of variance are given elsewhere (e.g., Rosenthal & Rosnow,

Table 11.3. *The blocking method of combining probabilities applied to the studies of Table 11.1*

Study	Control Mean	(n)	Experimental Mean	(n)	Mean	MS error
1	0.48	(21)	2.00	(21)	1.24	17.13
2	0.00	(31)	2.48	(31)	1.24	16.69
3	2.00	(6)	0.48	(6)	1.24	19.25
4	0.12	(16)	2.36	(16)	1.24	17.37
5	0.36	(11)	2.12	(11)	1.24	17.74
Mean	.592		1.888		1.24	17.64

Analysis of variance: unweighted means

Source	SS	df	MS	F
Treatments	4.1990	1	4.1990	2.98*
Studies	0.	4	0.[a]	—
Treatments × studies	5.2442	4	1.3110	—
Error		160	1.4110[b]	

*$Z = 1.70$, $p = .045$, one-tail.

[a]In the example constructed here and, more generally, in cases wherein the data from each study are standardized with zero mean and unit variance, the mean square for studies is always zero, that is, since the means of all studies have been set equal to each other (to zero) the between-studies SS and MS must equal zero.

[b]Computations are reviewed in the text.

1984, chapter 20). Basically, we perform our computations on the means of the control and experimental conditions of the five studies.

$$\text{Total } SS = \Sigma(M - \bar{M})^2 = (0.48 - 1.24)^2 + (2.00 - 1.24)^2 + \cdots$$
$$+ (0.36 - 1.24)^2 + (2.12 - 1.24)^2 = 9.4432 \quad (11.10)$$

$$\text{Row (studies) } SS = \Sigma[c(M_R - \bar{M})^2] = 2(1.24 - 1.24)^2 + \cdots$$
$$+ 2(1.24 - 1.24)^2 = 0 \quad (11.11)$$

$$\text{Column (treatments) } SS = \Sigma[r(M_C - \bar{M})^2]$$
$$= 5(.592 - 1.24)^2 + 5(1.888 - 1.24)^2$$
$$= 4.1990 \quad (11.12)$$

$$\text{Row} \times \text{Column } SS = \text{Total } SS - \text{Row } SS - \text{Column } SS$$
$$= 9.4432 - 0 - 4.1990 = 5.2442 \quad (11.13)$$

When divided by their appropriate *df* the Studies, Treatments, and Studies by Treatments SS's yield MS's of 0, 4.1990, and 1.3110, respectively.

The error term is obtained by dividing the *MS* error from the original one-way analysis of variance of the ten conditions (17.64) by the harmonic mean of the sample sizes, n_h. In this case $n_h = 12.5016$ so our error term is

$$\frac{17.64}{12.5016} = 1.4110$$

as shown in Table 11.3.

Choosing a method

Table 11.4 shows the advantages, limitations, and indications for use of each of the nine methods of combining probabilities. Various methods have special advantages under special circumstances. Suppose we were confronted by 200 studies, each with only the information provided that it did or did not reach a given alpha level. A counting method (χ^2) gives a very quick test, if not a very elegant or powerful estimate of overall probability. With so many studies to process we would probably decide against the blocking method on the grounds that the work required would not be justified by any special benefits. We would not be able to apply the basic method of adding probabilities for reasons given earlier. Most other methods are applicable, however.

If we were combining only a very few studies, we might favor the method of adding probabilities. We would avoid both the method of testing the mean *Z* and the counting methods, which do better on larger numbers of studies.

There is no "best" method under all conditions (Birnbaum, 1954), but the one that seems most serviceable under the largest range of conditions is that of adding *Z*'s, with or without weighting. When the number of studies is small, it can be suggested that at least two other procedures also be employed and the overall *p*'s emerging from all three be reported. When the number of studies is large, a useful combination would seem to be the method of adding *Z*'s combined with one or more of the counting methods as a check. Practical experience with the various methods suggests that there is only rarely a serious discrepancy among appropriately chosen methods. It goes without saying, of course, that any overall *p* that has been computed (or its associated test statistic with *df*) should be reported and not suppressed for being higher or lower than the investigator might like.

To make possible the computations described in this chapter, authors should routinely report the exact *t*, *F*, *Z*, or other test statistic along with its *df* or *N*, rather than simply making such vague statements as "*t* was significant at $p < .05$."

Table 11.4. *Advantages and limitations of nine methods of combining probabilities*

Method	Advantages	Limitations	Use when
1. Adding logs	Well-established historically	Cumulates poorly; can support opposite conclusions.	N of studies small (≤ 5)
2. Adding p's	Good power	Inapplicable when N of studies (or p's) large unless complex corrections are introduced.	N of studies small ($\Sigma p \leq 1.0$)
3. Adding t's	Unaffected by N of studies given minimum df per study	Inapplicable when t's based on very few df.	Studies not based on too few df
4. Adding Z's	Routinely applicable; simple	Assumes unit variance when under some conditions Type I or Type II errors may be increased.	Anytime
5. Adding weighted Z's	Routinely applicable, permits weighting	Assumes unit variance when under some conditions Type I or Type II errors may be increased.	Whenever weighting desired
6. Testing mean p	Simple	N of studies should not be less than four.	N of studies ≥ 4
7. Testing mean Z	No assumption of unit variance	Low power when N of studies small.	N of studies ≥ 5
8. Counting	Simple and robust	Large N of studies needed; may be low in power.	N of studies large
9. Blocking	Displays all means for inspection, thus facilitating search for *moderators* (variables altering the relationship between independent and dependent variables).	Laborious when N large; insufficient data may be available.	N of studies not too large

Reporting the test statistic along with an approximate p level also seems preferable to reporting the "exact" p level for several reasons: (1) the exact p level may be difficult to determine without a computer, (2) ambiguity about one-tail versus two-tail usage is avoided, and (3) the test statistic allows us to compute exact p as well as the effect size. Speaking of effect size, it would be highly desirable to the enterprise of comparing and combining research results if editors routinely required the report of an effect size (e.g., r, g, Δ, or d) for every test statistic reported.

Finally, it should be noted that even if we have established a low combined p, we have said absolutely nothing about the typical size of the effect the "existence" of which we have been examining. We owe it to our readers to give for each combined p estimate an estimate of the probable size of the effect in terms of a correlation coefficient, a σ unit, or some other estimate. This estimated effect size should be accompanied, when possible, by a confidence interval.

On not combining raw data

Sometimes it happens that the raw data of two or more studies are available. We have seen how these data could be appropriately combined in the method of blocking. There may, however, be a temptation to combine the raw data without first blocking or subdividing the data on the basis of the studies producing the data. The purpose of this section is to help avoid that temptation by showing the very misleading or even paradoxical results that can occur when raw data are pooled without blocking.

Table 11.5 shows the results of four studies in which the correlation between variables X and Y is shown for two subjects. The number of subjects per study makes no difference and the small number ($n = 2$) is employed here only to keep the example simple. For each of the four studies the correlation (r) between X and Y is -1.00. However, no matter how we combine the raw data of these four studies, the correlation is never negative again. Indeed, the range of r's is from zero (as when we pool the data between any two adjacent studies) to .80 (as when we pool the data from studies 1 and 4). The remainder of Table 11.5 shows the six different correlations that are possible (.00, .45, .60, .67, .72, .80) as a function of which studies are pooled.

How can these anomalous results be explained? Examination of the means of the X and Y variables for the four studies of Table 11.5 helps us understand. The means of the X and Y variables differ substantially from study to study and are substantially positively correlated. Thus, in study 1 the X and Y scores (although perfectly negatively correlated) are all quite low relative to the X and Y scores of study 4 which are all quite high (although also perfectly negatively correlated). Thus, *across* these studies in which the varia-

Table 11.5. *Effects of pooling raw data: four studies*

	Study 1		Study 2		Study 3		Study 4	
	X	Y	X	Y	X	Y	X	Y
Subject 1	2	0	4	2	6	4	8	6
Subject 2	0	2	2	4	4	6	6	8
Mean	1.0	1.0	3.0	3.0	5.0	5.0	7.0	7.0
r		−1.00		−1.00		−1.00		−1.00

Correlations obtained

When pooling:	Two studies			Three or four studies		
r =	.00	.60	.80	.45	.67	.72
Pooled studies:	1+2	1+3	1+4	1, 2, 3	1, 2, 3, 4	1, 2, 4
	2+3	2+4		2, 3, 4		1, 3, 4
	3+4					

tion is substantial, we have an overall positive correlation between variables *X* and *Y*. *Within* these studies, where the correlations are negative (−1.00) the variation in scores is relatively small, small enough to be swamped by the variation between studies.

Although there may be times when it is useful to array the data from multiple studies in order to see an overall pattern of results, or to see what might happen if we planned a single study with variation equivalent to that shown by a set of pooled studies, Table 11.5 serves as serious warning of how pooled raw data can lead to conclusions (though not necessarily "wrong") opposite to those obtained from individual, less variable studies.

Yule's or Simpson's Paradox. Over 80 years ago G. Udny Yule (1903) described a related problem in dealing with 2×2 tables of counts. He showed how two studies in which no relationship ($r = .00$) was found between the variables defined by the two rows and the two columns, could yield a positive correlation ($r = .19$) when the raw data were pooled. Similarly, Simpson (1951) showed how two studies with modest positive correlations (r's = .03 and .04) could yield a zero correlation when the raw data were pooled. Table 11.6 illustrates the problem described by Yule (1903), by Simpson (1951) and by others (e.g., Birch, 1963; Blyth, 1972; Fienberg, 1977; Glass, McGaw, & Smith, 1981; and Upton, 1978).

Table 11.6. *Effects of pooling tables of counts*

Example I	Study 1		Study 2		Pooled	
	Alive	Dead	Alive	Dead	Alive	Dead
Treatment	100	1,000	100	10	200	1,010
Control	10	100	1,000	100	1,010	200
Σ	110	1,100	1,100	110	1,210	1,210
	$r = 0$		$r = 0$		$r = .67$	

Example II	Study 1		Study 2		Pooled	
	Alive	Dead	Alive	Dead	Alive	Dead
Treatment	50	100	50	0	100	100
Control	0	50	100	50	100	100
Σ	50	150	150	50	200	200
	$r = .33$		$r = .33$		$r = 0$	

In Example I of Table 11.6 we see two studies showing zero correlation between the treatment condition and the outcome. When the raw data of these two studies are pooled, however, we find a dramatic correlation of .67 suggesting that the treatment was harmful. Note that in Study 1, only 9 percent of patients survived, while 91 percent received the treatment, whereas in Study 2, 91 percent of patients survived but only 9 percent received the treatment. It is these inequalities of row and column totals that lead to Yule's (or Simpson's) Paradoxes.

Example II of Table 11.6 shows two studies each obtaining a strong effect favoring the treatment condition ($r = .33$). When these two studies were pooled, however, these strong effects vanished. Note that in Study 1, only 25 percent of patients survived while 75 percent received the treatment, whereas in Study 2, 75 percent of patients survived but only 25 percent received the treatment. Had row and column totals been equal, the paradoxes of pooling would not have occurred.

The moral of the pooling paradoxes is clear. Except for the exploratory purposes mentioned above, raw data should *not* be pooled without blocking. In most cases, effect sizes and significance levels should be computed separately for each study and only then combined.

Special issues

Earlier in this chapter we saw that the method of adding Z's was perhaps the most generally serviceable method for combining probabilities. In the following section we provide procedures facilitating the use of this method.

Obtaining the value of Z

The method of adding Z's requires that we begin by converting the obtained one-tailed p level of each study to its equivalent Z. The value of Z is zero when the one-tailed p is .50, positive as p decreases from $p = .50$ to p close to zero, and negative as p increases from .50 to p close to unity. Thus a one-tailed p of .01 has an associated Z of 2.33, while a one-tailed p of .99 has an associated Z of -2.33. These values can be located in the table of probabilities associated with observed values of Z in the normal distribution found in most textbooks on statistics.

Unfortunately for the meta-analyst, few studies report the Z associated with their obtained p. Worse still, the obtained p's are often given imprecisely as $< .05$ or $< .01$, so that p might be .001 or .0001 or .00001. If p is all that is given in a study, all we can do is use a table of the normal distribution to find the Z associated with a reported p. Thus, one-tailed p's of .05, .01, and .001 are found to have associated Z's of 1.65, 2.33, and 3.09, respectively. (If a result is simply called "nonsignificant," and if no further information is available, we have little choice but to treat the result as a p of .50, $Z = 0.00$.)

Since p's reported in research papers tend to be imprecisely reported we can do a better job of combining p's by going back to the original test statistics employed, for example, t, F, or χ^2. Fortunately, many journals require that these statistics, along with their df, be reported routinely. The df for t and for the denominator of the F test in analysis of variance tell us about the size of the study. The df for χ^2 is analogous to the df for the numerator of the F test in analysis of variance and so tells us about the number of conditions, not the number of sampling units. Fortunately, the 1983 edition of the *Publication Manual* of the American Psychological Association has added a requirement that when reporting χ^2 test statistics the total N be given along with the df.

Test statistics. If a t test was employed, we can use a t table to find the Z associated with the obtained t. Suppose $t(20) = 2.09$ so that $p = .025$, one-tailed. We enter the t table at the row for $df = 20$ and read across to the t value of 2.09. Then we read down the column to the entry for $df = \infty$, which is the Z identical to the value of t with ∞ df (1.96). Suppose, however, that our t was 12.00 with 144 df. Even extended tables of t cannot help us when values of t are so large for substantial df (Federighi, 1959; Rosenthal & Rosnow, 1984). A very accurate estimation of Z from t is available for such circumstances (Wallace, 1959):

$$Z = \left[df \log_e \left(1 + \frac{t^2}{df} \right) \right]^{1/2} \left[1 - \frac{1}{2\,df} \right]^{1/2} \tag{11.14}$$

A very useful and conservative approximation to this formula is also available (Rosenthal & Rubin, 1979a):

$$Z = t \left(1 - \frac{t^2}{4\,df} \right) \tag{11.15}$$

This approximation works best when $t^2 < df$; when $t^2 = df$, this approximation tends to be 10 percent smaller than the Z obtained from equation 11.14.

If the test statistic employed was F (from analysis of variance) and df for the numerator was unity, we take the $[F]^{1/2}$ as t and proceed as we did in the case of t with df equal to the df of the denominator of the F ratio. We should note that F ratios of $df > 1$ in the numerator cannot be used in combining p levels to address a directional hypothesis.

When $[F]^{1/2}$ or $[\chi^2]^{1/2}$ is employed we must be sure that the Z is given the appropriate sign to indicate the direction of the effect.

Effect size estimates.   Sometimes we want to find Z for a study in which no test statistic is given (e.g., t, F, χ^2), but an effect size estimator such as r (including point biserial r and phi), g, Δ, or d is given along with a rough p level indicator such as $p < .05$. In those cases we can often get a serviceable direct approximation of Z by using the fact that $(\text{phi})^2 = \chi^2(1)/N$ so that $N(\text{phi})^2 = \chi^2(1)$ and $[N]^{1/2}(\text{phi}) = [\chi^2(1)]^{1/2} = Z$.

In the case of r or point biserial r, multiplying by $[N]^{1/2}$ will yield a generally conservative approximation to Z. A more accurate value can be obtained by solving for t in the equation:

$$t = \frac{r}{[1 - r^2]^{1/2}} \times [df]^{1/2} \quad \text{or} \quad t = \frac{r}{[1 - r^2]^{1/2}} \times [N - 2]^{1/2} \tag{6.3}$$

and then employing t to estimate Z as shown in equations 11.14 or 11.15.

We will not review here how to get t from the other effect size estimators but that information is found in equations 6.3–6.13 (Tables 6.1 and 6.2), 10.19, and 10.20.

The file drawer problem

Statisticians and behavioral researchers have long suspected that the studies published in the behavioral and social sciences are a biased sample of the studies that are actually carried out (Bakan, 1967; McNemar, 1960; Smart, 1964; Sterling, 1959). The extreme view of this problem, the *file drawer problem,* is that the journals are filled with the 5 percent of the studies that show type I errors, while the file drawers back at the lab are filled with the 95 percent of the studies that show nonsignificant (e.g., $p > .05$) results (Rosenthal, 1979a).

In the past, there was very little we could do to assess the net effect of studies tucked away in file drawers that did not make the magic .05 level (Nelson et al., 1985; Rosenthal & Gaito, 1963, 1964). Now, however, although no definitive solution to the problem is available, we can establish reasonable boundaries on the problem and estimate the degree of damage to any research conclusion that could be done by the file drawer problem. The fundamental idea in coping with the file drawer problem is simply to calculate the number of studies averaging null results that must be in the file drawers before the overall probability of a type I error can be just brought to any desired level of significance, say $p = .05$. This number of filed studies, or the tolerance for future null results, is then evaluated for whether such a tolerance level is small enough to threaten the overall conclusion drawn by the reviewer. If the overall level of significance of the research review will be brought down to the level of *just significant* by the addition of just a few more null results, the finding is not resistant to the file drawer threat.

Computation. To find the number (X) of new, filed, or unretrieved studies averaging null results required to bring the new overall p to any desired level, say, just significant at $p = .05$ ($Z = 1.645$), one simply writes:

$$1.645 = \frac{K\bar{Z}}{[K+X]^{1/2}} \tag{11.16}$$

where K is the number of studies combined and $\bar{Z}$ is the mean Z obtained for the K studies.

Rearrangement shows that

$$X = \frac{K[K\bar{Z}^2 - 2.706]}{2.706} \tag{11.17}$$

An alternative formula that may be more convenient when the sum of the Z's (ΣZ) is given rather than the mean Z, is as follows:

$$X = \frac{(\Sigma Z)^2}{2.706} - K \qquad (11.18)$$

One method based on counting rather than adding Z's may be easier to compute and can be employed when exact p levels are not available; but it is probably less powerful. If X is the number of new studies required to bring the overall p to .50 (not to .05), s is the number of summarized studies significant at $p < .05$ and n is the number of summarized studies not significant at .05, then

$$X = 19s - n \qquad (11.19)$$

where 19 is the ratio of the total number of nonsignificant (at $p > .05$) results to the number of significant (at $p \leq .05$) results expected when the null hypothesis is true.

Another conservative alternative when exact p levels are not available is to set $Z = .00$ for any nonsignificant result and to set $Z = 1.645$ for any result significant at $p < .05$.

The equations above all assume that each of the K studies is independent of all other $K - 1$ studies, at least in the sense of employing different sampling units. There are other senses of independence, however; for example, we can think of two or more studies conducted in a given laboratory as less independent than two or more studies conducted in different laboratories. Such nonindependence can be assessed by such procedures as intraclass correlations. Whether nonindependence of this type serves to increase type I or type II errors appears to depend in part on the relative magnitude of the Z's obtained from the studies that are "correlated" or "too similar." If the correlated Z's are, on the average, as high as or higher than the grand mean Z corrected for nonindependence, the combined Z we compute treating all studies as independent will be too large, leading to an increase in type I errors. If the correlated Z's are, on the average, clearly low relative to the grand mean Z corrected for nonindependence, the combined Z we compute treating all studies as independent will tend to be too small, leading to an increase in type II errors.

Illustration.   In 1969, ninety-four experiments examining the effects of interpersonal self-fulfilling prophecies were summarized (Rosenthal, 1969). The mean Z of these studies was 1.014, K was 94, and Z for the studies combined was:

$$\frac{\Sigma Z}{[K]^{1/2}} = \frac{K\bar{Z}}{[K]^{1/2}} = \frac{94(1.014)}{[94]^{1/2}} = 9.83$$

How many new, filed, or unretrieved studies (X) would be required to bring this very large Z down to a barely significant level ($Z = 1.645$)? From equation 11.17 of the preceding section:

$$X = \frac{K[K\bar{Z}^2 - 2.706]}{2.706} = \frac{94[94(1.014)^2 - 2.706]}{2.706} = 3263$$

One finds that 3,263 studies averaging null results ($\bar{Z} = .00$) must be crammed into file drawers before one would conclude that the overall results were due to sampling bias in the studies summarized by the reviewer. In a more recent summary of the same area of research (Rosenthal & Rubin, 1978a) the mean Z of 345 studies was 1.22, K was 345, and X was 65,123. Thus, over 65,000 unreported studies averaging a null result would have to exist somewhere before the overall results could reasonably be ascribed to sampling bias.

Guidelines for a tolerance level. At the present time, no firm guidelines can be given as to what constitutes an unlikely number of unretrieved and/ or unpublished studies. For some areas of research 100 or even 500 unpublished and unretrieved studies may be a plausible state of affairs while for others even ten or twenty seems unlikely. Probably any rough and ready guide should be based partly on K so that as more studies are known it becomes more plausible that other studies in that area may be in those file drawers. Perhaps we could regard as robust to the file drawer problem any combined results for which the tolerance level (X) reaches $5K + 10$. That seems a conservative but reasonable tolerance level; the $5K$ portion suggests that it is unlikely that the file drawers have more than five times as many studies as the reviewer, and the $+10$ sets the minimum number of studies that could be filed away at fifteen (when $K = 1$).

It appears that more and more reviewers of research literatures will be estimating average effect sizes and combined p's of the studies they summarize. It would be very helpful to readers if for each combined p they presented, reviewers also gave the tolerance for future null results associated with their overall significance level.

Appendix: Statistical Tables

Table 1 Table of standard normal deviates (Z)

				Second digit of Z					
Z	.00	.01	.02	.03	.04	.05	.06	.07	.08	.09
.0	.5000	.4960	.4920	.4880	.4840	.4801	.4761	.4721	.4681	.4641
.1	.4602	.4562	.4522	.4483	.4443	.4404	.4364	.4325	.4286	.4247
.2	.4207	.4168	.4129	.4090	.4052	.4013	.3974	.3936	.3897	.3859
.3	.3821	.3783	.3745	.3707	.3669	.3632	.3594	.3557	.3520	.3483
.4	.3446	.3409	.3372	.3336	.3300	.3264	.3228	.3192	.3156	.3121
.5	.3085	.3050	.3015	.2981	.2946	.2912	.2877	.2843	.2810	.2776
.6	.2743	.2709	.2676	.2643	.2611	.2578	.2546	.2514	.2483	.2451
.7	.2420	.2389	.2358	.2327	.2296	.2266	.2236	.2206	.2177	.2148
.8	.2119	.2090	.2061	.2033	.2005	.1977	.1949	.1922	.1894	.1867
.9	.1841	.1814	.1788	.1762	.1736	.1711	.1685	.1660	.1635	.1611
1.0	.1587	.1562	.1539	.1515	.1492	.1469	.1446	.1423	.1401	.1379
1.1	.1357	.1335	.1314	.1292	.1271	.1251	.1230	.1210	.1190	.1170
1.2	.1151	.1131	.1112	.1093	.1075	.1056	.1038	.1020	.1003	.0985
1.3	.0968	.0951	.0934	.0918	.0901	.0885	.0869	.0853	.0838	.0823
1.4	.0808	.0793	.0778	.0764	.0749	.0735	.0721	.0708	.0694	.0681
1.5	.0668	.0655	.0643	.0630	.0618	.0606	.0594	.0582	.0571	.0559
1.6	.0548	.0537	.0526	.0516	.0505	.0495	.0485	.0475	.0465	.0455
1.7	.0446	.0436	.0427	.0418	.0409	.0401	.0392	.0384	.0375	.0367
1.8	.0359	.0351	.0344	.0336	.0329	.0322	.0314	.0307	.0301	.0294
1.9	.0287	.0281	.0274	.0268	.0262	.0256	.0250	.0244	.0239	.0233
2.0	.0228	.0222	.0217	.0212	.0207	.0202	.0197	.0192	.0188	.0183
2.1	.0179	.0174	.0170	.0166	.0162	.0158	.0154	.0150	.0146	.0143
2.2	.0139	.0136	.0132	.0129	.0125	.0122	.0119	.0116	.0113	.0110
2.3	.0107	.0104	.0102	.0099	.0096	.0094	.0091	.0089	.0087	.0084
2.4	.0082	.0080	.0078	.0075	.0073	.0071	.0069	.0068	.0066	.0064
2.5	.0062	.0060	.0059	.0057	.0055	.0054	.0052	.0051	.0049	.0048
2.6	.0047	.0045	.0044	.0043	.0041	.0040	.0039	.0038	.0037	.0036
2.7	.0035	.0034	.0033	.0032	.0031	.0030	.0029	.0028	.0027	.0026
2.8	.0026	.0025	.0024	.0023	.0023	.0022	.0021	.0021	.0020	.0019
2.9	.0019	.0018	.0018	.0017	.0016	.0016	.0015	.0015	.0014	.0014
3.0	.0013	.0013	.0013	.0012	.0012	.0011	.0011	.0011	.0010	.0010
3.1	.0010	.0009	.0009	.0009	.0008	.0008	.0008	.0008	.0007	.0007
3.2	.0007									
3.3	.0005									
3.4	.0003									
3.5	.00023									
3.6	.00016									
3.7	.00011									
3.8	.00007									
3.9	.00005									
4.0*	.00003									

Note: All p values are one-tailed in this table.

* Additional values of Z are found in the bottom row of Table 3 since t values for $df = \infty$ are also Z values.

Source: Reproduced from S. Siegel, *Nonparametric Statistics*, McGraw-Hill, New York, 1956, p. 247, with the permission of the publisher.

Table 2 Summary table of t

df	$p = .9$	.8	.7	.6	.5	.4	.3	.2	.1	.05	.02	.01
1	.158	.325	.510	.727	1.000	1.376	1.963	3.078	6.314	12.706	31.821	63.657
2	.142	.289	.445	.617	.816	1.061	1.386	1.886	2.920	4.303	6.965	9.925
3	.137	.277	.424	.584	.765	.978	1.250	1.638	2.353	3.182	4.541	5.841
4	.134	.271	.414	.569	.741	.941	1.190	1.533	2.132	2.776	3.747	4.604
5	.132	.267	.408	.559	.727	.920	1.156	1.476	2.015	2.571	3.365	4.032
6	.131	.265	.404	.553	.718	.906	1.134	1.440	1.943	2.447	3.143	3.707
7	.130	.263	.402	.549	.711	.896	1.119	1.415	1.895	2.365	2.998	3.499
8	.130	.262	.399	.546	.706	.889	1.108	1.397	1.860	2.306	2.896	3.355
9	.129	.261	.398	.543	.703	.883	1.100	1.383	1.833	2.262	2.821	3.250
10	.129	.260	.397	.542	.700	.879	1.093	1.372	1.812	2.228	2.764	3.169
11	.129	.260	.396	.540	.697	.876	1.088	1.363	1.796	2.201	2.718	3.106
12	.128	.259	.395	.539	.695	.873	1.083	1.356	1.782	2.179	2.681	3.055
13	.128	.259	.394	.538	.694	.870	1.079	1.350	1.771	2.160	2.650	3.012
14	.128	.258	.393	.537	.692	.868	1.076	1.345	1.761	2.145	2.624	2.977
15	.128	.258	.393	.536	.691	.866	1.074	1.341	1.753	2.131	2.602	2.947
16	.128	.258	.392	.535	.690	.865	1.071	1.337	1.746	2.120	2.583	2.921
17	.128	.257	.392	.534	.689	.863	1.069	1.333	1.740	2.110	2.567	2.898
18	.127	.257	.392	.534	.688	.862	1.067	1.330	1.734	2.101	2.552	2.878
19	.127	.257	.391	.533	.688	.861	1.066	1.328	1.729	2.093	2.539	2.861
20	.127	.257	.391	.533	.687	.860	1.064	1.325	1.725	2.086	2.528	2.845
21	.127	.257	.391	.532	.686	.859	1.063	1.323	1.721	2.080	2.518	2.831
22	.127	.256	.390	.532	.686	.858	1.061	1.321	1.717	2.074	2.508	2.819
23	.127	.256	.390	.532	.685	.858	1.060	1.319	1.714	2.069	2.500	2.807
24	.127	.256	.390	.531	.685	.857	1.059	1.318	1.711	2.064	2.492	2.797
25	.127	.256	.390	.531	.684	.856	1.058	1.316	1.708	2.060	2.485	2.787
26	.127	.256	.390	.531	.684	.856	1.058	1.315	1.706	2.056	2.479	2.779
27	.127	.256	.389	.531	.684	.855	1.057	1.314	1.703	2.052	2.473	2.771
28	.127	.256	.389	.530	.683	.855	1.056	1.313	1.701	2.048	2.467	2.763
29	.127	.256	.389	.530	.683	.854	1.055	1.311	1.699	2.045	2.462	2.756
30	.127	.256	.389	.530	.683	.854	1.055	1.310	1.697	2.042	2.457	2.750
∞	.12566	.25335	.38532	.52440	.67449	.84162	1.03643	1.28155	1.64485	1.95996	2.32634	2.57582

Note: All p values are *two-tailed* in this table. Table 3 presents a more detailed table of t values for *one-tailed* $p \leq .25$.
Source: Reproduced from E. F. Lindquist, *Design and Analysis of Experiments in Psychology and Education*, Houghton Mifflin, Boston, 1953, p. 38, with the permission of the publisher.

Table 3 Extended table of *t*

df \ p	.25	.10	.05	.025	.01	.005	.0025	.001
1	1.000	3.078	6.314	12.706	31.821	63.657	127.321	318.30*
2	.816	1.886	2.920	4.303	6.965	9.925	14.089	22.32˙
3	.765	1.638	2.353	3.182	4.541	5.841	7.453	10.21˖
4	.741	1.533	2.132	2.776	3.747	4.604	5 598	7.17.
5	.727	1.476	2.015	2.571	3.365	4.032	4.773	5.89˙
6	.718	1.440	1.943	2.447	3.143	3.707	4.317	5.20▪
7	.711	1.415	1.895	2.365	2.998	3.499	4.029	4.78.
8	.706	1.397	1.860	2.306	2.896	3.355	3.833	4.50˙
9	.703	1.383	1.833	2.262	2.821	3.250	3.690	4.29˙
10	.700	1.372	1.812	2.228	2.764	3.169	3.581	4.144
11	.697	1.363	1.796	2.201	2.718	3.106	3.497	4.02˙
12	.695	1.356	1.782	2.179	2.681	3.055	3.428	3.93C
13	.694	1.350	1.771	2.160	2.650	3.012	3.372	3.85.
14	.692	1.345	1.761	2.145	2.624	2.977	3.326	3.78˙
15	.691	1.341	1.753	2.131	2.602	2.947	3.286	3.73˸
16	.690	1.337	1.746	2.120	2.583	2.921	3.252	3.68˓
17	.689	1.333	1.740	2.110	2.567	2.898	3.223	3.64˓
18	.688	1.330	1.734	2.101	2.552	2.878	3.197	3.61C
19	.688	1.328	1.729	2.093	2.539	2.861	3.174	3.57˹
20	.687	1.325	1.725	2.086	2.528	2.845	3.153	3.552
21	.686	1.323	1.721	2.080	2.518	2.831	3.135	3.527
22	.686	1.321	1.717	2.074	2.508	2.819	3.119	3.50˹
23	.685	1.319	1.714	2.069	2.500	2.807	3.104	3.48˹
24	.685	1.318	1.711	2.064	2.492	2.797	3.090	3.46˹
25	.684	1.316	1.708	2.060	2.485	2.787	3.078	3.45C
26	.684	1.315	1.706	2.056	2.479	2.779	3.067	3.43˹
27	.684	1.314	1.703	2.052	2.473	2.771	3.057	3.42˩
28	.683	1.313	1.701	2.048	2.467	2.763	3.047	3.408
29	.683	1.311	1.699	2.045	2.462	2.756	3.038	3.396
30	.683	1.310	1.697	2.042	2.457	2.750	3.030	3.385
35	.682	1.306	1.690	2.030	2.438	2.724	2.996	3.340▪
40	.681	1.303	1.684	2.021	2.423	2.704	2.971	3.307
45	.680	1.301	1.679	2.014	2.412	2.690	2.952	3.281
50	.679	1.299	1.676	2.009	2.403	2.678	2.937	3.261
55	.679	1.297	1.673	2.004	2.396	2.668	2.925	3.245
60	.679	1.296	1.671	2.000	2.390	2.660	2.915	3.232
70	.678	1.294	1.667	1.994	2.381	2.648	2.899	3.211
80	.678	1.292	1.664	1.990	2.374	2.639	2.887	3.195
90	.677	1.291	1.662	1.987	2.368	2.632	2.878	3.183
100	.677	1.290	1.660	1.984	2.364	2.626	2.871	3.174
200	.676	1.286	1.652	1.972	2.345	2.601	2.838	3.131
500	.675	1.283	1.648	1.965	2.334	2.586	2.820	3.107
1,000	.675	1.282	1.646	1.962	2.330	2.581	2.813	3.098
2,000	.675	1.282	1.645	1.961	2.328	2.578	2.810	3.094
10,000	.675	1.282	1.645	1.960	2.327	2.576	2.808	3.091
∞	.674	1.282	1.645	1.960	2.326	2.576	2.807	3.090

Note: All *p* values are one-tailed in this table. For *p* values > .25 see Table 2.

Table 3 (*Continued*)

df \ p	.0005	.00025	.0001	.00005	.000025	.00001
1	636.619	1,273.239	3,183.099	6,366.198	12,732.395	31,830.989
2	31.598	44.705	70.700	99.992	141.416	223.603
3	12.924	16.326	22.204	28.000	35.298	47.928
4	8.610	10.306	13.034	15.544	18.522	23.332
5	6.869	7.976	9.678	11.178	12.893	15.547
6	5.959	6.788	8.025	9.082	10.261	12.032
7	5.408	6.082	7.063	7.885	8.782	10.103
8	5.041	5.618	6.442	7.120	7.851	8.907
9	4.781	5.291	6.010	6.594	7.215	8.102
10	4.587	5.049	5.694	6.211	6.757	7.527
11	4.437	4.863	5.453	5.921	6.412	7.098
12	4.318	4.716	5.263	5.694	6.143	6.756
13	4.221	4.597	5.111	5.513	5.928	6.501
14	4.140	4.499	4.985	5.363	5.753	6.287
15	4.073	4.417	4.880	5.239	5.607	6.109
16	4.015	4.346	4.791	5.134	5.484	5.960
17	3.965	4.286	4.714	5.044	5.379	5.832
18	3.922	4.233	4.648	4.966	5.288	5.722
19	3.883	4.187	4.590	4.897	5.209	5.627
20	3.850	4.146	4.539	4.837	5.139	5.543
21	3.819	4.110	4.493	4.784	5.077	5.469
22	3.792	4.077	4.452	4.736	5.022	5.402
23	3.768	4.048	4.415	4.693	4.972	5.343
24	3.745	4.021	4.382	4.654	4.927	5.290
25	3.725	3.997	4.352	4.619	4.887	5.241
26	3.707	3.974	4.324	4.587	4.850	5.197
27	3.690	3.954	4.299	4.558	4.816	5.157
28	3.674	3.935	4.275	4.530	4.784	5.120
29	3.659	3.918	4.254	4.506	4.756	5.086
30	3.646	3.902	4.234	4.482	4.729	5.054
35	3.591	3.836	4.153	4.389	4.622	4.927
40	3.551	3.788	4.094	4.321	4.544	4.835
45	3.520	3.752	4.049	4.269	4.485	4.766
50	3.496	3.723	4.014	4.228	4.438	4.711
55	3.476	3.700	3.986	4.196	4.401	4.667
60	3.460	3.681	3.962	4.169	4.370	4.631
70	3.435	3.651	3.926	4.127	4.323	4.576
80	3.416	3.629	3.899	4.096	4.288	4.535
90	3.402	3.612	3.878	4.072	4.261	4.503
100	3.390	3.598	3.862	4.053	4.240	4.478
200	3.340	3.539	3.789	3.970	4.146	4.369
500	3.310	3.504	3.747	3.922	4.091	4.306
1,000	3.300	3.492	3.733	3.906	4.073	4.285
2,000	3.295	3.486	3.726	3.898	4.064	4.275
10,000	3.292	3.482	3.720	3.892	4.058	4.267
∞	3.291	3.481	3.719	3.891	4.056	4.265

Note: All p values are one-tailed in this table.

Table 3 (*Continued*)

df	.000005	.0000025	.000001	.0000005	.00000025	.0000001
1	63,661.977	127,323.954	318,309.886	636,619.772	1,273,239.545	3,183,098.86?
2	316.225	447.212	707.106	999.999	1,414.213	2,236.06?
3	60.397	76.104	103.299	130.155	163.989	222.57?
4	27.771	33.047	41.578	49.459	58.829	73.98?
5	17.807	20.591	24.771	28.477	32.734	39.34?
6	13.555	15.260	17.830	20.047	22.532	26.28?
7	11.215	12.437	14.241	15.764	17.447	19.93.
8	9.782	10.731	12.110	13.257	14.504	16.32?
9	8.827	9.605	10.720	11.637	12.623	14.04?
10	8.150	8.812	9.752	10.516	11.328	12.49?
11	7.648	8.227	9.043	9.702	10.397	11.38?
12	7.261	7.780	8.504	9.085	9.695	10.55?
13	6.955	7.427	8.082	8.604	9.149	9.90?
14	6.706	7.142	7.743	8.218	8.713	9.40?
15	6.502	6.907	7.465	7.903	8.358	8.98?
16	6.330	6.711	7.233	7.642	8.064	8.64?
17	6.184	6.545	7.037	7.421	7.817	8.35?
18	6.059	6.402	6.869	7.232	7.605	8.11?
19	5.949	6.278	6.723	7.069	7.423	7.90?
20	5.854	6.170	6.597	6.927	7.265	7.72?
21	5.769	6.074	6.485	6.802	7.126	7.56?
22	5.694	5.989	6.386	6.692	7.003	7.42?
23	5.627	5.913	6.297	6.593	6.893	7.29?
24	5.566	5.845	6.218	6.504	6.795	7.18?
25	5.511	5.783	6.146	6.424	6.706	7.08?
26	5.461	5.726	6.081	6.352	6.626	6.993
27	5.415	5.675	6.021	6.286	6.553	6.910
28	5.373	5.628	5.967	6.225	6.486	6.835
29	5.335	5.585	5.917	6.170	6.426	6.765
30	5.299	5.545	5.871	6.119	6.369	6.701
35	5.156	5.385	5.687	5.915	6.143	6.447
40	5.053	5.269	5.554	5.768	5.983	6.266
45	4.975	5.182	5.454	5.659	5.862	6.130
50	4.914	5.115	5.377	5.573	5.769	6.025
55	4.865	5.060	5.315	5.505	5.694	5.942
60	4.825	5.015	5.264	5.449	5.633	5.873
70	4.763	4.946	5.185	5.363	5.539	5.768
80	4.717	4.896	5.128	5.300	5.470	5.691
90	4.682	4.857	5.084	5.252	5.417	5.633
100	4.654	4.826	5.049	5.214	5.376	5.587
200	4.533	4.692	4.897	5.048	5.196	5.387
500	4.463	4.615	4.810	4.953	5.094	5.273
1,000	4.440	4.590	4.781	4.922	5.060	5.236
2,000	4.428	4.578	4.767	4.907	5.043	5.218
10,000	4.419	4.567	4.756	4.895	5.029	5.203
∞	4.417	4.565	4.753	4.892	5.026	5.199

Note: All p values are one-tailed in this table.
Standard normal deviates (Z) corresponding to t can be estimated quite accurately from:

$$Z = \left[df \log_e \left(1 + \frac{t^2}{df} \right) \right]^{1/2} \left[1 - \frac{1}{2df} \right]^{1/2}$$

Source: Reproduced from E. T. Federighi, Extended tables of the percentage points of Student's distribution, *Journal of the American Statistical Association*, 1959, *54*, 683–688, with the permission of th? publisher.

Table 4 Table of F

df_2	p	df_1 1	2	3	4	5	6	8	12	24	∞
1	.001	405284	500000	540379	562500	576405	585937	598144	610667	623497	636619
	.005	16211	20000	21615	22500	23056	23437	23925	24426	24940	25465
	.01	4052	4999	5403	5625	5764	5859	5981	6106	6234	6366
	.025	647.79	799.50	864.16	899.58	921.85	937.11	956.66	976.71	997.25	1018.30
	.05	161.45	199.50	215.71	224.58	230.16	233.99	238.88	243.91	249.05	254.32
	.10	39.86	49.50	53.59	55.83	57.24	58.20	59.44	60.70	62.00	63.33
	.20	9.47	12.00	13.06	13.73	14.01	14.26	14.59	14.90	15.24	15.58
2	.001	998.5	999.0	999.2	999.2	999.3	999.3	999.4	999.4	999.5	999.5
	.005	198.50	199.00	199.17	199.25	199.30	199.33	199.37	199.42	199.46	199.51
	.01	98.49	99.00	99.17	99.25	99.30	99.33	99.36	99.42	99.46	99.50
	.025	38.51	39.00	39.17	39.25	39.30	39.33	39.37	39.42	39.46	39.50
	.05	18.51	19.00	19.16	19.25	19.30	19.33	19.37	19.41	19.45	19.50
	.10	8.53	9.00	9.16	9.24	9.29	9.33	9.37	9.41	9.45	9.49
	.20	3.56	4.00	4.16	4.24	4.28	4.32	4.36	4.40	4.44	4.48
3	.001	167.5	148.5	141.1	137.1	134.6	132.8	130.6	128.3	125.9	123.5
	.005	55.55	49.80	47.47	46.20	45.39	44.84	44.13	43.39	42.62	41.83
	.01	34.12	30.81	29.46	28.71	28.24	27.91	27.49	27.05	26.60	26.12
	.025	17.44	16.04	15.44	15.10	14.89	14.74	14.54	14.34	14.12	13.90
	.05	10.13	9.55	9.28	9.12	9.01	8.94	8.84	8.74	8.64	8.53
	.10	5.54	5.46	5.39	5.34	5.31	5.28	5.25	5.22	5.18	5.13
	.20	2.68	2.89	2.94	2.96	2.97	2.97	2.98	2.98	2.98	2.98
4	.001	74.14	61.25	56.18	53.44	51.71	50.53	49.00	47.41	45.77	44.05
	.005	31.33	26.28	24.26	23.16	22.46	21.98	21.35	20.71	20.03	19.33
	.01	21.20	18.00	16.69	15.98	15.52	15.21	14.80	14.37	13.93	13.46
	.025	12.22	10.65	9.98	9.60	9.36	9.20	8.98	8.75	8.51	8.26
	.05	7.71	6.94	6.59	6.39	6.26	6.16	6.04	5.91	5.77	5.63
	.10	4.54	4.32	4.19	4.11	4.05	4.01	3.95	3.90	3.83	3.76
	.20	2.35	2.47	2.48	2.48	2.48	2.47	2.47	2.46	2.44	2.43
5	.001	47.04	36.61	33.20	31.09	29.75	28.84	27.64	26.42	25.14	23.78
	.005	22.79	18.31	16.53	15.56	14.94	14.51	13.96	13.38	12.78	12.14
	.01	16.26	13.27	12.06	11.39	10.97	10.67	10.29	9.89	9.47	9.02
	.025	10.01	8.43	7.76	7.39	7.15	6.98	6.76	6.52	6.28	6.02
	.05	6.61	5.79	5.41	5.19	5.05	4.95	4.82	4.68	4.53	4.36
	.10	4.06	3.78	3.62	3.52	3.45	3.40	3.34	3.27	3.19	3.10
	.20	2.18	2.26	2.25	2.24	2.23	2.22	2.20	2.18	2.16	2.13
6	.001	35.51	27.00	23.70	21.90	20.81	20.03	19.03	17.99	16.89	15.75
	.005	18.64	14.54	12.92	12.03	11.46	11.07	10.57	10.03	9.47	8.88
	.01	13.74	10.92	9.78	9.15	8.75	8.47	8.10	7.72	7.31	6.88
	.025	8.81	7.26	6.60	6.23	5.99	5.82	5.60	5.37	5.12	4.85
	.05	5.99	5.14	4.76	4.53	4.39	4.28	4.15	4.00	3.84	3.67
	.10	3.78	3.46	3.29	3.18	3.11	3.05	2.98	2.90	2.82	2.72
	.20	2.07	2.13	2.11	2.09	2.08	2.06	2.04	2.02	1.99	1.95
7	.001	29.22	21.69	18.77	17.19	16.21	15.52	14.63	13.71	12.73	11.69
	.005	16.24	12.40	10.88	10.05	9.52	9.16	8.68	8.18	7.65	7.08
	.01	12.25	9.55	8.45	7.85	7.46	7.19	6.84	6.47	6.07	5.65
	.025	8.07	6.54	5.89	5.52	5.29	5.12	4.90	4.67	4.42	4.14
	.05	5.59	4.74	4.35	4.12	3.97	3.87	3.73	3.57	3.41	3.23
	.10	3.59	3.26	3.07	2.96	2.88	2.83	2.75	2.67	2.58	2.47
	.20	2.00	2.04	2.02	1.99	1.97	1.96	1.93	1.91	1.87	1.83
8	.001	25.42	18.49	15.83	14.39	13.49	12.86	12.04	11.19	10.30	9.34
	.005	14.69	11.04	9.60	8.81	8.30	7.95	7.50	7.01	6.50	5.95
	.01	11.26	8.65	7.59	7.01	6.63	6.37	6.03	5.67	5.28	4.86
	.025	7.57	6.06	5.42	5.05	4.82	4.65	4.43	4.20	3.95	3.67
	.05	5.32	4.46	4.07	3.84	3.69	3.58	3.44	3.28	3.12	2.93
	.10	3.46	3.11	2.92	2.81	2.73	2.67	2.59	2.50	2.40	2.29
	.20	1.95	1.98	1.95	1.92	1.90	1.88	1.86	1.83	1.79	1.74
9	.001	22.86	16.39	13.90	12.56	11.71	11.13	10.37	9.57	8.72	7.81
	.005	13.61	10.11	8.72	7.96	7.47	7.13	6.69	6.23	5.73	5.19
	.01	10.56	8.02	6.99	6.42	6.06	5.80	5.47	5.11	4.73	4.31
	.025	7.21	5.71	5.08	4.72	4.48	4.32	4.10	3.87	3.61	3.33
	.05	5.12	4.26	3.86	3.63	3.48	3.37	3.23	3.07	2.90	2.71
	.10	3.36	3.01	2.81	2.69	2.61	2.55	2.47	2.38	2.28	2.16
	.20	1.91	1.94	1.90	1.87	1.85	1.83	1.80	1.76	1.72	1.67

233

Table 4 (*Continued*)

df_2	p	1	2	3	4	5	6	8	12	24	∞
10	.001	21.04	14.91	12.55	11.28	10.48	9.92	9.20	8.45	7.64	6.76
	.005	12.83	9.43	8.08	7.34	6.87	6.54	6.12	5.66	5.17	4.64
	.01	10.04	7.56	6.55	5.99	5.64	5.39	5.06	4.71	4.33	3.91
	.025	6.94	5.46	4.83	4.47	4.24	4.07	3.85	3.62	3.37	3.08
	.05	.4.96	4.10	3.71	3.48	3.33	3.22	3.07	2.91	2.74	2.54
	.10	3.28	2.92	2.73	2.61	2.52	2.46	2.38	2.28	2.18	2.06
	.20	1.88	1.90	1.86	1.83	1.80	1.78	1.75	1.72	1.67	1.62
11	.001	19.69	13.81	11.56	10.35	9.58	9.05	8.35	7.63	6.85	6.00
	.005	12.23	8.91	7.60	6.88	6.42	6.10	5.68	5.24	4.76	4.23
	.01	9.65	7.20	6.22	5.67	5.32	5.07	4.74	4.40	4.02	3.60
	.025	6.72	5.26	4.63	4.28	4.04	3.88	3.66	3.43	3.17	2.88
	.05	4.84	3.98	3.59	3.36	3.20	3.09	2.95	2.79	2.61	2.40
	.10	3.23	2.86	2.66	2.54	2.45	2.39	2.30	2.21	2.10	1.97
	.20	1.86	1.87	1.83	1.80	1.77	1.75	1.72	1.68	1.63	1.57
12	.001	18.64	12.97	10.80	9.63	8.89	8.38	7.71	7.00	6.25	5.42
	.005	11.75	8.51	7.23	6.52	6.07	5.76	5.35	4.91	4.43	3.90
	.01	9.33	6.93	5.95	5.41	5.06	4.82	4.50	4.16	3.78	3.36
	.025	6.55	5.10	4.47	4.12	3.89	3.73	3.51	3.28	3.02	2.72
	.05	4.75	3.88	3.49	3.26	3.11	3.00	2.85	2.69	2.50	2.30
	.10	3.18	2.81	2.61	2.48	2.39	2.33	2.24	2.15	2.04	1.90
	.20	1.84	1.85	1.80	1.77	1.74	1.72	1.69	1.65	1.60	1.54
13	.001	17.81	12.31	10.21	9.07	8.35	7.86	7.21	6.52	5.78	4.97
	.005	11.37	8.19	6.93	6.23	5.79	5.48	5.08	4.64	4.17	3.65
	.01	9.07	6.70	5.74	5.20	4.86	4.62	4.30	3.96	3.59	3.16
	.025	6.41	4.97	4.35	4.00	3.77	3.60	3.39	3.15	2.89	2.60
	.05	4.67	3.80	3.41	3.18	3.02	2.92	2.77	2.60	2.42	2.21
	.10	3.14	2.76	2.56	2.43	2.35	2.28	2.20	2.10	1.98	1.85
	.20	1.82	1.83	1.78	1.75	1.72	1.69	1.66	1.62	1.57	1.51
14	.001	17.14	11.78	9.73	8.62	7.92	7.43	6.80	6.13	5.41	4.60
	.005	11.06	7.92	6.68	6.00	5.56	5.26	4.86	4.43	3.96	3.44
	.01	8.86	6.51	5.56	5.03	4.69	4.46	4.14	3.80	3.43	3.00
	.025	6.30	4.86	4.24	3.89	3.66	3.50	3.29	3.05	2.79	2.49
	.05	4.60	3.74	3.34	3.11	2.96	2.85	2.70	2.53	2.35	2.13
	.10	3.10	2.73	2.52	2.39	2.31	2.24	2.15	2.05	1.94	1.80
	.20	1.81	1.81	1.76	1.73	1.70	1.67	1.64	1.60	1.55	1.48
15	.001	16.59	11.34	9.34	8.25	7.57	7.09	6.47	5.81	5.10	4.31
	.005	10.80	7.70	6.48	5.80	5.37	5.07	4.67	4.25	3.79	3.26
	.01	8.68	6.36	5.42	4.89	4.56	4.32	4.00	3.67	3.29	2.87
	.025	6.20	4.77	4.15	3.80	3.58	3.41	3.20	2.96	2.70	2.40
	.05	4.54	3.68	3.29	3.06	2.90	2.79	2.64	2.48	2.29	2.07
	.10	3.07	2.70	2.49	2.36	2.27	2.21	2.12	2.02	1.90	1.76
	.20	1.80	1.79	1.75	1.71	1.68	1.66	1.62	1.58	1.53	1.46
16	.001	16.12	10.97	9.00	7.94	7.27	6.81	6.19	5.55	4.85	4.06
	.005	10.58	7.51	6.30	5.64	5.21	4.91	4.52	4.10	3.64	3.11
	.01	8.53	6.23	5.29	4.77	4.44	4.20	3.89	3.55	3.18	2.75
	.025	6.12	4.69	4.08	3.73	3.50	3.34	3.12	2.89	2.63	2.32
	.05	4.49	3.63	3.24	3.01	2.85	2.74	2.59	2.42	2.24	2.01
	.10	3.05	2.67	2.46	2.33	2.24	2.18	2.09	1.99	1.87	1.72
	.20	1.79	1.78	1.74	1.70	1.67	1.64	1.61	1.56	1.51	1.43
17	.001	15.72	10.66	8.73	7.68	7.02	6.56	5.96	5.32	4.63	3.85
	.005	10.38	7.35	6.16	5.50	5.07	4.78	4.39	3.97	3.51	2.98
	.01	8.40	6.11	5.18	4.67	4.34	4.10	3.79	3.45	3.08	2.65
	.025	6.04	4.62	4.01	3.66	3.44	3.28	3.06	2.82	2.56	2.25
	.05	4.45	3.59	3.20	2.96	2.81	2.70	2.55	2.38	2.19	1.96
	.10	3.03	2.64	2.44	2.31	2.22	2.15	2.06	1.96	1.84	1.69
	.20	1.78	1.77	1.72	1.68	1.65	1.63	1.59	1.55	1.49	1.42
18	.001	15.38	10.39	8.49	7.46	6.81	6.35	5.76	5.13	4.45	3.67
	.005	10.22	7.21	6.03	5.37	4.96	4.66	4.28	3.86	3.40	2.87
	.01	8.28	6.01	5.09	4.58	4.25	4.01	3.71	3.37	3.00	2.57
	.025	5.98	4.56	3.95	3.61	3.38	3.22	3.01	2.77	2.50	2.19
	.05	4.41	3.55	3.16	2.93	2.77	2.66	2.51	2.34	2.15	1.92
	.10	3.01	2.62	2.42	2.29	2.20	2.13	2.04	1.93	1.81	1.66
	.20	1.77	1.76	1.71	1.67	1.64	1.62	1.58	1.53	1.48	1.40

Table 4 (*Continued*)

df_2	p	1	2	3	4	5	6	8	12	24	∞
19	.001	15.08	10.16	8.28	7.26	6.61	6.18	5.59	4.97	4.29	3.52
	.005	10.07	7.09	5.92	5.27	4.85	4.56	4.18	3.76	3.31	2.78
	.01	8.18	5.93	5.01	4.50	4.17	3.94	3.63	3.30	2.92	2.49
	.025	5.92	4.51	3.90	3.56	3.33	3.17	2.96	2.72	2.45	2.13
	.05	4.38	3.52	3.13	2.90	2.74	2.63	2.48	2.31	2.11	1.88
	.10	2.99	2.61	2.40	2.27	2.18	2.11	2.02	1.91	1.79	1.63
	.20	1.76	1.75	1.70	1.66	1.63	1.61	1.57	1.52	1.46	1.39
20	.001	14.82	9.95	8.10	7.10	6.46	6.02	5.44	4.82	4.15	3.38
	.005	9.94	6.99	5.82	5.17	4.76	4.47	4.09	3.68	3.22	2.69
	.01	8.10	5.85	4.94	4.43	4.10	3.87	3.56	3.23	2.86	2.42
	.025	5.87	4.46	3.86	3.51	3.29	3.13	2.91	2.68	2.41	2.09
	.05	4.35	3.49	3.10	2.87	2.71	2.60	2.45	2.28	2.08	1.84
	.10	2.97	2.59	2.38	2.25	2.16	2.09	2.00	1.89	1.77	1.61
	.20	1.76	1.75	1.70	1.65	1.62	1.60	1.56	1.51	1.45	1.37
21	.001	14.59	9.77	7.94	6.95	6.32	5.88	5.31	4.70	4.03	3.26
	.005	9.83	6.89	5.73	5.09	4.68	4.39	4.01	3.60	3.15	2.61
	.01	8.02	5.78	4.87	4.37	4.04	3.81	3.51	3.17	2.80	2.36
	.025	5.83	4.42	3.82	3.48	3.25	3.09	2.87	2.64	2.37	2.04
	.05	4.32	3.47	3.07	2.84	2.68	2.57	2.42	2.25	2.05	1.81
	.10	2.96	2.57	2.36	2.23	2.14	2.08	1.98	1.88	1.75	1.59
	.20	1.75	1.74	1.69	1.65	1.61	1.59	1.55	1.50	1.44	1.36
22	.001	14.38	9.61	7.80	6.81	6.19	5.76	5.19	4.58	3.92	3.15
	.005	9.73	6.81	5.65	5.02	4.61	4.32	3.94	3.54	3.08	2.55
	.01	7.94	5.72	4.82	4.31	3.99	3.76	3.45	3.12	2.75	2.31
	.025	5.79	4.38	3.78	3.44	3.22	3.05	2.84	2.60	2.33	2.00
	.05	4.30	3.44	3.05	2.82	2.66	2.55	2.40	2.23	2.03	1.78
	.10	2.95	2.56	2.35	2.22	2.13	2.06	1.97	1.86	1.73	1.57
	.20	1.75	1.73	1.68	1.64	1.61	1.58	1.54	1.49	1.43	1.35
23	.001	14.19	9.47	7.67	6.69	6.08	5.65	5.09	4.48	3.82	3.05
	.005	9.63	6.73	5.58	4.95	4.54	4.26	3.88	3.47	3.02	2.48
	.01	7.88	5.66	4.76	4.26	3.94	3.71	3.41	3.07	2.70	2.26
	.025	5.75	4.35	3.75	3.41	3.18	3.02	2.81	2.57	2.30	1.97
	.05	4.28	3.42	3.03	2.80	2.64	2.53	2.38	2.20	2.00	1.76
	.10	2.94	2.55	2.34	2.21	2.11	2.05	1.95	1.84	1.72	1.55
	.20	1.74	1.73	1.68	1.63	1.60	1.57	1.53	1.49	1.42	1.34
24	.001	14.03	9.34	7.55	6.59	5.98	5.55	4.99	4.39	3.74	2.97
	.005	9.55	6.66	5.52	4.89	4.49	4.20	3.83	3.42	2.97	2.43
	.01	7.82	5.61	4.72	4.22	3.90	3.67	3.36	3.03	2.66	2.21
	.025	5.72	4.32	3.72	3.38	3.15	2.99	2.78	2.54	2.27	1.94
	.05	4.26	3.40	3.01	2.78	2.62	2.51	2.36	2.18	1.98	1.73
	.10	2.93	2.54	2.33	2.19	2.10	2.04	1.94	1.83	1.70	1.53
	.20	1.74	1.72	1.67	1.63	1.59	1.57	1.53	1.48	1.42	1.33
25	.001	13.88	9.22	7.45	6.49	5.88	5.46	4.91	4.31	3.66	2.89
	.005	9.48	6.60	5.46	4.84	4.43	4.15	3.78	3.37	2.92	2.38
	.01	7.77	5.57	4.68	4.18	3.86	3.63	3.32	2.99	2.62	2.17
	.025	5.69	4.29	3.69	3.35	3.13	2.97	2.75	2.51	2.24	1.91
	.05	4.24	3.38	2.99	2.76	2.60	2.49	2.34	2.16	1.96	1.71
	.10	2.92	2.53	2.32	2.18	2.09	2.02	1.93	1.82	1.69	1.52
	.20	1.73	1.72	1.66	1.62	1.59	1.56	1.52	1.47	1.41	1.32
26	.001	13.74	9.12	7.36	6.41	5.80	5.38	4.83	4.24	3.59	2.82
	.005	9.41	6.54	5.41	4.79	4.38	4.10	3.73	3.33	2.87	2.33
	.01	7.72	5.53	4.64	4.14	3.82	3.59	3.29	2.96	2.58	2.13
	.025	5.66	4.27	3.67	3.33	3.10	2.94	2.73	2.49	2.22	1.88
	.05	4.22	3.37	2.98	2.74	2.59	2.47	2.32	2.15	1.95	1.69
	.10	2.91	2.52	2.31	2.17	2.08	2.01	1.92	1.81	1.68	1.50
	.20	1.73	1.71	1.66	1.62	1.58	1.56	1.52	1.47	1.40	1.31
27	.001	13.61	9.02	7.27	6.33	5.73	5.31	4.76	4.17	3.52	2.75
	.005	9.34	6.49	5.36	4.74	4.34	4.06	3.69	3.28	2.83	2.29
	.01	7.68	5.49	4.60	4.11	3.78	3.56	3.26	2.93	2.55	2.10
	.025	5.63	4.24	3.65	3.31	3.08	2.92	2.71	2.47	2.19	1.85
	.05	4.21	3.35	2.96	2.73	2.57	2.46	2.30	2.13	1.93	1.67
	.10	2.90	2.51	2.30	2.17	2.07	2.00	1.91	1.80	1.67	1.49
	.20	1.73	1.71	1.66	1.61	1.58	1.55	1.51	1.46	1.40	1.30

Table 4 (*Continued*)

df_2 \ df_1 → p ↓	1	2	3	4	5	6	8	12	24	∞
28 .001	13.50	8.93	7.19	6.25	5.66	5.24	4.69	4.11	3.46	2.70
.005	9.28	6.44	5.32	4.70	4.30	4.02	3.65	3.25	2.79	2.25
.01	7.64	5.45	4.57	4.07	3.75	3.53	3.23	2.90	2.52	2.06
.025	5.61	4.22	3.63	3.29	3.06	2.90	2.69	2.45	2.17	1.83
.05	4.20	3.34	2.95	2.71	2.56	2.44	2.29	2.12	1.91	1.65
.10	2.89	2.50	2.29	2.16	2.06	2.00	1.90	1.79	1.66	1.48
.20	1.72	1.71	1.65	1.61	1.57	1.55	1.51	1.46	1.39	1.30
29 .001	13.39	8.85	7.12	6.19	5.59	5.18	4.64	4.05	3.41	2.64
.005	9.23	6.40	5.28	4.66	4.26	3.98	3.61	3.21	2.76	2.21
.01	7.60	5.42	4.54	4.04	3.73	3.50	3.20	2.87	2.49	2.03
.025	5.59	4.20	3.61	3.27	3.04	2.88	2.67	2.43	2.15	1.81
.05	4.18	3.33	2.93	2.70	2.54	2.43	2.28	2.10	1.90	1.64
.10	2.89	2.50	2.28	2.15	2.06	1.99	1.89	1.78	1.65	1.47
.20	1.72	1.70	1.65	1.60	1.57	1.54	1.50	1.45	1.39	1.29
30 .001	13.29	8.77	7.05	6.12	5.53	5.12	4.58	4.00	3.36	2.59
.005	9.18	6.35	5.24	4.62	4.23	3.95	3.58	3.18	2.73	2.18
.01	7.56	5.39	4.51	4.02	3.70	3.47	3.17	2.84	2.47	2.01
.025	5.57	4.18	3.59	3.25	3.03	2.87	2.65	2.41	2.14	1.79
.05	4.17	3.32	2.92	2.69	2.53	2.42	2.27	2.09	1.89	1.62
.10	2.88	2.49	2.28	2.14	2.05	1.98	1.88	1.77	1.64	1.46
.20	1.72	1.70	1.64	1.60	1.57	1.54	1.50	1.45	1.38	1.28
40 .001	12.61	8.25	6.60	5.70	5.13	4.73	4.21	3.64	3.01	2.23
.005	8.83	6.07	4.98	4.37	3.99	3.71	3.35	2.95	2.50	1.93
.01	7.31	5.18	4.31	3.83	3.51	3.29	2.99	2.66	2.29	1.80
.025	5.42	4.05	3.46	3.13	2.90	2.74	2.53	2.29	2.01	1.64
.05	4.08	3.23	2.84	2.61	2.45	2.34	2.18	2.00	1.79	1.51
.10	2.84	2.44	2.23	2.09	2.00	1.93	1.83	1.71	1.57	1.38
.20	1.70	1.68	1.62	1.57	1.54	1.51	1.47	1.41	1.34	1.24
60 .001	11.97	7.76	6.17	5.31	4.76	4.37	3.87	3.31	2.69	1.90
.005	8.49	5.80	4.73	4.14	3.76	3.49	3.13	2.74	2.29	1.69
.01	7.08	4.98	4.13	3.65	3.34	3.12	2.82	2.50	2.12	1.60
.025	5.29	3.93	3.34	3.01	2.79	2.63	2.41	2.17	1.88	1.48
.05	4.00	3.15	2.76	2.52	2.37	2.25	2.10	1.92	1.70	1.39
.10	2.79	2.39	2.18	2.04	1.95	1.87	1.77	1.66	1.51	1.29
.20	1.68	1.65	1.59	1.55	1.51	1.48	1.44	1.38	1.31	1.18
120 .001	11.38	7.31	5.79	4.95	4.42	4.04	3.55	3.02	2.40	1.56
.005	8.18	5.54	4.50	3.92	3.55	3.28	2.93	2.54	2.09	1.43
.01	6.85	4.79	3.95	3.48	3.17	2.96	2.66	2.34	1.95	1.38
.025	5.15	3.80	3.23	2.89	2.67	2.52	2.30	2.05	1.76	1.31
.05	3.92	3.07	2.68	2.45	2.29	2.17	2.02	1.83	1.61	1.25
.10	2.75	2.35	2.13	1.99	1.90	1.82	1.72	1.60	1.45	1.19
.20	1.66	1.63	1.57	1.52	1.48	1.45	1.41	1.35	1.27	1.12
∞ .001	10.83	6.91	5.42	4.62	4.10	3.74	3.27	2.74	2.13	1.00
.005	7.88	5.30	4.28	3.72	3.35	3.09	2.74	2.36	1.90	1.00
.01	6.64	4.60	3.78	3.32	3.02	2.80	2.51	2.18	1.79	1.00
.025	5.02	3.69	3.12	2.79	2.57	2.41	2.19	1.94	1.64	1.00
.05	3.84	2.99	2.60	2.37	2.21	2.09	1.94	1.75	1.52	1.00
.10	2.71	2.30	2.08	1.94	1.85	1.77	1.67	1.55	1.38	1.00
.20	1.64	1.61	1.55	1.50	1.46	1.43	1.38	1.32	1.23	1.00

Source: Reproduced from E. F. Lindquist, *Design and Analysis of Experiments in Psychology and Education*, Houghton Mifflin, Boston, 1953, pp. 41–44, with the permission of the publisher.

236

Table 5 Table of χ^2

df	\multicolumn{14}{c}{Probability}
	.99	.98	.95	.90	.80	.70	.50	.30	.20	.10	.05	.02	.01	.001
1	.0157	.0628	.00393	.0158	.0642	.148	.455	1.074	1.642	2.706	3.841	5.412	6.635	10.827
2	.0201	.0404	.103	.211	.446	.713	1.386	2.408	3.219	4.605	5.991	7.824	9.210	13.815
3	.115	.185	.352	.584	1.005	1.424	2.366	3.665	4.642	6.251	7.815	9.837	11.345	16.268
4	.297	.429	.711	1.064	1.649	2.195	3.357	4.878	5.989	7.779	9.488	11.668	13.277	18.465
5	.554	.752	1.145	1.610	2.343	3.000	4.351	6.064	7.289	9.236	11.070	13.388	15.086	20.517
6	.872	1.134	1.635	2.204	3.070	3.828	5.348	7.231	8.558	10.645	12.592	15.033	16.812	22.457
7	1.239	1.564	2.167	2.833	3.822	4.671	6.346	8.383	9.803	12.017	14.067	16.622	18.475	24.322
8	1.646	2.032	2.733	3.490	4.594	5.527	7.344	9.524	11.030	13.362	15.507	18.168	20.090	26.125
9	2.088	2.532	3.325	4.168	5.380	6.393	8.343	10.656	12.242	14.684	16.919	19.679	21.666	27.877
10	2.558	3.059	3.940	4.865	6.179	7.267	9.342	11.781	13.442	15.987	18.307	21.161	23.209	29.588
11	3.053	3.609	4.575	5.578	6.989	8.148	10.341	12.899	14.631	17.275	19.675	22.618	24.725	31.264
12	3.571	4.178	5.226	6.304	7.807	9.034	11.340	14.011	15.812	18.549	21.026	24.054	26.217	32.909
13	4.107	4.765	5.892	7.042	8.634	9.926	12.340	15.119	16.985	19.812	22.362	25.472	27.688	34.528
14	4.660	5.368	6.571	7.790	9.467	10.821	13.339	16.222	18.151	21.064	23.685	26.873	29.141	36.123
15	5.229	5.985	7.261	8.547	10.307	11.721	14.339	17.322	19.311	22.307	24.996	28.259	30.578	37.697
16	5.812	6.614	7.962	9.312	11.152	12.624	15.338	18.418	20.465	23.542	26.296	29.633	32.000	39.252
17	6.408	7.255	8.672	10.085	12.002	13.531	16.338	19.511	21.615	24.769	27.587	30.995	33.409	40.790
18	7.015	7.906	9.390	10.865	12.857	14.440	17.338	20.601	22.760	25.989	28.869	32.346	34.805	42.312
19	7.633	8.567	10.117	11.651	13.716	15.352	18.338	21.689	23.900	27.204	30.144	33.687	36.191	43.820
20	8.260	9.237	10.851	12.443	14.578	16.266	19.337	22.775	25.038	28.412	31.410	35.020	37.566	45.315
21	8.897	9.915	11.591	13.240	15.445	17.182	20.337	23.858	26.171	29.615	32.671	36.343	38.932	46.797
22	9.542	10.600	12.338	14.041	16.314	18.101	21.337	24.939	27.301	30.813	33.924	37.659	40.289	48.268
23	10.196	11.293	13.091	14.848	17.187	19.021	22.337	26.018	28.429	32.007	35.172	38.968	41.638	49.728
24	10.856	11.992	13.848	15.659	18.062	19.943	23.337	27.096	29.553	33.196	36.415	40.270	42.980	51.179
25	11.524	12.697	14.611	16.473	18.940	20.867	24.337	28.172	30.675	34.382	37.652	41.566	44.314	52.620
26	12.198	13.409	15.379	17.292	19.820	21.792	25.336	29.246	31.795	35.563	38.885	42.856	45.642	54.052
27	12.879	14.125	16.151	18.114	20.703	22.719	26.336	30.319	32.912	36.741	40.113	44.140	46.963	55.476
28	13.565	14.847	16.928	18.939	21.588	23.647	27.336	31.391	34.027	37.916	41.337	45.419	48.278	56.893
29	14.256	15.574	17.708	19.768	22.475	24.577	28.336	32.461	35.139	39.087	42.557	46.693	49.588	58.302
30	14.953	16.306	18.493	20.599	23.364	25.508	29.336	33.530	36.250	40.256	43.773	47.962	50.892	59.703

Note: For larger values of df, the expression $\sqrt{2\chi^2} - \sqrt{2df - 1}$ may be used as a normal deviate with unit variance, remembering that the probability for χ^2 corresponds with that of a single tail of the normal curve.

Source: Reproduced from E. F. Lindquist, *Design and Analysis of Experiments in Psychology and Education*, Houghton Mifflin, Boston, 1953, p. 29, with the permission of the publisher.

Table 6 Significance levels of r

(N-2)	Probability level				
	.10	.05	.02	.01	.001
1	.988	.997	.9995	.9999	1.000
2	.900	.950	.980	.990	.999
3	.805	.878	.934	.959	.991
4	.729	.811	.882	.917	.974
5	.669	.754	.833	.874	.951
6	.622	.707	.789	.834	.925
7	.582	.666	.750	.798	.898
8	.550	.632	.716	.765	.872
9	.521	.602	.685	.735	.847
10	.497	.576	.658	.708	.823
11	.476	.553	.634	.684	.801
12	.458	.532	.612	.661	.780
13	.441	.514	.592	.641	.760
14	.426	.497	.574	.623	.742
15	.412	.482	.558	.606	.725
16	.400	.468	.542	.590	.708
17	.389	.456	.528	.575	.693
18	.378	.444	.516	.561	.679
19	.369	.433	.503	.549	.665
20	.360	.423	.492	.537	.652
22	.344	.404	.472	.515	.629
24	.330	.388	.453	.496	.607
25	.323	.381	.445	.487	.597
30	.296	.349	.409	.449	.554
35	.275	.325	.381	.418	.519
40	.257	.304	.358	.393	.490
45	.243	.288	.338	.372	.465
50	.231	.273	.322	.354	.443
55	.220	.261	.307	.338	.424
60	.211	.250	.295	.325	.408
65	.203	.240	.284	.312	.393
70	.195	.232	.274	.302	.380
75	.189	.224	.264	.292	.368
80	.183	.217	.256	.283	.357
85	.178	.211	.249	.275	.347
90	.173	.205	.242	.267	.338
95	.168	.200	.236	.260	.329
100	.164	.195	.230	.254	.321
125	.147	.174	.206	.228	.288
150	.134	.159	.189	.208	.264
175	.124	.148	.174	.194	.248
200	.116	.138	.164	.181	.235
300	.095	.113	.134	.148	.188
500	.074	.088	.104	.115	.148
1000	.052	.062	.073	.081	.104
2000	.037	.044	.052	.058	.074

Note: All p values are two-tailed in this table.

Source: Reproduced from H. M. Walker and J. Lev, *Statistical Inference*, Holt, New York, 1953, p. 470, with the permission of the author and publisher.

Table 7 Table of Fisher's z transformation of r

Second digit of r

r	.00	.01	.02	.03	.04	.05	.06	.07	.08	.09
.0	.000	.010	.020	.030	.040	.050	.060	.070	.080	.090
.1	.100	.110	.121	.131	.141	.151	.161	.172	.182	.192
.2	.203	.213	.224	.234	.245	.255	.266	.277	.288	.299
.3	.310	.321	.332	.343	.354	.365	.377	.388	.400	.412
.4	.424	.436	.448	.460	.472	.485	.497	.510	.523	.536
.5	.549	.563	.576	.590	.604	.618	.633	.648	.662	.678
.6	.693	.709	.725	.741	.758	.775	.793	.811	.829	.848
.7	.867	.887	.908	.929	.950	.973	.996	1.020	1.045	1.071
.8	1.099	1.127	1.157	1.188	1.221	1.256	1.293	1.333	1.376	1.422

Third digit of r

r	.000	.001	.002	.003	.004	.005	.006	.007	.008	.009
.90	1.472	1.478	1.483	1.488	1.494	1.499	1.505	1.510	1.516	1.522
.91	1.528	1.533	1.539	1.545	1.551	1.557	1.564	1.570	1.576	1.583
.92	1.589	1.596	1.602	1.609	1.616	1.623	1.630	1.637	1.644	1.651
.93	1.658	1.666	1.673	1.681	1.689	1.697	1.705	1.713	1.721	1.730
.94	1.738	1.747	1.756	1.764	1.774	1.783	1.792	1.802	1.812	1.822
.95	1.832	1.842	1.853	1.863	1.874	1.886	1.897	1.909	1.921	1.933
.96	1.946	1.959	1.972	1.986	2.000	2.014	2.029	2.044	2.060	2.076
.97	2.092	2.109	2.127	2.146	2.165	2.185	2.205	2.227	2.249	2.273
.98	2.298	2.323	2.351	2.380	2.410	2.443	2.477	2.515	2.555	2.599
.99	2.646	2.700	2.759	2.826	2.903	2.994	3.106	3.250	3.453	3.800

Note: z is obtained as $\frac{1}{2}\log_e \frac{(1 + r)}{(1 - r)}$.

Source: Reprinted by permission from *Statistical Methods* by George W. Snedecor and William G. Cochran, 7th ed. (c) 1980 by the Iowa State University Press, Ames, Iowa 50010.

Table 8 Table of r equivalents of Fisher's z

z	.00	.01	.02	.03	.04	.05	.06	.07	.08	.09
.0	.000	.010	.020	.030	.040	.050	.060	.070	.080	.090
.1	.100	.110	.119	.129	.139	.149	.159	.168	.178	.187
.2	.197	.207	.216	.226	.236	.245	.254	.264	.273	.282
.3	.291	.300	.310	.319	.327	.336	.345	.354	.363	.371
.4	.380	.389	.397	.405	.414	.422	.430	.438	.446	.454
.5	.462	.470	.478	.485	.493	.500	.508	.515	.523	.530
.6	.537	.544	.551	.558	.565	.572	.578	.585	.592	.598
.7	.604	.611	.617	.623	.629	.635	.641	.647	.653	.658
.8	.664	.670	.675	.680	.686	.691	.696	.701	.706	.711
.9	.716	.721	.726	.731	.735	.740	.744	.749	.753	.757
1.0	.762	.766	.770	.774	.778	.782	.786	.790	.793	.797
1.1	.800	.804	.808	.811	.814	.818	.821	.824	.828	.831
1.2	.834	.837	.840	.843	.846	.848	.851	.854	.856	.859
1.3	.862	.864	.867	.869	.872	.874	.876	.879	.881	.883
1.4	.885	.888	.890	.892	.894	.896	.898	.900	.902	.903
1.5	.905	.907	.909	.910	.912	.914	.915	.917	.919	.920
1.6	.922	.923	.925	.926	.928	.929	.930	.932	.933	.934
1.7	.935	.937	.938	.939	.940	.941	.942	.944	.945	.946
1.8	.947	.948	.949	.950	.951	.952	.953	.954	.954	.955
1.9	.956	.957	.958	.959	.960	.960	.961	.962	.963	.963
2.0	.964	.965	.965	.966	.967	.967	.968	.969	.969	.970
2.1	.970	.971	.972	.972	.973	.973	.974	.974	.975	.975
2.2	.976	.976	.977	.977	.978	.978	.978	.979	.979	.980
2.3	.980	.980	.981	.981	.982	.982	.982	.983	.983	.983
2.4	.984	.984	.984	.985	.985	.985	.986	.986	.986	.986
2.5	.987	.987	.987	.987	.988	.988	.988	.988	.989	.989
2.6	.989	.989	.989	.990	.990	.990	.990	.990	.991	.991
2.7	.991	.991	.991	.992	.992	.992	.992	.992	.992	.992
2.8	.993	.993	.993	.993	.993	.993	.993	.994	.994	.994
2.9	.994	.994	.994	.994	.994	.995	.995	.995	.995	.995

Note: r is obtained as $\dfrac{e^{2z} - 1}{e^{2z} + 1}$.

Source: Reprinted by permission from *Statistical Methods* by George W. Snedecor and William G. Cochran, 7th ed. (c) 1980 by the Iowa State University Press, Ames, Iowa 50010.

References

Adcock, C. J. 1960. A note on combining probabilities. *Psychometrika* 25: 303-5.

Allport, F. H. 1924. *Social psychology.* Boston: Houghton-Mifflin.

American Psychological Association. 1983. *Publication manual of the American Psychological Association.* 3d ed. Washington, D.C.: Author.

Argyle, M. 1975. *Bodily communication.* New York: International Universities Press.

Armor, D. J. 1974. Theta reliability and factor scaling. In H. L. Costner (ed.), *Sociological methodology 1973-1974.* San Francisco: Jossey-Bass.

Armor, D. J. and Couch, A. S. 1972. *Data-Text primer: An introduction to computerized social data analysis.* New York: Free Press.

Bailey, K. D. 1974. Cluster analysis. In D. R. Heise (ed.), *Sociological Methodology 1975,* 59-128. San Francisco: Jossey-Bass.

Bakan, D. 1967. *On method.* San Francisco: Jossey-Bass.

Barnett, V. and Lewis, T. 1978. *Outliers in statistical data.* New York: John Wiley and Sons.

Bem, S. L. 1974. The measurement of psychological androgyny. *Journal of Consulting and Clinical Psychology* 42: 155-62.

Birch, M. W. 1963. Maximum likelihood in three-way contingency tables. *Journal of the Royal Statistical Society* B: 25, 220-33.

Birnbaum, A. 1954. Combining independent tests of significance. *Journal of the American Statistical Association* 49: 559-74.

Blanck, P. D.; Buck, R. W.; and Rosenthal, R. (eds.). 1986. *Nonverbal communication in the clinical context.* University Park, Pa.: Pennsylvania State University Press.

Blanck, P. D. and Rosenthal, R. 1984. Mediation of interpersonal expectancy effects: Counselor's tone of voice. *Journal of Educational Psychology* 76: 418-26.

Blanck, P. D.; Rosenthal, R.; and Vannicelli, M. 1986. *Talking to and about patients: The therapist's tone of voice.* In P. D. Blanck; R. Buck; and R. Rosenthal (eds.), *Nonverbal communication in the clinical context,* 99-143. University Park, Pa.: Pennsylvania State University Press.

Blyth, C. R. 1972. On Simpson's paradox and the sure-thing principle. *Journal of the American Statistical Association* 67: 364-6.

Brozek, J. and Tiede, K. 1952. Reliable and questionable significance in a series of statistical tests. *Psychological Bulletin* 49: 339-41.

Brunswick, E. 1956. *Perception and the representative design of psychological experiments.* Berkeley: University of California Press.

Buck, R. 1975. Nonverbal communication of affect in children. *Journal of Personality and Social Psychology* 31: 644-53.

1979. Individual differences in nonverbal sending accuracy and electrodermal responding: The externalizing-internalizing dimension. In R. Rosenthal (ed.), *Skill in nonverbal communication: Individual differences,* 140-70. Cambridge, Mass.: Oelgeschlager, Gunn and Hain.

Clark, H. H. 1973. The language-as-fixed-effect fallacy: A critique of language statistics in psychological research. *Journal of Verbal Learning and Verbal Behavior* 12: 335–59.

Cline, V. B. 1964. Interpersonal perception. In B. A. Maher (ed.), *Progress in Experimental Personality Research: Volume 1,* 221–84. New York: Academic Press.

Cochran, W. G. 1954. Some methods for strengthening the common χ^2 tests. *Biometrics* 10: 417–51.

Cochran, W. G. and Cox, G. M. 1957. *Experimental designs.* 2d ed. New York: Wiley. (First corrected printing, 1968.)

Cohen, J. 1962. The statistical power of abnormal-social psychological research: A review. *Journal of Abnormal and Social Psychology* 65: 145–53.

1965. Some statistical issues in psychological research. In B. B. Wolman (ed.), *Handbook of clinical psychology.* New York: McGraw-Hill.

1969. *Statistical power analysis for the behavioral sciences.* New York: Academic Press.

1977. *Statistical power analysis for the behavioral sciences.* rev. ed. New York: Academic Press.

Coombs, C. H.; Dawes, R. M.; and Tversky, A. 1970. *Mathematical psychology: An elementary introduction.* Englewood Cliffs, N.J.: Prentice-Hall.

Cooper, H. M. 1981. On the significance of effects and the effects of significance. *Journal of Personality and Social Psychology* 41: 1013–18.

1984. *The integrative research review: A systematic approach.* Beverly Hills, Calif.: Sage.

Cunningham, M. R. 1977. Personality and the structure of the nonverbal communication of emotion. *Journal of Personality* 45: 564–84.

Darwin, C. 1965. *The expression of the emotions in man and animals.* Chicago: University of Chicago Press. (Originally published, 1872.)

Davitz, J. R. 1964. *The communication of emotional meaning.* New York: McGraw-Hill.

DePaulo, B. M. and Rosenthal, R. 1979a. Ambivalence, discrepancy, and deception in nonverbal communication. In R. Rosenthal (ed.), *Skill in nonverbal communication,* 204–248. Cambridge, Mass.: Oelgeschlager, Gunn and Hain.

1979b. Telling lies. *Journal of Personality and Social Psychology* 37: 1713–22.

1982. Measuring the development of sensitivity to nonverbal communication. In C. E. Izard (ed.), *Measuring emotions in infants and children,* 208–47. New York: Cambridge University Press.

DePaulo, B. M.; Rosenthal, R.; Eisenstat, R. A.; Rogers, P. L.; and Finkelstein, S. 1978. Decoding discrepant nonverbal cues. *Journal of Personality and Social Psychology* 36: 313–23.

DiMatteo, M. R. 1979. Nonverbal skill and the physician-patient relationship. In R. Rosenthal (ed.), *Skill in nonverbal communication: Individual differences,* 104–34. Cambridge, Mass.: Oelgeschlager, Gunn and Hain.

Eagly, A. H. and Carli, L. L. 1981. Sex of researchers and sex-typed communications as determinants of sex differences in influenceability: A meta-analysis of social influence studies. *Psychological Bulletin* 90: 1–20.

Edgington, E. S. 1972a. An additive method for combining probability values from independent experiments. *Journal of Psychology* 80: 351–63.

1972b. A normal curve method for combining probability values from independent experiments. *Journal of Psychology* 82: 85–9.

Ekman, P. 1965a. Communication through nonverbal behavior: A source of information about an interpersonal relationship. In S. S. Tomkins and C. Izard (eds.), *Affect, cognition and personality.* New York: Springer.

1965b. Differential communication of affect by head and body cues. *Journal of Personality and Social Psychology* 2: 725–35.

1973. Cross-cultural studies of facial expression. In P. Ekman (ed.), *Darwin and facial expression: A century of research in review.* New York: Academic Press.

Ekman, P. and Friesen, W. V. 1969. Nonverbal leakage and clues to deception. *Psychiatry* 32: 88–106.

1974. Detecting deception from the body or face. *Journal of Personality and Social Psychology* 29: 288–98.

Ekman, P.; Friesen, W. V.; and Ellsworth, P. 1972. *Emotion in the human face: Guidelines for research and an integration of findings.* New York: Pergamon Press.

Ekman, P.; Friesen, W. V.; and Scherer, K. R. 1976. Body movement and voice pitch in deceptive interaction. *Semiotica* 16:1: 23–7.

Federighi, E. T. 1959. Extended tables of the percentage points of Student's *t*-distribution. *Journal of the American Statistical Association* 54: 683–88.

Fienberg, S. E. 1977. *The analysis of cross-classified categorical data.* Cambridge, Mass.: The MIT Press.

Fisher, R. A. 1932. *Statistical methods for research workers.* 4th ed. London: Oliver and Boyd.

1938. *Statistical methods for research workers.* 7th ed. London: Oliver and Boyd.

Friedman, H. 1968. Magnitude of experimental effect and a table for its rapid estimation. *Psychological Bulletin* 70: 245–51.

Friedman, H. S. 1976. About face: The role of facial expressions of emotion in the verbal communication of meaning. Unpublished doctoral dissertation, Harvard University.

1978. The relative strength of verbal versus nonverbal cues. *Personality and Social Psychology Bulletin* 4: 147–50.

1979a. The interactive effects of facial expressions of emotion and verbal messages on perceptions of affective meaning. *Journal of Experimental Social Psychology* 15: 453–69.

1979b. The concept of skill in nonverbal communication: Implications for understanding social interaction. In R. Rosenthal (ed.), *Skill in nonverbal communication: Individual differences,* 2–27. Cambridge, Mass.: Oelgeschlager, Gunn and Hain.

Glass, G. V. 1976a, April. *Primary, secondary, and meta-analysis of research.* Paper presented at the meeting of the American Educational Research Association, San Francisco.

1976b. Primary, secondary, and meta-analysis of research. *Educational Researcher* 5: 3–8.

1980. Summarizing effect sizes. In R. Rosenthal (ed.), *New directions for methodology of social and behavioral science: Quantitative assessment of research domains,* 13–31. San Francisco: Jossey-Bass.

Glass, G. V; McGaw, B.; and Smith, M. L. 1981. *Meta-analysis in social research.* Beverly Hills, Calif.: Sage.

Green, B. F. and Tukey, J. W. 1960. Complex analyses of variance: General problems. *Psychometrika* 25: 127–52.

Guilford, J. P. 1954. *Psychometric methods.* 2d ed. New York: McGraw-Hill.

Guilford, J. P. and Fruchter, B. 1978. *Fundamental statistics in psychology and education.* 6th ed. New York: McGraw-Hill.

Guttman, L. 1966. Order analysis of correlation matrices. In R. B. Cattell (ed.), *Handbook of multivariate experimental psychology,* 438–58. Chicago: Rand McNally.

Hall, J. A. 1979. Gender, gender roles, and nonverbal communication skills. In R. Rosenthal (ed.), *Skill in nonverbal communication: Individual differences,* 32–67. Cambridge, Mass.: Oelgeschlager, Gunn and Hain.

1980. Gender differences in nonverbal communication skills. In R. Rosenthal (ed.), *New directions for methodology of social and behavioral science: Quantitative assessment of research domains,* 63–77. San Francisco: Jossey-Bass.

1984. *Nonverbal sex differences.* Baltimore, Md.: The Johns Hopkins University Press.

Hammond, K. R. 1954. Representative vs. systematic design in clinical psychology. *Psychological Bulletin* 51, 150–59.

Harris, M. J. and Rosenthal, R. 1985. The mediation of interpersonal expectancy effects: 31 meta-analyses. *Psychological Bulletin* 97: 363–86.

Hedges, L. V. 1981. Distribution theory for Glass's estimator of effect size and related estimators. *Journal of Educational Statistics* 6: 107–28.

1982a. Estimation of effect size from a series of independent experiments. *Psychological Bulletin* 92: 490–99.

1982b. Fitting categorical models to effect sizes from a series of experiments. *Journal of Educational Statistics* 7: 119–37.

Hedges, L. V. and Olkin, I. 1985. *Statistical methods for meta-analysis.* New York: Academic Press.

Hsu, L. M. 1980. Tests of differences in *p* levels as tests of differences in effect sizes. *Psychological Bulletin* 88: 705–708.

Huber, P. J. 1981. *Robust statistics.* New York: John Wiley and Sons.

Hunter, J. E.; Schmidt, F. L.; and Jackson, G. B. 1982. *Meta-analysis: Cumulating research findings across studies.* Beverly Hills, Calif.: Sage.

Izard, C. E. 1971. *The face of emotion.* New York: Appleton-Century-Crofts.

1977. *Human emotions.* New York: Plenum.

Jones, L. V. and Fiske, D. W. 1953. Models for testing the significance of combined results. *Psychological Bulletin* 50: 375–82.

Judd, C. M. and Kenny, D. A. 1981. *Estimating the effects of social interventions.* New York: Cambridge University Press.

Kaplan, A. 1964. *The conduct of inquiry: Methodology for behavioral science.* Scranton, Pa.: Chandler.

Kim, J.-O. 1975. Factor analysis. In N. H. Nie; C. H. Hull; J. G. Jenkins; K. Steinbrenner; and D. H. Bent (eds.), *SPSS: Statistical package for the social sciences.* 2d ed., pp. 468–514. New York: McGraw-Hill.

Kim, K. H. and Roush, F. W. 1980. *Mathematics for social scientists.* New York: Elsevier.

Knapp, M. L. 1978. *Nonverbal communication in human interaction.* 2d ed. New York: Holt, Rinehart and Winston.

Kolata, G. B. 1981. Drug found to help heart attack survivors. *Science* 214: 774–5.

Kraemer, H. C. and Andrews, G. 1982. A nonparametric technique for meta-analysis effect size calculation. *Psychological Bulletin* 91: 404–12.

Krauth, J. 1983. Nonparametric effect size estimation: A comment on Kraemer and Andrews. *Psychological Bulletin* 94: 190–92.

Lamb, W. K and Whitla, D. K. 1983. *Meta-analysis and the integration of research findings: A trend analysis and bibliography prior to 1983.* Unpublished manuscript, Harvard University, Cambridge.

Lancaster, H. O. 1961. The combination of probabilities: An application of orthonormal functions. *Australian Journal of Statistics* 3: 20–33.

Lazarsfeld, P. F. and Henry, N. W. 1968. *Latent structure analysis.* Boston: Houghton Mifflin.

Light, R. J. and Pillemer, D. B. 1984. *Summing up: The science of reviewing research*. Cambridge, Mass.: Harvard University Press.

Littlepage, G. and Pineault, T. 1978. Verbal, facial, and paralinguistic cues to the detection of truth and lying. *Personality and Social Psychology Bulletin* 4: 461–64.

Maier, N. R. F. and Thurber, J. A. 1968. Accuracy of judgments of deception when an interview is watched, heard, and read. *Personnel Psychology* 21: 23–30.

Mayo, R. J. 1978. Statistical considerations in analyzing the results of a collection of experiments. *The Behavioral and Brain Sciences* 3: 400–1.

McNemar, Q. 1960. At random: Sense and nonsense. *American Psychologist* 15: 295–300.

Mehrabian, A. 1970. A semantic space for nonverbal behavior. *Journal of Consulting and Clinical Psychology* 35: 248–57.

Milmoe, S.; Novey, M. S.; Kagan, J.; and Rosenthal, R. 1968. The mother's voice: Postdictor of aspects of her baby's behavior. *Proceedings of the 76th Annual Convention of the American Psychological Association*, 463–4.

Milmoe, S.; Rosenthal, R.; Blane, H. T.; Chafetz, M. E.; and Wolf, I. 1967. The doctor's voice: Postdictor of successful referral of alcoholic patients. *Journal of Abnormal Psychology* 72: 78–84.

Mosteller, F. 1968. Association and estimation in contingency tables. *Journal of the American Statistical Association* 63: 1–28.

Mosteller, F. M. and Bush, R. R. 1954. Selected quantitative techniques. In G. Lindzey (ed.), *Handbook of social psychology*, Vol. 1. Theory and method, 289–334. Cambridge, Mass.: Addison-Wesley.

Mosteller, F. and Rourke, R. E. K. 1973. *Sturdy statistics*. Reading, Mass.: Addison-Wesley.

Mosteller, F. and Tukey, J. W. 1977. *Data analysis and regression*. Reading, Mass.: Addison-Wesley.

Mulaik, S. A. 1972. *The foundations of factor analysis*. New York: McGraw-Hill.

Mullen, B. and Rosenthal, R. 1985. *BASIC meta-analysis: Procedures and programs*. Hillsdale, N.J.: Erlbaum.

Nasby, W.; Hayden, B.; and DePaulo, B. M. 1980. Attributional bias among aggressive boys to interpret unambiguous social stimuli as displays of hostility. *Journal of Abnormal Psychology* 89: 459–68.

Nelson, N.; Rosenthal, R.; and Rosnow, R. L. 1986. Interpretation of significance levels and effect sizes by psychological researchers. *American Psychologist* 41: 1299–1301.

Nunnally, J. C. 1978. *Psychometric theory*. 2d ed. New York: McGraw-Hill.

Osgood, C. E. 1966. Dimensionality of the semantic space for communication via facial expressions. *Scandinavian Journal of Psychology* 7: 1–30.

Rimland, B. 1979. Death knell for psychotherapy? *American Psychologist* 34: 192.

Rogers, P. L.; Scherer, K. R.; and Rosenthal, R. 1971. Content-filtering human speech: A simple electronic system. *Behavior Research Methods and Instrumentation* 3: 16–18.

Rosenthal, R. 1964. Effects of the experimenter on the results of psychological research. In B. A. Maher (ed.), *Progress in experimental personality research*, Vol. 1, 79–114. New York: Academic Press.

1966. *Experimenter effects in behavioral research*. New York: Appleton-Century-Crofts.

1967. Covert communication in the psychological experiment. *Psychological Bulletin* 67: 356–67.

1969. Interpersonal expectations. In R. Rosenthal and R. L. Rosnow (eds.), *Artifact in behavioral research*, 181–277. New York: Academic Press.

1973. Estimating effective reliabilities in studies that employ judges' ratings. *Journal of Clinical Psychology* 29: 342–5.

1974. *On the social psychology of the self-fulfilling prophecy: Further evidence for Pygmalion effects and their mediating mechanisms,* Module 53. New York: MSS Modular Publications.

1976. *Experimenter effects in behavioral research.* Enlarged edition. New York: Irvington Publishers, Halsted Press Division of Wiley.

1978. Combining results of independent studies. *Psychological Bulletin* 85: 185–93.

1979a. The "file drawer problem" and tolerance for null results. *Psychological Bulletin* 86: 638–41.

1979b. Replications and their relative utilities. *Replications in Social Psychology* 1(1): 15–23.

(ed.). 1979c. *Skill in nonverbal communication: Individual differences.* Cambridge, Mass.: Oelgeschlager, Gunn and Hain.

(ed.). 1980. *New directions for methodology of social and behavioral science: Quantitative assessment of research domains.* No. 5. San Francisco: Jossey-Bass.

1982. Conducting judgment studies. In K. R. Scherer and P. Ekman (eds.), *Handbook of methods in nonverbal behavior research,* 287–361. New York: Cambridge University Press.

1984. *Meta-analytic procedures for social research.* Beverly Hills, Calif.: Sage.

1985. From unconscious experimenter bias to teacher expectancy effects. In J. B. Dusek; V. C. Hall; and W. J. Meyer (eds.), *Teacher expectancies.* Hillsdale, N.J.: Erlbaum.

Rosenthal, R.; Blanck, P. D.; and Vannicelli, M. 1984. Speaking to and about patients: Predicting therapists' tone of voice. *Journal of Consulting and Clinical Psychology* 52: 679–86.

Rosenthal, R. and DePaulo, B. M. 1979a. Sex differences in accommodation in nonverbal communication. In R. Rosenthal (ed.), *Skill in nonverbal communication: Individual differences,* 68–103. Cambridge, Mass.: Oelgeschlager, Gunn and Hain.

1979b. Sex differences in eavesdropping on nonverbal cues. *Journal of Personality and Social Psychology* 37: 273–85.

1980. Encoders vs. decoders as units of analysis in research in nonverbal communication. *Journal of Nonverbal Behavior* 5: 92–103.

Rosenthal, R.; Fode, K. L.; Friedman, C. J.; and Vikan, L. L. 1960. Subjects' perception of their experimenter under conditions of experimenter bias. *Perceptual and Motor Skills* 11: 325–31.

Rosenthal, R. and Gaito, J. 1963. The interpretation of levels of significance by psychological researchers. *Journal of Psychology* 55: 33–8.

1964. Further evidence for the cliff effect in the interpretation of levels of significance. *Psychological Reports* 15: 570.

Rosenthal, R.; Hall, J. A.; DiMatteo, M. R.; Rogers, P. L.; and Archer, D. 1979. *Sensitivity to nonverbal communication: The PONS test.* Baltimore, Md.: The Johns Hopkins University Press.

Rosenthal, R.; Hall, J. A.; and Zuckerman, M. 1978. The relative equivalence of senders in studies of nonverbal encoding and decoding. *Environmental Psychology and Nonverbal Behavior* 2: 161–6.

Rosenthal, R. and Jacobson, L. 1968. *Pygmalion in the classroom.* New York: Holt, Rinehart and Winston.

Rosenthal, R. and Rosnow, R. L. 1975a. *Primer of methods for the behavioral sciences.* New York: Wiley.

1975b. *The volunteer subject.* New York: Wiley-Interscience.

1984. *Essentials of behavioral research: Methods and data analysis.* New York:

McGraw-Hill.

1985. *Contrast analysis: Focused comparisons in the analysis of variance.* New York: Cambridge University Press.

Rosenthal, R. and Rubin, D. B. 1978a. Interpersonal expectancy effects: The first 345 studies. *The Behavioral and Brain Sciences* 3: 377–86.

1978b. Issues in summarizing the first 345 studies of interpersonal expectancy effects. *The Behavioral and Brain Sciences* 3: 410–15.

1979a. Comparing significance levels of independent studies. *Psychological Bulletin* 86: 1165–8.

1979b. A note on percent variance explained as a measure of the importance of effects. *Journal of Applied Social Psychology* 9: 395–6.

1980. Comparing within- and between-subjects studies. *Sociological Methods and Research* 9: 127–36.

1982a. Comparing effect sizes of independent studies. *Psychological Bulletin* 92: 500–4.

1982b. A simple, general purpose display of magnitude of experimental effect. *Journal of Educational Psychology* 74: 166–9.

Rummel, R. J. 1970. *Applied factor analysis.* Evanston, Ill.: Northwestern University Press.

Scherer, K. R. 1970. *Non-verbale Kommunikation.* Hamburg: Helmut Buske Verlag.

1971. Randomized-splicing: A note on a simple technique for masking speech content. *Journal of Experimental Research in Personality* 5: 155–9.

1978. Personality inference from voice quality: The loud voice of extroversion. *European Journal of Social Psychology* 8: 467–87.

1979a. Acoustic concomitants of emotional dimensions: Judging affect from synthesized tone sequences. In S. Weitz (ed.), *Nonverbal communication: Readings with commentary.* 2d ed., 249–53. New York: Oxford University Press.

1979b. Voice and speech correlates of perceived social influence in simulated juries. In H. Giles and R. St. Clair (eds.), *Language and social psychology,* 88–120. Oxford: Basil Blackwell.

1982. Methods of research on vocal communication: Paradigms and parameters. In K. R. Scherer and P. Ekman (eds.), *Handbook of methods in nonverbal behavior research,* 136–98. New York: Cambridge University Press.

Scherer, K. R.; Koivumaki, J.; and Rosenthal, R. 1972. Minimal cues in the vocal communication of affect: Judging emotions from content-masked speech. *Journal of Psycholinguistic Research* 1: 269–85.

Scherer, K. R. and Oshinsky, J. S. 1977. Cue utilization in emotion attribution from auditory stimuli. *Motivation and Emotion* 1: 331–46.

Scherer, K. R.; Rosenthal, R.; and Koivumaki, J. 1972. Mediating interpersonal expectancies via vocal cues: Differential speech intensity as a means of social influence. *European Journal of Social Psychology* 2: 163–75.

Scherer, K. R.; Scherer, U.; Hall, J. A.; and Rosenthal, R. 1977. Differential attribution of personality based on multi-channel presentation of verbal and nonverbal cues. *Psychological Research* 39: 221–47.

Shepard, R. N.; Romney, A. K.; and Nerlove, S. B. (eds.). 1972. *Multidimensional scaling,* 2 vols. New York: Seminar Press.

Siegel, S. 1956. *Nonparametric statistics.* New York: McGraw-Hill.

Simpson, E. H. 1951. The interpretation of interaction in contingency tables. *Journal of the Royal Statistical Society, B* 13: 238–41.

Smart, R. G. 1964. The importance of negative results in psychological research. *Canadian Psychologist* 5a: 225–32.

Smith, M. L. and Glass, G. V. 1977. Meta-analysis of psychotherapy outcome studies. *American Psychologist* 32: 752–60.

Smith, M. L.; Glass, G. V; and Miller, T. I. 1980. *The benefits of psychotherapy.* Baltimore: The Johns Hopkins University Press.

Snedecor, G. W. and Cochran, W. G. 1967. *Statistical methods.* 6th ed. Ames, Iowa: Iowa State University Press.

1980. *Statistical methods.* 7th ed. Ames, Iowa: Iowa State University Press.

Spence, J. T. and Helmreich, R. 1978. *Masculinity and femininity: Their psychological dimensions, correlates, and antecedents.* Austin: University of Texas Press.

Sterling, T. D. 1959. Publication decisions and their possible effects on inferences drawn from tests of significance – or vice versa. *Journal of the American Statistical Association* 54: 30–34.

Stouffer, S. A.; Suchman, E. A.; DeVinney, L. C.; Star, S. A.; and Williams, R. M., Jr. 1949. *The American soldier: Adjustment during army life,* Vol I. Princeton, N.J.: Princeton University Press.

Tomkins, S. S. and McCarter, R. 1964. What and where are the primary affects? Some evidence for a theory. *Perceptual and Motor Skills* 18: 119–58.

Torgerson, W. S. 1958. *Theory and methods of scaling.* New York: Wiley.

Tukey, J. W. 1977. *Exploratory data analysis.* Reading, Mass.: Addison-Wesley.

Uno, Y.; Koivumaki, J. H.; and Rosenthal, R. 1972. Unintended experimenter behavior as evaluated by Japanese and American observers. *Journal of Social Psychology* 88: 91–106.

Upton, G. J. G. 1978. *The analysis of cross-tabulated data.* New York: Wiley.

Walker, H. M. and Lev, J. 1953. *Statistical inference.* New York: Holt.

Wallace, D. L. 1959. Bounds on normal approximations to Student's and the chi-square distributions. *Annals of Mathematical Statistics* 30: 1121–30.

Weitz, S. 1979. Commentary. In R. Rosenthal (ed.), *Skill in nonverbal communication: Individual differences.* Cambridge, Mass.: Oelgeschlager, Gunn and Hain.

Wickens, T. D. and Keppel, G. 1983. On the choice of design and of test statistic in the analysis of experiments with sampled materials. *Journal of Verbal Learning and Verbal Behavior* 22: 296–309.

Wilkinson, B. 1951. A statistical consideration in psychological research. *Psychological Bulletin* 48: 156–8.

Winer, B. J. 1971. *Statistical principles in experimental design.* 2d ed. New York: McGraw-Hill.

Yule, G. U. 1903. Notes on the theory of association of attributes in statistics. *Biometrika* 2: 121–34.

Zelen, M. and Joel, L. S. 1959. The weighted compounding of two independent significance tests. *Annals of Mathematical Statistics* 30: 885–95.

Zuckerman, M.; DeFrank, R. S.; Hall, J. A.; Larrance, D. T.; and Rosenthal, R. 1979. Facial and vocal cues of deception and honesty. *Journal of Experimental Social Psychology* 15: 378–96.

Zuckerman, M.; Hall, J. A.; DeFrank, R. S.; and Rosenthal, R. 1976. Encoding and decoding of spontaneous and posed facial expressions. *Journal of Personality and Social Psychology* 34: 966–77.

Zuckerman, M. and Larrance, D. T. 1979. Individual differences in perceived encoding and decoding abilities. In R. Rosenthal (ed.), *Skill in nonverbal communication: Individual differences,* 171–203. Cambridge, Mass.: Oelgeschlager, Gunn and Hain.

Zuckerman, M.; Larrance, D. T.; Hall, J. A.; DeFrank, R. S.; and Rosenthal, R. 1979. Posed and spontaneous communication of emotion via facial and vocal cues. *Journal of Personality* 47: 712–33.

Zuckerman, M.; Lipets, M. S.; Koivumaki, J. H.; and Rosenthal, R. 1975. Encoding and decoding nonverbal cues of emotion. *Journal of Personality and Social Psychology* 32: 1068–76.

Name index

Subject index